Barnsley: A Study in l

"Geoff Cook lent me *Barnsley: A Study in Football 1*
sitting, while Gatting and Emburey were playing t
music, and everyone else was sleepily re-reading tl
Frank Keating *The Guardian*

"There is something about Barnsley, something that seems to bring out the artist in a writer ... *Barnsley: A Study in Football 1953-59* seems a fancy title, but then, to use rather flippant terms, it is a fancy book. It attempts, indeed succeeds, in going beyond the bare facts and figures and getting behind the scenes within a football club."
Jon Culley *Sheffield Morning Telegraph*

"Using his father's extraordinary memory as a starting point, Andrew Ward set out with Ian Alister to interview as many of the old players, directors, office staff, coaches and coach-drivers, journalists, fans and laundry ladies as they could trace ... There emerges a story as absorbing as any a novelist might have conjured up ... The book is nostalgic, humorous and affectionate, though rarely sentimental."
Phil Shaw *Time Out*

"Although Ward and Alister are not writing from vivid personal memory, their long and loving labours of research over five years have produced the next best thing. They write with skill, clarity and humour, and there are richly enjoyable portrayals of players such as Johnny Kelly, a Scottish winger of great individual talent."
Patrick Barclay *The Guardian*

"The book chronicles the years at Barnsley, when the Blanchflowers and the dreamers had departed, and Tim Ward, ex-England and Derby County, arrived and eventually took over as manager. Moreover, and more importantly, it is the obituary to an epoch when great performers earned £15 a week."
Michael Parkinson *The Sunday Times*

"It doesn't follow the usual format of the football history, and instead is rather more of a documentary drama in which the story of Barnsley in the period under review unfolds with the immediacy of a novel. The authors have produced a document rich in humour and drama, and the flavour and atmosphere of the time and the place have been recaptured in splendid style."
Keith Farnsworth *Quality*

Other books published by Crowberry

Armed with a Football: A Memoir of Tim Ward, Footballer and Father

The Boys from up the Hill: An Oral History of Oxford United

Barnsley

A Study in Football 1953 - 59

Second Edition

Ian Alister and Andrew Ward

Crowberry

FIRST PUBLISHED 1981
SECOND EDITION 1997

Published in Great Britain by Crowberry, PO Box 623, Oxford, OX2 6DA, England.

Cover pictures
TOP *Barnsley FC first team on 2nd September 1953*
Back row: Norman Smith, "Joe" Thomas, Harry May, Harry Hough, George Spruce and Syd "Skinner" Normanton. Front row: Gavin Smith, Tommy Lumley, Doug Kelly, Bobby Brown and Frank Pattison. *(Barnsley Chronicle)*
BOTTOM *Group picture at the beginning of the 1958-59 season*
Back row: Bryan Matthews, David Barber, Frank Bartlett, Harry Hough, Bob Wood, Colin Swift and John Short. Front row: Arthur Kaye, Norman Smith, Lol Chappell, Malcolm Graham and John McCann. *(Barnsley Chronicle)*

ISBN 0 9507568 3 0 Second Edition
(ISBN 0 9507568 0 6 First Edition)

Cover design: Ian Nixon. Page design and production: Nichola Nixon, Oxford
Text from first edition scanned by Phil Armstrong, Sheffield
Printed in Great Britain by Hillman Printers, Frome, Somerset

This is not a playing history of Barnsley Football Club. It is the story of six seasons from the viewpoint of the individuals who made up the club in the 1950s. Although there is a background of dates, facts and figures from newspaper and club records, most of the material is drawn from interviews with seventy players who actually pulled on the red shirt of Barnsley, and with many others who worked behind the scenes.

Most football books deal with rich and famous clubs. Few touch upon the life of the ordinary player or the everyday workings of a club. This book records the reality of professional football in the 1950s. It was an important era too soon forgotten.

Other books by Andrew Ward

The Boys from up the Hill
(with Geron Swann)

Kicking and Screaming: An Oral History of Football in England
(with Rogan Taylor)

The Day of the Hillsborough Disaster: A Narrative Account
(with Rogan Taylor and Tim Newburn)

Armed with a Football

Three Sides of the Mersey: An Oral History of Everton, Liverpool and Tranmere Rovers
(with Rogan Taylor and John Williams)

Sports Shots

The Derby County Story, 1884-1991
(with Anton Rippon)

Knowabout Soccer
(with Trevor Spindler)

Soccer's Strangest Matches

Cricket's Strangest Matches

Horse-racing's Strangest Races

Golf's Strangest Rounds

Scotland the Team

The Manchester City Story

The Authors

When this book was first written, in 1979-80, Ian Alister and Andrew Ward were both teaching at Cambridge College of Further Education. Ian Alister still lives and works in Cambridge. Andrew Ward is now a free-lance writer.

Authors' Acknowledgements

This title was first published in 1981 as an antidote to books about *great* footballers playing *great* matches for *great* clubs. In late 1979 and early 1980 we talked at length to more than a hundred people connected to Barnsley Football Club in the fifties. The majority of the interviews took place in South Yorkshire, though we visited places as far afield as Barnstaple, Margate, Grimsby, Chester, Chelmsford, Blackpool and Edinburgh.

Wherever we went we had a vibrant response to our work. Initially men and women might be hesitant or sceptical about their capacity to recall events of a quarter of a century before; but the more we talked the more interested they became, and it was not unusual to find other family members adding comments or memories. We learned that people's thoughts and memories really matter. When they are revived, and indeed enhanced, it keeps alive an ongoing feeling of community.

Sadly, not all our interviewees are now alive. However, we would like to repeat the names of those we interviewed because they are the heart and soul of this book, and we will always be grateful for the way they welcomed us: Sybil Allenby, Ron Archer, Trevor Archer, Frank Bartlett, Jimmy Baxter, Frank Beaumont, Alma Bell, Barrie Betts, Reg Bonson, Colin Brookes, Ted Brown, Lol Chappell, Gordon Duggins, John Edgar, Arthur Gill, Peter Gillott, Arthur Glover, Malcolm Graham, Dorothy and Ralph Grimes, Harold Hackney, Rev. Norman Hallam, Chief Superintendent Harrison, Benny Hill, Barry Hines, John Hirst, Malcolm Hirst, Tommy Holmes, Joe Hooley, Olly Hopkins, Harry Hough, Billy Houghton, Morris Hudson, John Jarman, Ray John, Lily Johnson, Bryn Jones, Arthur Kaye, Doug Kelly, Johnny Kelly, Ernest Knowles, Roy Lax, Geoff Lees, Don Leeson, Tommy Lumley, Jackie Lunn, John McCann, Malcolm McCullough, Eddie McMorran, Baron Mason of Barnsley, Bryan Matthews, Harry May, Peter Mulligan, Len Noad, Syd Normanton, Harry O'Hara, Gordon Pallister, Ralph Potter, Bryn Price, Arthur Raynor, Leslie Richards, Ron Riches, Norman Rimmington, Phil Roscoe, Arthur "Chippy" Rowe, Harold Rushforth, Roy Sawyer, Fred Semley, Duncan Sharp, Mary Sheridan, Bob Shotton, Ron Smillie, Bob Smith, Gavin Smith, Norman Smith, George Spruce, Lawrence Stafford, John Stainsby, Ernest Steele, John Steele, Syd Storey, Brian Summerfield, Colin Swift, Joe Thomas, Joe Thorpe, Albion Turner, John Uprichard, John Vest, Jack Walls, Henry Walters, Nancy and Tim Ward, Fred Whittlestone, Peter Whyke, Bob Wood, David Wright.

We would also like to thank those who have helped with this edition: Phil Armstrong, Ian and Nichola Nixon, Ewan Smith and, especially, Jan Ayton.

The photographs in this book have been reproduced by kind permission of the *Barnsley Chronicle.*

Contents

Preface to 1997 Edition

This edition of *Barnsley: A Study in Football 1953-59* is essentially the same as the first. We have made a few changes to the text and have introduced different photographs. Our designers have also upgraded the original fanzine-style production. As Michael Parkinson said of the first edition, "It looks like it was printed in someone's back bedroom with the police knocking on the door." He wasn't far wrong. But now we have moved to the front room.

Throughout the period covered by the book, a win earned a team two points (rather than three) in the Football League standings. If two or more teams had the same number of points, positions were decided on goal average (goals scored divided by goals conceded). In the old Second Division two clubs were promoted and two relegated. However, only the champions of the Third Division (North) and Third Division (South) were promoted.

Foreword to 1981 Edition

Rt. Hon. Roy Mason MP

now Baron Mason of Barnsley

It is a pleasure for me to write a few words on the subject of Barnsley Football Club. The club has always been part of my life. Week after week I have gone to great lengths to ensure I could be there, at Oakwell, whether it be from the pits, Parliament or even abroad. In my early teens I used to walk from Carlton to Barnsley and back again because I couldn't afford the bus fare.

Later, in the 1940s, I had to work all Friday morning and then also do the night shift to be free for the match. After the Saturday shift it would be impossible to get home, get bathed, get to the bus stop, queue, and still make the kick-off. Wives would wait outside the ground or in town with sandwiches and there were many black faces in the crowd, straight from the pit in their pit muck.

Everything revolved around "the game", including family harmony. If the team won, the wife and kids could relax, otherwise they would do well to keep out of the way. The repercussions of the result spilt over into Monday in happiness or misery at work. The chatter of victory undoubtedly helped production in the mines and factories.

I became friendly with Danny Blanchflower during his time with the club. We were studying economic theory together at Barnsley Mining and Technical College – indeed we shared the same desk. Danny was mad about football and talked it non-stop. Once he even stopped me at Barnsley bus station, pulled out a piece of chalk and drew some patterns of play on the wall. He soon showed me how he could get full-back Dave Lindsay into the Scotland team.

I was elected MP for Barnsley in March 1953, within a week of Tim Ward's appointment as manager. When the club sent me a complimentary ticket for the directors' box they didn't realise what a keen supporter I was and how much I would value this privilege. I continued to make time at week-ends. When I was Secretary of State for Northern Ireland I had to fly to RAF Finningley where I was met by a car which took me to the match. By this time my protection team were swelling the numbers in the directors' box, and my wife, on the basis of "if you can't beat 'em, join 'em", had also become a fervent football supporter.

My involvement with the club stretches back to the days of Angus Seed and the portly Joe Richards, with his big cigars and favourite drink of whisky and milk. After becoming an MP my interest in the club's image and development became even greater – speaking on their behalf in Parliament, travelling away, meeting other clubs' directors, presenting the occasional match ball; in general, showing my face and backing Barnsley.

The present board is not dominated by one man as was the case under Joe Richards. They have wide experience and a strong personal involvement with all the club's teams. They have taken some exciting decisions, both in the appointment of managers and the provision of money to buy players. This has led to success on the field which has brought the return of crowds and an atmosphere inside Oakwell hardly seen since Second Division days.

It is an interesting time to look back at what made Barnsley a force to be reckoned with in the 1940s and 1950s. Everyone will have their memories of going to Oakwell, but not many people will know anything of what went on behind the scenes. This book looks at the club in all its aspects, many of them so very different from what we see today. One thing remains the same. There are still men on the terrace who thirst for Saturday to come, planning their week accordingly. That part of it will always go on.

All Barnsley supporters will want to dig into this treasure-chest of memories of their football idols, their strengths and their weaknesses. Memories will be jogged and recollections will come flooding back. It is a fascinating account of the Barnsley club written in a most attractive conversational style. It is a classic and unique reference work that anybody who professes to know Oakwell's history will be proud to possess, indeed he cannot afford to be without.

June 1981

Prologue

August 1945 - March 1953

Monday 13th August 1945

"We can offer him a job, Mrs Baxter," said Angus Seed, sitting comfortably inside a Scottish miner's house in Fife. "There are a lot of pit vacancies in Barnsley."

"Jimmy must make his own mind up, Mr Seed. It's his life and it's up to him what he makes of it."

Like most mothers she would have liked her son out of the pits, but she knew that as a Bevin boy he would have to continue underground to earn his exemption from National Service. She could hardly believe her son could play football. Once, after a rare visit to watch him, she had chided him that he didn't even walk out like a footballer, although she was the first to notice how frequently he wore out boots.

Seed was reasonably encouraged. Mr Baxter was sitting quietly in a corner, taking no part in the discussion. It meant he had only to persuade the player, and that was a process in which the Barnsley manager had much experience and success. Seed had been raised in a mining community in County Durham and now, at 52, he cut the warm fatherly figure necessary to entice players to Barnsley; and players were always needed. In 1939 his side had won the championship of Division Three (North), but now, after six years of interrupted careers he had to rebuild if the impetus were to be maintained.

"This sounds like Jimmy now," said Mrs Baxter.

The door opened, and as Jimmy Baxter came in, his father slipped out to avoid any part in the negotiation. Angus Seed stood up. He might have had cause to regret taking his scout's recommendation. James Cunningham Baxter was 5ft 7 ½in, the smallest member of the family. A few months from his 20th birthday, he stood slight and slouched, dusty and dirty from a Monday's work at the pit.

"This is Mr Seed, Jimmy, he's from, er ..."

"Barnsley," interjected Seed politely. *Barnsley*. It meant very little to Jimmy Baxter although he knew that the Yorkshire club had been showing an interest in him for some time. The name "Seed" was more familiar, since Angus Seed's younger brother, Jimmy, had managed Charlton Athletic from Third to First Division in successive seasons.

"We've got quite a few Scots at Barnsley," Seed told Baxter, "And we can find you some nice digs." Seed then played his trump card. "There's a position at Wharncliffe Woodmoor Colliery waiting for you, Jimmy."

Seed saw Baxter as another Johnny Lang, whom he had signed from Aberdeen for £2,000 in 1937. Baxter had been playing in Dunfermline Athletic's wartime inside-forward trio alongside Billy Liddell and Jimmy Logie, but their clubs, Liverpool and Arsenal, were not in mining communities and therefore less able to accommodate a pit worker. Baxter himself would have liked to go to Dundee but they couldn't match the £3,000 transfer fee that Barnsley were prepared to pay. It would be a new Dunfermline record.

"Oakwell's a wonderful pitch," continued Seed, "It's a happy atmosphere and you'll like the people." He spoke sincerely, though he knew of days when Barnsley snowed soot or rained ink. There was a risk in saying "Come to Barnsley and the place will grow on you," because sometimes players came and the place fell on them. But most stayed to discover the warmth of the people and the rugged, undulating beauty of the region.

"I'd like you to play against Manchester United," said Seed, "They're playing at Maine Road since Old Trafford caught it in an air-raid." Seed arranged for Baxter and his father to travel to Barnsley on the Friday before the match. There they could stay in the White Hart Hotel in Peel Street, which Seed ran with his wife.

Throughout the war Angus Seed had struggled to put together a team of part-timers and guest players, sometimes counting heads in the dressing-room rather than selecting a team. Strangers might try a bluff to gain 30 shillings appearance money and there was no way of checking names. "I've played for Aldershot," was a favourite. It was not the same Aldershot as between 1927 and 1937 when Seed was manager there. In wartime many famous players were stationed in the area and the club's status rose accordingly.

Seed looked forward to stability and progress. So did the mass of men and women who had just given Clement Attlee and Labour a landslide victory in the general election. But Jimmy Baxter posed an immediate problem, finding the travelling, training and faster football too much. Within a week he was back at East End Park playing for Dunfermline on a match-to-match basis, sending one or two telegrams to Barnsley to say he had an injured leg or back. Angus Seed was not unused to players' homesickness and at first he simply waited for Baxter to come back and take up his job in the pit. But as Christmas approached, questions began to be asked. Seed travelled to Scotland and returned with his player. Jimmy Baxter started work at Wharncliffe Woodmoor in the first week of December.

Despite the continuing difficulties caused by rationing, the immediate post-war years offered many welcome prospects to Barnsley people. The nationalisation of coal promised a remedy to the many ills of a miner's existence. Strikes were expected to decline; wages, pit safety and job security were expected to increase. Throughout the country more and more people were attending football matches and Barnsley miners were no exception.

By the end of 1948 buses were bulging with Barnsley fans. They clung tightly as buses rolled in from mining villages, perhaps eight or ten hanging on the platform. They tumbled from trains at Bunkers Hill and toppled down the embankment to walk along Oakwell Lane. They cycled through the throng and paid twopence to store bicycles in front gardens while they watched the game. Others had to walk. In 1947–48 Barnsley attendances averaged 21,050 for home League matches.

Angus Seed had assembled an exceptional team. Since the great FA Cup win of 1912 they had acquired the nickname "battling Barnsley". West Brom had enjoyed the affections of neutrals in that final, it being generally believed that Barnsley had used unduly rough methods to dispose of Swindon, the last hopes of the south.

In 1949 the legacy was apparent in the strategic advice delivered from the stands: "give it sum clog", "booit it" and "get rid". But Seed had also signed skilful players. In defence there was the experienced Gordon Pallister, a survivor of the 1938–39 side that won the Third Division (North) by 11 points and conceded only 34 goals. In front of him Seed had conjured up something of a spectacle – Jimmy Baxter and Danny Blanchflower, with George Robledo leading the attack. On the right wing was Gavin Smith, whose speed encouraged the usual phrase "he can catch pigeons". In fact he had a more practical speciality – racing a bus from one stop to the next. At outside-left was the main attraction, Scottish international Johnny Kelly. A winger of great individual talent would really bring in the crowds, as Stanley Matthews proved everywhere he went, and Kelly was a cheeky, effervescent entertainer. If he had a fault, it was allowing his man to recover with a view to beating him again. The spectators seldom complained.

On Saturday evenings the Barnsley streets became a sea of *Green 'Uns* as the fanatics read the *Sheffield Star* reports. They met their wives and, depending on their mood after the match, took a night on the town, perhaps a meal at the bus station cafe and a visit to one of the eight cinemas or a dance-hall. Occasionally a man could be seen reading the *Green 'Un* behind his partner's back as they waltzed. The club had introduced cheaper season tickets for ladies in a bid to attract them to the match. "Never marry a miner," mothers told their daughters, worrying about the insecurity and isolation of the miner's life, but most recognised that they would. "I don't mind what you do," said fathers to their sons, "as long as you don't go down the pit," but most recognised that they would.

When schoolboys weren't piling into Oakwell they were playing in parks and in streets empty of cars. Anything would substitute for a leather-cased football – rags, cans, tennis balls or a pig's bladder of water; goalposts were coats, sticks, gateways or, best of all, a gable-end.

At school there was an unusual level of encouragement. During the war, with most male teachers away, women such as Gaynor Lawrence at Smithies had come forward to coach young lads. Now, Harold Rushforth was out every evening organising junior football at Raley. Within weeks of his demobilisation from the RAF in 1945 he had been asked to manage Barnsley Boys. After a poor first season he had been joined by Ted Davies and they planned a full fixture list. On Boxing Day 1946 they entertained Leicester Boys, holders of the English Schools' Trophy, at Oakwell. The venture made a profit of £146. Within 18 months they had reached the semi-finals of the competition themselves, producing two schoolboy internationals – Frank Levitt and Arthur Kaye. In 1949 they won the competition in a two-leg final against Derby Boys. The game at Oakwell was watched by 27,700, and the club showed their interest in youth development by organising a celebration at the Queen's Hotel for the boys and their parents, presenting the boys with blazer badges. The club took the unprecedented step of offering to sign the whole team. Phil Roscoe, Colin Swift and Frank Levitt were invited on to the groundstaff and the others were offered amateur forms. Despite competing offers, all accepted apart from Levitt. He lived between Barnsley and Sheffield and opted for Sheffield Wednesday. His groundstaff place went to Doug Kelly, the Don and Dearne Valley Boys' centre-forward.

These new signings had hardly seen the ultimate authority at Oakwell – chairman Joe Richards. Though small in physical stature he cut an impressive figure in his chauffeur-driven Rolls-Bentley puffing a double Corona cigar, and there was no doubting the extent of his influence in the club.

His livelihood, like most people's in Barnsley, was coal. Born in 1888 he had started as a miner at Barnsley Main, where his father was manager. After breaking his leg badly in an accident with a pit tub Richards moved above ground, progressing rapidly until at the age of 32 he was secretary and sales manager, as well as a newly-elected director of Barnsley FC. Richards then consolidated both interests with various senior posts in the coal and coking industry, a second spell as chairman of the football club and membership of the Football League Management Committee.

His business methods were well illustrated by the sale of George Robledo in January 1949. Barnsley had just been knocked out of the FA Cup and it was agreed that their Chilean-born centre-forward should become the club's first major post-war sale. The next thing the directors knew was when their chairman rang to say "George Martin and Stan Seymour are coming for him." What the Newcastle officials didn't realise was that Richards expected them to buy wing-half Ted Robledo as well – "to keep his brother company," as their mother had put it during a forceful interview at Oakwell.

When the Barnsley directors met at the Royal Hotel most of them thought that a price of £25,000 had been settled for the two players. "Why don't we ask £26,500?" asked one director, mentioning the figure fed to him by Joe Richards. It was agreed.

"You're putting a poor price on Ted," said Richards when Newcastle offered £20,000. This was true. They had not come for him and expected to get him free, but there was no negotiation. Newcastle signed the Robledos for £26,500 and other clubs, such as Sheffield Wednesday, were upset to find the players sold without ever having been on the open market; and Sheffield Wednesday was the one club George Robledo had always wanted to play for.

Joe Richards also served on the FA Council, which gave him an opportunity to broaden his experience of the game. In the summer of 1950 the England team were booked for the World Cup in Brazil, but another FA party toured Canada, and Richards was chosen to accompany it. It was a two-month affair with many banquets and receptions, an unusual chance to break down traditional social barriers between players and officials. The Barnsley chairman got on particularly well with one senior professional, Tim Ward, even strolling onto the pitch before one game when Ward was captain to discuss a last-minute hitch in arrangements. A normal enough incident, but it would have been unthinkable at Oakwell where even the chairman's appearances in the dressing-room were rare and formal, with Richards looking very much as though he had just stepped out of an Austin Reed shop window.

Joe Richards took a personal hand in many signings, especially as Angus Seed's health grew poorer. Some of these were far from straightforward. When he travelled with director John Hirst to sign Cecil McCormack there were two fees to be agreed – one with McCormack's present side, non-League Chelmsford City, and another with his previous club, Middlesbrough, who held his League registration.

McCormack proved to be a prodigious goalscorer. In 1949–50 he got 33 goals, a record for Barnsley, and although the club were unable to capitalise on several good starts, they maintained a consistent position in the middle of Division Two. However, the situation in March 1951 was not so healthy and saw a series of significant transfer deals. On Thursday 15th Joe Richards completed two transactions at the Midland Hotel, Derby. Danny Blanchflower, so long an ardent critic of the training methods employed at Barnsley, went to Aston Villa for £15,000, while Eddie Murphy was signed from Northampton on the strength of his outstanding showing against Barnsley in the FA Cup. But that was by no means the end of the proceedings.

Friday 16th March 1951

It was the night of the transfer deadline. A player signed later than midnight could not play for his new club in matches affecting that season's honours or relegation. At 8 pm Tim Ward of Derby County was at home babysitting his two-year-old son while his wife was at the cinema. There was a knock at the door. Jack Nicholas, Derby County's chief scout, entered with some news. At 6.30 that evening Derby County had been approached by Barnsley to release their international wing-half. The size of the offer had agreeably surprised Derby, who earlier in the day had signed defender Charlie Revell from Charlton Athletic.

Tim Ward was taken aback. He had been with Derby for 14 years. Now he had four hours to decide whether to join a Second Division club and move to a town he had never visited. What's more, his wife was out.

"What's Derby's position?" he asked.

"We're prepared to let you go," replied Nicholas, "I've got a number here, where you can reach Mr Richards, if you're interested, Tim."

Ward felt annoyed at Derby's willingness to release him, although it did not show in his calm exterior. He asked Nicholas for the number and walked to a neighbour's house to make the call. It was a telephone call he would not have contemplated had he not known Joe Richards. It was the first time the two men had talked since the Canadian tour. They exchanged pleasantries and then Richards quickly reached the business. Ward listened. The terms were not as good as at Derby and below the £14 a week maximum. But Ward wanted to coach and eventually manage, and he felt that staying with Derby was not the best way to achieve this. He knew he would have to move at some stage.

"That's fine by me, Mr Richards," said Ward, "But I'm really looking for a coaching opportunity."

"Well, we want you as a player right now. We can still go down," said Richards, "But Angus Seed's been in poor health and there's a good chance he'll need someone to help him."

Ward accepted the move on that basis. Minutes before, he had not considered leaving Derby County. He was picked to play against Arsenal the following day and had even collected the complimentary tickets he had promised to a friend. Now he seemed destined to move to Barnsley who tomorrow would play Notts County in the Second Division.

The two clubs moved to the next stage of their deal. John Hirst, a Barnsley butcher, was the director designated to complete the signing. Hirst was surprised when he learned that Ward was available. Being an admirer of the player, his journey to the Portland Hotel, Chesterfield, was a pleasant task – despite the fog.

Tim Ward, meanwhile, needed a babysitter. He persuaded Granville Sandford, a local shopkeeper, and explained hurriedly, "I've got to go to Chesterfield to sign for Barnsley." Then Ward joined the Derby officials for the trip.

The meeting was swift since the details were already settled. It took a round of drinks, from which Ward abstained, and a round of signatures. Ward was now a Barnsley player. At 11.30 John Hirst picked up the telephone for an important part of the transaction. "I want to send a time-dated telegram," said Hirst, "It's to Football League Headquarters at Preston … registration of Tim Ward transferred from Derby County to Barnsley."

It did not matter how long the telegram took to arrive. Barnsley had covered themselves and Ward could play the following day. Joseph Richards was proud when he heard the news. He had brought an England international to Barnsley.

His administrative career was helping the club.

However, when Nancy Ward returned from the pictures she was surprised to see Granville Sandford. "Where's Tim?" she asked, speaking loudly, for she knew the shopkeeper was slightly deaf.

"He's gone to sign for Chesterfield."

"He's done what?"

It came as a shock to Nancy Ward, who had never lived outside Derby. She sat down, switched on the Murphy wireless and waited. An hour passed and she went to bed, but was still awake when her husband returned.

"You're never going to Chesterfield," she greeted him.

"No, Barnsley."

"Barnsley: Oh dear, where's Barnsley?"

"I'm not sure."

"I hope it's a nice place," said Nancy Ward.

"I'm sure it will be," said her husband, "Mr Richards is a gentleman." He looked at the clock. It was hours past his normal Friday bedtime. "I'd better get some sleep now. I've got a train to catch at nine in the morning." He settled down, but as he did so he remembered that he still had complimentary tickets for Derby's game. He would have to leave them with someone in the morning.

During the following weeks Barnsley collected points that saw them to safety, but Tim Ward's domestic arrangements had to catch up later. Ward continued to train at Derby. His wife dreaded the move and Derby people's impression of Barnsley did nothing to set her mind at rest. Ward himself had been surprised at his first sight of the town through the window of Joe Richards' Rolls-Bentley, which had met him at Sheffield station. The Wards finally moved to Barnsley in October 1951, when they set up home in Huddersfield Road. It was a semi-detached house specially bought by the club. The rent was £1 a week.

By March 1952, problems on the field were the same as the previous year, and again the club moved to beat the transfer deadline. John Steele, coach of Barnsley Juniors, was sent to Swindon to watch Charlton Athletic's Tommy Lumley in a reserve match. Steele was hesitant in his report, feeling that Lumley would not give his best for 90 minutes. Nevertheless Angus Seed went ahead and purchased Lumley from his brother Jimmy Seed for £4,500. The little inside-forward responded with 7 goals in 10 games and relegation was narrowly avoided.

When the 1951–52 season ended, Tim Ward was asked to coach the Barnsley A team in the Yorkshire League. Because he was given responsible tasks, such as scouting and coaching, Ward was viewed with some suspicion. People assumed there was an ulterior motive in his move from Derby. There were rumours that he would be the next manager, and the southerner from Cheltenham was only accepted slowly.

At the start of the 1952–53 season, Barnsley's 40 Second Division seasons were six more than any other Football League club, but this tradition had to be maintained every year. They were losing the players who had steadied their post-war position. Cecil McCormack had been sold to Notts County for £20,000. Then

Preston signed Jimmy Baxter for a further £20,000. Preston's chairman, Nat Buck, no giant himself, paced around the uncomfortable Baxter, muttering "He's very small, very small ..." It was seven years since Angus Seed had sat in the house in Fife with the same misgivings.

October 1952 was too early for the club to enjoy the full benefit of signing the 1948 and 1949 school-leavers – although Kaye, Archer and Smillie had all played in the Second Division. Angus Seed had to sign players to halt a bad start to the season. There was no point waiting until the transfer deadline because Barnsley had collected only 6 points from 12 games. It was the last thing Seed needed for his health, which had failed so much that he had now relinquished his secretarial duties to Raymond Vicary.

Angus Seed approached his friend Tom Whittaker, Arsenal's manager, about Norman Smith, a wing-half kept out of the first team by internationals Forbes, Mercer and Macaulay. There was no doubting Smith's ability. He had served an apprenticeship in the Arsenal academy and was much admired, although he did seem slightly injury-prone. They called him "Legs" at Arsenal, for he was slight, spindly and had lost three of his four cartilages although only 28-years-old. This left his legs looking mildly concave.

Seed found he needed all his persistence and charm to lure Smith away from the attractions of London life; he offered a first-team place and the full £750 benefit. Smith signed. The following Friday, Seed met him at Doncaster station in his Austin Twelve, and on the journey to the Royal Hotel he continued his overtures: "We've got a good inside-left in Tommy Taylor ... he'll play for England one day ... and a great centre-forward, McMorran, Irish international ... if only he thought he was in a green shirt every week."

Unfortunately, both the relegation struggle and Seed's illness became chronic. One December day, Seed walked into the Barnsley boot-room, where the coaches held conversations in bad weather. "Do you know," he said, "I'd be the happiest man in Barnsley if I died today." He was continually taking tablets to ease the pain of his bronchitis.

January was no help. Barnsley lost all four League matches. In the FA Cup they recovered from three down to beat Brighton 4–3, but their interest in the competition ended at Plymouth on the last day of the month. On the return journey, Angus Seed was so ill that he was taken from the train at Gloucester. He died in the early hours of 7th February, the day after his 60th birthday.

Barnsley had lost a major football figure. Angus Seed left supporters with many memories. He left the club with a youth policy, a resource as highly valued as coal, but he also left a team rooted at the bottom of Division Two. The club's status was seriously threatened.

Trainer Bob Shotton took charge of the team in consultation with Joe Richards. Tim Ward was one strong candidate for the job of manager, but he was the junior of four trainer/coaches who met to discuss selection: Shotton, Steele, assistant trainer Eddie Fleetwood and Ward.

Three weeks went by and there was no sign of the year's first win. Nor did anything happen about the vacant managership. The rumour re-emerged that

Ward had been bought to take over from Seed. Tim Ward, however, remained unconvinced.

Barnsley ended February in the same way they ended January – with a long haul to Plymouth. They travelled on the Friday and Tim Ward was with the team. At Birmingham, West Brom manager Vic Buckingham boarded the same train. Buckingham was one of several managers interested in Tommy Taylor, scorer of 19 of Barnsley's 39 Second Division goals. He took Ward aside on the train, and after a brief chat, offered him a job as his assistant at West Brom. It was certainly worth considering.

The next evening, having lost 4–0, Barnsley took the train home in low spirits. On the way back they passed through Exeter, a city which could hardly have been more dissimilar to Barnsley. But their football clubs had something in common. Both had no manager. Norman Kirkman had just left Exeter for Bradford Park Avenue. The following week Tim Ward received a telephone call from Len Noad, a *Weekly News* journalist. The Exeter job was Ward's if he wanted it – player/manager.

Ward approached Joe Richards, who said that the club wouldn't stand in the way. So Tim Ward travelled to Exeter and met the club's directors. He was offered the job and accepted. He started immediately.

Meanwhile the Barnsley directors were busy. Attendances were falling and would drop still further in the lower division. New blood would be needed to revive interest. To an astute businessman like Joseph Richards it amounted to a severe financial headache. If the club were to realise large sums for any of their players then March was the best time, before the transfer deadline.

"If somebody doesn't decide soon, I'm going down the pit," said Tommy Taylor, besieged with offers but apparently content in his home town. On 4th March he fetched £29,999 from Manchester United. United manager Matt Busby had not wanted to hang a £30,000 tag on the player and he gave the odd £1 to Barnsley FC receptionist Lily Wilby, who had served the tea.

In the same week Barnsley sold Eddie McMorran to Doncaster Rovers for £8,000, and in the wave of publicity which surrounded the sales, Tim Ward was almost forgotten. Then Ward was suddenly informed of a hitch in his proposed move. Barnsley still held his playing registration, so after eight days as Exeter manager, back he came.

Ward was invited to apply for the manager's job at Barnsley. He did so and waited. Financially, he would be better off at Barnsley, who offered a salary of £1,000 a year, but both jobs were an improvement on the £10 a week he had been earning as A team player/coach. However, Ward felt some loyalty to Exeter, who considerately kept their post vacant while the Barnsley issue was settled. That took three board meetings. The applications were sifted and a short-list of four drawn up – Ward, former captain Gordon Pallister, Alf Young and Crewe manager Harry Catterick – and then an appointment was made.

The Detergent of the Day

Chapter One

Tuesday 31st March 1953

Belgrave Road at 9.45 in the morning. At the bottom of the steep slope stood Oakwell, a resplendent red and white in contrast to the darker colours of Barnsley Main Colliery behind. Footballers were walking nonchalantly to the ground from digs, club houses or the bus station. Then two of them jumped out of their skins as a loud motor horn blasted right behind them. They turned to see the impish face of Johnny Kelly grinning over the steering-wheel. It was one of his favourite tricks to turn off the engine of his van, pull it up onto the pavement and coast down silently after unsuspecting colleagues. Indeed it was a fright in itself to travel in the van, an apparent deathtrap flatback with string holding the doors in place, obviously accustomed to bouncing over the subsidence-ridden roads of Barnsley.

The players grouped and crossed Grove Street, and without deviating they passed through the players' entrance. Then they pushed open the swing-doors to walk under the main stand. One post-war player was famed for his party-piece of knocking these doors open with his head – until the day the trainer reversed the hinges and the player laid himself out.

Instead of immediately changing for training, the players were asked to congregate in the billiard room where they gathered around a billiard table that had been brought from the White Hart Hotel by Angus Seed. Chairman Joe Richards entered to make an announcement. "As a result of last night's board meeting," started Richards, "the directors have appointed Mr Ward as our new manager. We hope you will give him all your support. Mr Ward will have the full backing of the directors." Richards looked around. "Would you like to say anything, Mr Ward?"

"Well, just to say that those of you who know me as 'Tim' will have to call me 'Boss' from now on."

There was no real reaction of surprise. The appointment, though delayed, had been rumoured and predicted, even though there had been some misunderstanding.

When Tim Ward started his new job on 31st March 1953, he took over a team that were bottom of the Second Division. In fact they were more than just bottom, they were welded bottom. In 35 games they had totalled 17 points. If they won their last seven games, and either Hull or Lincoln lost their last eight, then Barnsley had a chance of avoiding relegation ... providing Southampton did badly. It seemed like the drop to the Third Division (North).

On his first day Tim Ward established himself in the club's only office, which was shared with secretary Raymond Vicary and receptionist Lily Wilby. Both Vicary and Ward stayed until after the Tuesday evening training session. Vicary had insisted on being present to advise Ward in his first major business – signing a part-time professional. It needed three copies of the contract and a reminder that the player should produce his birth certificate. This was required by the Football League's Provident Fund, for a share-out at the age of 35 of a percentage of a retired player's earnings in football.

The player concerned was a young lad from Hall Green who only a few weeks previously had been recommended by former player Arthur Glover for a game in the A team. Ward was playing that day. In the wilds of windy Thorne, playing against Doncaster A, Ward had been impressed with the ginger-haired youngster's speed off the mark and his lethal left foot. Ward put his arm around him after the game and congratulated him. He then watched his progress into the Central League team. Now was the time for action. Ward sent for him, signatures were inserted and the following day's date used. It was Tim Ward's first signing. Malcolm Graham. April Fool's Day 1953.

Malcolm Graham worked in a local colliery. This was common among Barnsley's part-time professionals, who found football an opportunity for a break after work. At the other end of the scale was Johnny Kelly, at 32 more experienced in life and living away from home. Kelly was unusual among the full-time players in that he owned his own transport. He used his flatback for a bleach business which he ran from stables near the Mason's Arms, Worsbrough Dale.

Kelly was the instigator of Kelzone, the detergent of the day. For the last seven years he had made it in a bath. It was a simple mixture of sodium hydrochlorate and water. He measured the strength of the mixture with a twaddell and then syphoned it into bottles, a tricky procedure that could lead to mouthfuls of bleach. He finished by sticking special labels on the bottles.

Footballers occasionally visited the stables out of curiosity, bringing empty bottles on request.

Kelly collected the acid from Widnes, one of many detours in his monthly trips home to Scotland, for which the club paid his expenses. The journeys regularly clocked 400 miles rather than 250, as he unfailingly collected hitch-hikers and made stops for Barnsley footballers returning to homes in the north. He had been the owner of many vehicles and they were always safer than they looked: one had its engine held on by ropes; an Austin Twelve had an unusual registration – AGE 100; and another had a loose steering-wheel which Kelly would hand to an unsuspecting passenger at a safe speed, saying "Can you take the wheel for a minute?"

Most of the bleach went to the Co-op, where £25 worth of Kelzone sales per week were assured by Barnsley director Horace Pickering OBE, a retired Co-op secretary. In addition Kelly placed an advertisement in the Barnsley programme, recommending his product to "loyal supporters". More than one director's wife used it dutifully. But Kelly did not make much money. It simply filled in his time.

Johnny Kelly was missing a thumb and two fingers from his right hand following a construction site accident as a youth. More recently he had needed three knee operations, having suffered his worst injury in a tackle with Bill Ellerington on a frosty Southampton pitch in 1951. Yet it was against Southampton that Kelly had played some of his best games, tormenting Alf Ramsey. And he was soon to be needed against them again. The hectic Easter programme meant Barnsley would play Blackburn twice and Southampton at home.

Saturday 4th April 1953

Thirty minutes passed without a goal. It was a terrible game. Fellow-strugglers Southampton were the visitors and it was four months since Barnsley's last win, but Tim Ward, sitting in the Oakwell trainer's box, was still believing in the miracles of new managers. If Captain Hunt thought Mount Everest could be climbed then perhaps anything was possible. It was Ward's first home game in charge, yet already he had stamped his authority on certain players, severely rebuking senior professional Syd Normanton for calling him "Tim" and not "Boss" in a momentary slip.

From his low position, almost on the halfway line, Ward watched with trainer Bob Shotton. The two men were almost level with Southampton left-back Peter Sillett when he intercepted a kicked clearance from Barnsley goalkeeper Jack Walls. Sillett booted the ball back first-time, and those on the sidelines waited, powerless. The players watched too as the stranded Walls backtracked across his penalty area. The ball from Sillett, whether a centre, clearance or shot, looped a long way and drifted into the Barnsley net. It was the only goal. Relegation was unavoidable.

With relegation assured, Tim Ward could concentrate on evaluating the playing staff and preparing for the next season. Results continued to be bad. Each week a new

Oakwell record for post-war low attendances was being created, and only 3,155 saw the season's last game against Fulham, when Lumley's late equaliser brought Ward his first point. Even the Barnsley Challenge Cup Final between Winn Street and Shipcroft United attracted a 4,136 attendance. So while Jimmy Baxter of Preston was missing a Championship medal on goal average, Barnsley were finishing with only five wins and just 18 points.

One of Tim Ward's first major tasks was the season's retained list, the list of professionals he wished to keep for the following season. The manager was responsible for selecting the names while Joe Richards and his directors fixed the fees for those released. The club, however, would retain the player's Football League registration unless they had agreed the transfer. They had no power to prevent a player moving outside the League though they would keep his League registration.

Tim Ward wanted players who would produce their ability consistently for Barnsley in a style he favoured. He believed in team-work and admired the push-and-run strategy of the 1951 Tottenham Hotspur Championship team: "Don't just kick the ball, pass it. Play the game simply, accurately, quickly."

Ward retained 32 players. In addition he signed six young players as part-time professionals, including youth international Peter Gillott and three members of the 1950 Barnsley Boys team – Ted Brown, Trevor Archer and Harold Sidebottom. The youngsters had survived intense teenage competition.

Consider the competition. In 1949 the club had signed a team of 15-year-olds to add to other promising youngsters. In 1950 they signed another team of 15-year-olds, so when Barnsley won the Northern Intermediate League in 1951 there were more than 30 youngsters striving for a game. Training sessions were enormous. Kit had been rationed by the government and still was by the club; one full-time player even took it home for safe-keeping.

When Don Leeson, a goalkeeper from Askern, played a trial in 1952, he was one of 80 young hopefuls. The numbers were pruned and John Steele alternated between two goalkeepers before deciding on Leeson for Barnsley Juniors. It was a major competitive process just to reach Barnsley's fourth team.

Tim Ward, having released seven professionals, brought his staff to 38 with the signing of the six youngsters. None of the 38 came from as far south as Ward himself. In fact 25 came from the Barnsley area and almost all of these had fathers working in local collieries. Scotland accounted for five and the north-east a further four. Excluding John Jarman, who was brought up in the Midlands, no player came from south of Chester, George Spruce's home town. The other two were Lancastrians, club captain Norman Smith and Joe Thomas, who had been raised locally and had played for Yorkshire Boys.

It would be over two months before the staff re-grouped for the next season. In the meantime wages needed agreeing and players needed to be imported and exported. Attendance receipts had slumped and the Third Division was a less attractive proposition. Barnsley's newly-elected MP, Roy Mason, was quick to take an interest in the affairs of the club he had followed since he was a boy. On 20th May in a debate on the Finance Bill he raised the question of entertainment tax and the part it played in forcing the sales of Blanchflower, McCormack, Baxter, McMorran and Taylor. Mason stressed that Yorkshire miners should have the opportunity to watch first-class football during their leisure hours, and that this would no doubt be reflected in higher productivity. Entertainment tax of 3½d on a 1/9 admission charge had a substantial effect on the balancing of the books. With the income from attendances steadily falling, it was clear to Joe Richards that selling players was the only available method of stabilising finances.

Effect of Transfers on Overall Annual Profit (£s)

Source: Barnsley Football Club balance-sheets

Year ending 31st May	Fees Paid £	Fees Received £	Profit £
1945	2,110	-	119
1946	7,350	1,800	1,845
1947	9,345	5,200	3,184
1948	6,225	1,350	5,160
1949	28,870	32,535	2,616
1950	980	2,550	(3,409) (loss)
1951	40,040	46,075	4,487
1952	21,890	20,700	(4,508) (loss)
1953	23,870	36,675	1,338

NB Certain transfer fees were paid in instalments.

Norman Smith, back in Lancashire for the summer, received a registered letter from Joe Richards. The Football League maximum weekly wage was £14 (£10 close-season) but when Smith moved from the Arsenal to Barnsley his wages stayed constant, below the maximum. The incentives were first-team football and an immediate benefit. But now he learned of a 10/- reduction in his Third Division terms.

Norman Smith's abilities were not confined to the football field. In his schooldays his annual visits to Blackpool had taught him enough to entertain at Christmas shows. Then during the war – which he ended as a rear-gunner in Lancaster bombers – he learned a selection of card tricks and eventually joined the Magic Circle in London. Smith was also ambidextrous. Not only could he compose a convincing reply, but he could do so with either hand or with elegant medieval handwriting. He wrote back to Richards saying he did not see how he could perform "10 bob worse" on the field. He waited, knowing he had no alternative work available.

Joe Richards replied. Times were hard, but Smith's terms could stay the same – providing he did not broadcast them. Smith felt this fair, since these were the terms of his transfer. Terms were between player and club, not player and players. Recent signings had led to discrepancies such that players opened wage packets in all corners of Oakwell. The directors now wished to standardise wages, which suited Tim Ward's ethic of teamwork. But standardisation between players in the same team was a slow job.

In 1948, when Tommy Lumley signed for Charlton Athletic, he willingly underwent a drop in wages to be a professional footballer. From £7 a week (£6 close-season) his wages had steadily risen to the £14 maximum. But his new offer was slightly different, £12 a week plus £2 if in the first team. The board were anxious to curb the possibility of players being content to play in the Reserves at the same wage. Lumley suffered in this standardisation and he was upset, remembering his part when Barnsley avoided relegation in his first season. He refused his terms. The directors refused his transfer request. Lumley held out ... and then he re-signed. He really had very little option.

Harry May, 25, was an unusual player in that his five seasons as a professional had taken him to Cardiff and Swindon as well as Barnsley. He believed that football would not reward him for staying in one place, while moving to different areas also helped him learn about transport and anything to do with the export trade, which was where he saw his future. This was why he went back to his native Glasgow to work for British Railways in the summer of 1953, at the end of his first season at Barnsley. He was on the transfer list at his own request and in some doubt as to whether to continue as a professional player at all, but he received an encouraging letter from Tim Ward and the offer of a club house at 25/- a week.

May was familiar with the work of the Players' and Trainers' Union since he had been their representative at his two previous clubs. But in 1953 the union took their pressure for two continuing demands – removal of the maximum wage and freedom of contract – as far as an Industrial Disputes Tribunal which eventually sat on 26th July and raised the maximum wage to £15 (£12 close-season). However, this mattered little to players who were not earning. The most important date in the calendar of all footballers was 30th June. This was when the one-year contract ended and another began, or in some cases didn't begin.

Harry O'Hara, 22, spent the summer back in his home of Ryhope, County Durham. After four years part-time at Barnsley – including two in the army – O'Hara was on the transfer list. The fee was initially £1,000 but no club came. It was a high fee for a player who had played only six times for the Reserves and never for the first team, although Bob Shotton would point to first-team lists and say, "That's where you should be." But O'Hara, a prolific goalscorer in the A team, had not treated his football as seriously as his ability first suggested.

He received a second letter which reduced his fee to £500 but still no club came. June brought the prospect of joining the nation's 430,000 unemployed, but fortunately O'Hara had a trade as a plumber. He reverted to this and played football for Dalton Colliery Welfare in the Wearside League. His Football League registration stayed with Barnsley.

Six other players left the club, including experienced wingers Johnny Kelly and Gavin Smith. Kelly was retained but requested a return to Scotland. Joe Richards set a fee of £2,500 and Kelly was signed by Bob Shankly, manager of

Falkirk. Kelly now began making round trips in reverse to continue his Kelzone production.

Ted Davison, manager of Sheffield United, and Raich Carter, manager of Leeds United, showed interest in Gavin Smith but they were unwilling to match Barnsley's £3,000 evaluation. This fee was reduced to £1,000, but when Smith visited Joseph Richards to discuss a further reduction he met with a firm if flattering refusal. "You're worth some money, Gavin," Richards told him. So by the start of the next season Smith was without a club.

The only transfer-listed player to remain in the Football League was Matt McNeil, who signed for Brighton. Tommy Blenkinsopp, like McNeil a costly signing, joined Blyth Spartans and left behind memories of the 10 traumatic times he had played for Barnsley. For all these players the summer brought concern over where the next contract would come from.

Monday 29th June 1953

Henry Walters' career as a footballer had started during the war at Wolverhampton Wanderers, who ran a successful nursery at Wath upon Dearne under a local man, Mark Crook. Since then Walters had spent seven years with Walsall in the Third Division (South). It meant a lot of travelling from his home in Brampton, but for the past two seasons he'd had a car, bought with the £250 he received as a benefit for five years' service. Now, at the age of 28, he'd asked for a transfer. The request had been granted, and he'd been told to try and find a club himself. In three days he would be out of work.

His car was vital. First he drove six miles to Barnsley, the nearest League club. Tim Ward listened as the player explained his situation but he made no promises. The name "Walters" meant nothing to him.

Walters got back into his car and headed for Sheffield. Wednesday were in the First Division and he saw manager Eric Taylor. United, the Second Division champions, were on tour in Germany, so there was no prospect there.

Five more miles took Walters to his last stop – Rotherham United's ground, Millmoor. Andy Smailes, the manager, was encouraging, which was more than could be said for the surroundings. The office was just a wooden hut, and getting there was like completing an obstacle course. "I hope I don't go there," thought Henry Walters as he drove home.

He began to plan an excursion for the next day, starting with the two Bradford clubs. That would make five managers he had sounded out, but there was nothing definite. There were 10 clubs within 20 miles of his home, the nearest two in the heart of coal-mining areas. It was the reverse of the old saying "you could go down any pit shaft and find a top-class footballer". Here you could look into a Second Division dressing-room and several full-time miners would come out.

Henry Walters' car did in fact prove his salvation. He was cleaning it one night when the chief wages clerk from Cortonwood Colliery stopped and offered Walters his old joinery job. The only condition was that he play cricket for

Cortonwood. Since that was no hardship he jumped at the chance of a regular income.

Tim Ward, meanwhile, did his homework. He had never seen Walters play so he telephoned three people, including Stan Cullis of Wolves. "He's a great bloke," said one. "I don't know how they can let him go," said another, "he's the only player they've got at Walsall." Walsall had finished bottom of their division for two seasons. In the circumstances Ward liked all that he heard.

John Steele and Eddie Fleetwood arranged for Walters to meet Ward, and the player was offered full-time terms, even without a trial. Walters explained he had taken his old job back and it was agreed that he should become a part-time professional.

In the brief conversation that followed, Ward and Walters struck up the instant camaraderie that often occurred in football. They sensed their similarities: wing-half play, cricket and the same sense of humour. Ward recognised from the twinkle in Walters' bright blue eyes that his comments were understood and appreciated. Walters began to look forward to playing football again – until he broke a bone in his hand when batting against Denaby.

While Tim Ward strengthened his defence almost by accident, he was making a determined effort concerning his attack. With Taylor and McMorran transferred, Ward was interested in Bobby Brown, Shrewsbury Town's 27-year-old leading goalscorer. At Derby County, Ward had known both Brown and Shrewsbury's manager, Sammy Crooks, the second most capped England player between the wars.

Ward opened negotiations and they extended into his fortnight's holiday, which was taken at Skegness YMCA with his wife and four-year-old son. Twice Ward made day trips back to Barnsley, but each time Crooks had failed to find Brown. It transpired that the Scottish inside-forward was also on holiday, at Ingoldmells, only three miles along the coast from Skegness. Bobby Brown signed for Barnsley in a caravan. It was the end of Ward's summer signings, although there were other players he would have liked.

Friday 28th August 1953

Tim Ward parked his black Morris Eight and walked into Doncaster railway station. He bought a penny platform ticket and passed through the barrier. He was early for the train and would have to wait for winger Arthur Kaye, who had been playing cricket at Aldershot. Players on National Service like Kaye only cost the club £1 a week plus a match fee, but they could cause the manager headaches over travel arrangements.

It was the eve of the season's first home match, and there was a chance that Kaye might not make it. Ward hoped that the cricket game had finished early enough for him to catch the train. Kaye, now 21, was a prodigy. Although only 5ft 4in, and not easy to spot in a station crowd, he was brave and tenacious. To full-backs he appeared as wide as he was tall and if they took the ball from him they were chased in outrage.

So far Barnsley had played three successive away games, an unusual opening caused by the season starting midweek; matches originally fixed for FA Cup final day had been brought forward to mid-August, the same week that Len Hutton's team recaptured the Ashes. Two draws and one defeat meant that Barnsley were romping the "games without a win" table in the *Daily Express*. It was now 26 games since their last win, but at Chester it was prevented only by a last-minute goal from Willy Windle, Chester's "wide-awake winger". Tim Ward was pleased with the start, particularly the pattern produced by his right-wing triangle: right-half Norman Smith, inside-right Tommy Lumley and outside-right Arthur Kaye. It was worth waiting for Kaye. Ward paced the platform, hands in pockets, his feet pointing inwards as he walked.

When the train arrived there was no Arthur Kaye. Tim Ward left the station and drove back to Barnsley. It gave him half an hour to think about his team for the match with Bradford Park Avenue. He arrived home after midnight and thought for a further hour before he had a plan. He would start early the next morning and try to re-sign Gavin Smith, hoping the Scot was still in town. Having made his decision and realising it was no use thinking longer, Ward fell asleep.

Supporters arriving for the next day's game had reason to be surprised. They found a threepenny reduction in admission charges in all parts of Oakwell: paddock (2/-), terrace (2/6), wing stand (3/6) and centre stand (5/-). They found that Arthur Kaye was absent. They noticed that Kaye's place was taken by Gavin Smith. Lastly the spectators saw a different style of play.

Here at Oakwell was the influence of push-and-run. It was epitomised by Ward's first-choice centre-half, George Spruce. He was so far removed from the classic robust stopper that Bob Shotton furnished him with especially large shin-pads when he was signed for £10,000 from Wrexham in 1952. His elegant legs thus appeared more fearsome and although certainly tough-tackling, Spruce would dribble along the edge of his own penalty area looking for a pass rather than use the "big boot". An immensely popular man, Spruce was a constructive centre-half.

Perhaps the biggest surprise for the faithful followers of recent Barnsley football was the result. Barnsley beat Bradford 2–1 to record their first win in 27 outings. Then they proceeded to win the next two games.

Monday 21st September 1953

Lap, lap, lap, lap, lap, lap, lap, lap, lap, lap, lap, lap, lap, lap, lap, lap … round and round Oakwell they went on stamina training. The pre-season walks had given way to lapping around the pitch. Soon they would have played enough games to carry their fitness through the season, but now they ran. And if a player wanted a hard morning he ran with Harry Hough, the first-team goalkeeper. Hough was a versatile athlete and as strong as an ox. He led the training and set the pace.

Trainer Bob Shotton either ran in the opposite direction to the players or he stood in the centre-circle watching them. He ensured that they ran in pairs, not groups, so stopping chatter and yet retaining competition. Inevitably there were some stragglers for Shotton to study as an amateur psychologist.

"Close up at the back, now," he shouted, "Come on, Tommy ... speed it up at the front."

Shotton, previously a player with Leeds, Hartlepools and mainly Barnsley, was used to making his own decisions. He had lost his parents when young, his father being killed at 42 in the pit. Shotton was a strict disciplinarian who set standards. He expected players to be ready for training by 10 am. If they were two minutes late then he sent them to the manager without sympathy. He was teetotal and a non-smoker, and he wanted his players to show the same self-control, which most of them did.

"Let's see you do the last lap in 60 seconds," he shouted as the players came past again, "Come on. Athletes can do it." His training methods emphasised lapping. This suited some players, who knew where they stood and felt the benefit in their Saturday games. Yet it annoyed others, who felt it was like painting the same wall twice.

"How many's this, twenty?" a player asked his running partner, "If I had a penny for every lap, I'd be able to retire." He was glad to reach the end.

"Somebody talked on that one," said Bob Shotton, "You can't run if you're talking ... do another lap, and no cutting corners."

It was this sort of routine that had resulted in a transfer request from Danny Blanchflower in 1951. The Irishman demanded more time with the ball, saying that practice made perfect. "Golfers practice with a golf ball," he told Angus Seed, who didn't always believe in this sort of training. Seed argued that players starved of the ball would be hungry for it on Saturdays.

Blanchflower left. The lapping continued. Tim Ward saw that lapping had its place, but he also wanted players to see the ball, and he admired Blanchflower's image at the club. With the weather warm and Oakwell perfect, Ward occasionally took players out on to the pitch. After the drawn home game with Crewe, Ward tried to reconstruct the opposition's goal, scored by Betts from 20 yards. He asked where Betts had struck the ball from and received four different answers. He asked where the ball had hit the post before going in, and again he received four differing responses. Ward now realised that part of his job was to keep a mental record of the game, to use his keen eye, his perspective and his good memory for small points. As a manager he must study harder, free from involvement and physical tiredness. His talent for detail was a hallmark of professionalism, but it sometimes led him to bring up a player's mistake long after the game, which could cause worry and resentment.

The players returned from their extra lap. Some looked like marathon runners, with legs like jelly. They could see the stand swimming, eight wobbly pillars, which on match days seemed designed to conceal as much of the goalmouths as possible. But they held up the roof and the triangular obtrusion which carried, in white letters, the reminder of where they were – Barnsley Football Club.

"I don't know, you'll never make footballers," said Bob Shotton to some of the late-comers.

Barnsley picked up 15 points from the first 12 games. Their September form met the traditional target for promotion – one point away and two points at home. This would have to be sustained because only the champions qualified for promotion.

Saturday 3rd October 1953

The Workington game looked comfortable and Barnsley built a two-goal lead. Joe Thomas had the ball on the edge of his own penalty area. The right-back moved forward a couple of paces and looked for the short pass that characterised the new Barnsley style.

"Get it up t'field," shouted a spectator, who was surprised to see no Syd Normanton, dropped from team after a win against Hartlepools. No explanation was apparent, just the feeling that the times were changing.

Thomas, seemingly frail at 10 stone, pushed the ball forward for Norman Smith and ran alongside for the return. When it came, Thomas played the ball hurriedly towards Tommy Lumley, the next step in the move. Thomas was on one leg when Workington wing-half Joe Johnson collided with him. Bob Shotton and Tim Ward suddenly saw Thomas flying across the track towards their trainer's box. They jumped to cushion the impact but Thomas connected with the solid concrete structure. Spectators in the centre stand stood up. Spectators on the terrace craned forward. Shotton started to separate the red cinders from splashes of blood. "Gravel rash," they called it on the terrace. Thomas had split the back of his head and his knee. Badly shaken, he was carried to the dressing-room. His team-mates followed him a minute later, since it was then half-time.

Joe Thomas thought his leg was broken, but Shotton and physiotherapist Fred Semley were more concerned about his head. They ruled Thomas out of the rest of the game and Fred Semley drove him to Beckett Hospital for precautionary X-rays while supporters were left to shout "Come on the ten men" as Barnsley continued to a 4–2 win.

Fred Semley had a car and knew the town well. He had been appointed in 1948 after his father had treated players as private patients. In that year, first-team trainer Tom Wilson had died suddenly and Bob Shotton had been left with a large playing staff. Since then, Semley had been at Barnsley's beck and call, perhaps being telephoned at midnight when players returned from an away game. His job involved answering two major questions: what was wrong with a player and how soon could he be fit?

In Joe Thomas' case there was no serious injury and a week's treatment meant that he was passed fit for the following Saturday, when the promotion battle resumed. Two things caused concern – Port Vale's cast-iron defence and Barnsley's inability to win away. It was 21 games since an away win and they needed one in the next game – at Halifax on 10th October – if they were to recover lost ground that put them in third place.

1	Port Vale	14 – 23
2	Crewe	14 – 18
3	Barnsley	13 – 17

Halifax Town included a new signing for their match with Barnsley. Ironically the player had just completed a month's trial with Barnsley Reserves. He was the Reverend Norman Hallam. A Methodist minister who played football professionally was a unique combination, and there were various problems to this double life. One in particular was being away on a Saturday, the day he was most in demand for weddings and funerals.

Hallam had recently moved from the Potteries to Rossington, near Doncaster, where he was given two churches that formed part of the Coalfield Mission. It was an important challenge but, with several happy seasons at Port Vale behind him, he felt impelled to continue his football career.

Saturday 10th October 1953

It was 15 minutes before kick-off at the Shay. Tim Ward walked outside to distribute some complimentary tickets and saw Gerry Henry, the Halifax manager, pacing up and down like an expectant father.

"What's the matter, Gerry?" asked Ward.

"It's the ball, Tim. They bring it from the Co-op already blown up, and we owe them so much money that they might not send it this week."

Tim Ward joined him, walking up and down. A few more minutes passed, then a boy on a bicycle weaved towards them, balancing a football on the handlebars.

"Where've you been?" asked Henry, taking the ball quickly.

"Sorry, I got caught in the traffic."

A crowd of 8,000 was gathering. It was like the scene captured by Lowry in his painting "Going to the Match", which had recently been successful in an FA sponsored competition. The two managers walked back and barely had time for their customary few words before the teams lined up.

John Savage, the 6ft 2in Halifax goalkeeper, dominated his penalty area and dwarfed opposing forwards. The directors' box was littered with representatives from other clubs watching him. A sale seemed close and footballs would arrive more readily – for a time.

Savage put on a show, saving shot after shot as Barnsley got on top. He looked unbeatable, then Priestley made a goal for Murphy and Halifax were in the lead; but after 87 minutes Savage had no chance when Chappell equalised. The match went into injury time with referee Gerrard from Preston checking his watch. Gerry Henry rose from his position near the touch-line and picked up the bucket of water that accompanied trainer Alan Ure's magic sponge.

"That's it now," said Henry, throwing the water over the edge of the pitch. He turned to the bench and added, "I'll get a bomb for this goalie."

As Gerry Henry turned to face the pitch, Gavin Smith burst through and shot. Savage moved to save but this time it was too much for him. He could only parry, knocking the ball clumsily into the air. Tommy Lumley, who had only come to stretch his legs, scored with ease. There was hardly time to kick off again.

Gerry Henry was furious. He threw the bucket onto the field and kicked it up and down the touch-line. His team had lost and the value of a star player might have fallen by important pounds. For Barnsley it was their first away win in 22 attempts.

Bill Capel-Kirby, a sports reporter on the *Empire News*, was checking his pools coupon that Saturday evening. He had seven draws. Only one game had let him down. He knew one of the managers involved and decided to telephone him.

"Oh, hello Bill, what have I done now?"

You were my eighth draw and you go and win away."

"Yes, we got the winner in injury time."

"Oh no, not injury time," groaned the reporter.

On the following Monday afternoon the first team set off for Scotland. When Johnny Kelly signed for Falkirk in the summer, Barnsley had agreed to play a midweek friendly under the Falkirk floodlights, their first appearance in these conditions. Lights were banned at League matches though several English and Scottish grounds possessed them. They were considered a gimmick by some, too expensive by most, and suffered from continual teething troubles; 40 bulbs, each of a thousand watts, installed 30 feet above the pitch was the norm, some types fixed on pylons and others hauled up by rope and pulley for the game. All the systems were low enough and bright enough to dazzle players regularly.

Doncaster had fixed floodlights to the grandstands, and they were especially low to avoid distracting pilots approaching the nearby airfield. Undeterred, Doncaster Rovers staged friendlies and took the field wearing fluorescent orange shirts. They flashed around like Belisha beacons. The grass had never looked greener – except at the edges of the penalty areas which were lost in deep shadow. There were other subtle differences and the increased amount of oxygen in the night air was said to help some players' stamina. Everyone had to adapt.

Tim Ward asked his captain Norman Smith if he had ever played under floodlights. "Yes, Boss," replied Smith, "At Arsenal. And if I win the toss tomorrow night I'll play with the moon at our backs."

At Brockville Park, Falkirk, Barnsley conceded an early goal but adapted well. "They're coming through like Indians," said a bemused Falkirk defender as Lumley, Brown and Chappell exploited weaknesses. The result was a 3–1 win for Barnsley and a hat trick for Larratt Chappell. This earned Chappell the match ball, which had to be periodically dipped in whitening during the game.

"We should be able to get a few more of these matches," said Tim Ward after the game. The first-team players were pleased and optimistic. Ward, a top-class player in his day, was now seen as a go-ahead young manager, introducing a modern style of play, organising a floodlit match and other friendlies to replace training. The club was working more closely with the Supporters' Club and there were small alterations to the Barnsley kit. The socks had been changed to all-red and there was talk of badges on the red shirts.

The facilities at Barnsley seemed fine when compared with those of some opponents. The next away trip was to Accrington on 24th October and the players were brought face to face with the full horror of the late Angus Seed's words. "You'll be up the slope at Accrington," he had said, when relegation was just a threat. Now the reality started – two dressing-rooms with just a thin partition in between. There was a narrow pitch, at the side of which stood a form for the manager and trainer to sit on. On this occasion they watched players tumble around on a greasy surface. Even the normally mild-mannered Tim Ward became upset at some of the tackling as Barnsley lost 3–0.

For Ward, Norman Smith and Tommy Lumley, it was the first exposure to such grim facilities. When Smith arrived from Arsenal with his card tricks and general dexterity, he had at first been branded as a "fly boy". In time his personality won over both players and town, and he had become captain soon after his arrival, albeit by a haphazard procedure; Bob Shotton had simply arrived in the dressing-room, picked up the ball and asked for suggestions. Tommy Lumley had spoken up for Smith who had proved very suitable.

One break in the Third Division (North) routine came with the FA Cup draw. After beating York City 5–2 in the regionally-drawn first round, Barnsley were paired away to Norwich City, which offered a chance of gauging the strength of the Third Division (South). John Uprichard of the *Sheffield Star* wrote that the southern section on the whole provided more "footballing" sides as opposed to some of the "bootballing" sides of the northern section, and yet Barnsley were becoming a northern exception. "Keep playing good football," Ward told them, "the results will come."

All clubs hoped for a passage through to the third round, when the top two divisions would enter the tournament. Large attendances were important, even away, because FA Cup receipts were shared equally between the two teams and the FA Cup pool, which was split among clubs at the season's end. This was a different cash allocation from League games, where the home team took 80% after deductions had been made for expenses and entertainment tax. So the FA Cup meant something special and this was evident right from the start.

A Forest of Players

Chapter Two

Friday llth December 1954

At 2 pm the Yorkshire Traction bus headed out of Barnsley. It was bound for Norwich. The journey was 168 miles and driver Joe Thorpe knew it well from pre-war Midland League days when Norwich Reserves played Barnsley at the Nest. Thorpe had seen the Barnsley team showing the FA Cup outside the Clarence Hotel in 1912 and he had been driving them since 1927. He used this experience to calculate travel time, based on an average speed of 25 miles per hour and an hour for each meal. He often suggested the hotel when he consulted with secretary Raymond Vicary two days before an away game. Today, Thorpe had arrived typically early at Oakwell and he had helped Bob Shotton check the contents of the skip. Shotton took a spare set of all kit and he had a check-list for the medical case, which even included whisky in case of serious injuries. The whisky was stored in one of two lead lotion bottles – to stop players daring to guess.

The bus was a Leyland Tiger, known as a "Duck" for its resemblance to wartime landing craft. Its registration was DHE 561, and the club always chartered the same bus, which had card tables inserted at the start of the season. Joe Thorpe was always cheerful and helpful, an all-round asset to the club. He drove the bus with a temperament that guaranteed security. "Joe will get us back safely," players would comment, whatever the weather, and several times he had brought them back through treacherous conditions despite permission to stay overnight.

The "Duck" was driven through dusk and into the East Anglian dark. That didn't worry Joe Thorpe, who had driven the team during the war when milestones were buried in ditches, signposts were taken out or turned round – to confuse enemy paratroopers – and lights were not allowed to extend more than 22 feet in the blackout. Thorpe drove over Sutton Bridge and pointed out its crazy sign: "Please dip headlights because of passing ships." He stopped the bus for tea at a transport cafe near King's Lynn and then started on the last leg to Norwich.

Henry Walters sat at the front of the bus. Walters had always been a bad traveller. As a boy he was lucky if he completed the bus journey from Brampton to Oakwell without feeling sick. He had travelled a lot, both while working in London during the war and in the Third Division (South) days with Walsall, but he was still careful to simply watch the scenery and talk to the driver. Thorpe drove steadily, knowing that some players travelled badly. Ted Robledo had been his worst passenger, but not as bad as one player with another club who travelled a day in advance to allow time to recover.

Joe Thorpe drove into the narrow streets of Swaffham, where a large department store stood watch over a tight town centre. Thorpe wrestled with the steering-wheel of the big and clumsy "Duck" and swung the bus round, always in complete control although one or two players shut their eyes.

"'Aberdashery please, Joe," said Henry Walters from the front.

Joe Thorpe had never had an accident. His team bus had arrived late just once, in unavoidable circumstances at Bury. One of his worst moments had come earlier in the present season on the Darlington expedition. The main entrance to Feethams was via the adjoining cricket ground, a sharp turn from a narrow street. Most drivers left the bus outside and the skip was wheeled on a trolley, but Joe Thorpe drove in. Some players shouted from the back. They thought he wouldn't get out and they were nearly right. After the game Thorpe had to shunt up and down for half an hour, inch by inch, as spectators watched the cricket game. Despite his great admiration for Joe Thorpe's abilities, *Barnsley Chronicle* sports editor Benny Hill couldn't see how the coach was going to get out. "We 'll have to take the wall down," he remarked to John Uprichard of the *Sheffield Star.* The reserve, Maurice Jackson, was asked to get out and shout instructions, but after a while he gave up and sat down to watch the cricket, thinking he'd be there till stumps were drawn. Thorpe got the "Duck" out in the end, but not without a cracked mirror and slight damage to the rear of the bus. It was a testimony of Joe Thorpe's high reputation that this relatively minor incident became part of the folklore of Barnsley away trips. If ever someone wanted to upset him after that he just whispered "Darlington".

They reached the Royal Hotel, Norwich, at about 9 pm. It was only the second overnight trip of the season. The previous week, for the game at Barrow, they had stayed at Milnthorpe. The hotel was on a hill, at a busy crossroads with traffic lights. Lorries hauled themselves up the slope all night, gears grinding, brakes squealing. Clubs usually passed on such information about hotels and Raymond Vicary had made arrangements for players to have quiet rooms at the back.

"Have we got time for the pictures, Boss?" asked a player, tongue-in-cheek as he stepped from the bus at Norwich, "I hope we can find something as good as last week."

The other players laughed. They had enjoyed themselves at a flea-pit in Milnthorpe, trying not to trip over the balcony – which was one step higher than the stalls – and then sitting on benches. The screen was a white sheet and the film was the 1938 version of "Robin Hood". *Barnsley Chronicle* reporter Alan Ridgill linked the film and the match for his report. Barnsley had played like Robin Hood and his merry men, fighting off the foe against all odds and then stealing the winner through "marksman" Bobby Brown.

These overnight trips gave the players a prolonged time together. They could share conversation, entertainment, meals and the company of the manager and trainer. Some of them, such as Henry Walters and Joe Thomas, had taken Friday off work, which meant a substantial drop in wages. The weekly bonus in the mines was paid on a "six for five" basis. If you worked all five shifts you received six days' pay. Missing one shift therefore meant that you lost a third of your normal wage packet. There was certainly a conflict of interests, with both Tim Ward and the NUM president Sir William Lowther calling for more effort and support.

The players went to bed early and knew what to expect the following day: a morning walk, a light lunch such as boiled fish or poached eggs, and no smoking afterwards. They were not sure, however, exactly what to expect from playing a Third Division (South) team in the second round of the FA Cup.

There was no happy ending to the overnight stay. Despite a half-time lead, again through Bobby Brown, Barnsley lost 2–1 at Norwich, watched by a 20,655 crowd. It left the players "concentrating on the League". The time was right. The next match was at home to leaders Port Vale, who had conceded only eight goals. Remember, only one went up.

1	Port Vale	22 – 37
2	Gateshead	22 – 29
3	Bradford City	21 – 28
4	Barnsley	21 – 27
5	Stockport	22 – 26

The day that Barnsley lost 1–0 to Port Vale was 19th December, a frosty, wintry Saturday. Week after week Barnsley fielded four teams and this Saturday was no exception. (In 1949–50 they had even fielded a fifth side, the B team, in the Hatchard League.) The true fanatic followed the club and not just the first team. An example was Saturday Sam, whom the players named after a cartoon character in the *Weekly News.*

Saturday Sam was small and stocky, with horn-rimmed spectacles, flat cap and mucky raincoat. He carried Barnsley favours – red and white rosette, rattle and scarf – and the players debated whether he wore them in bed. He was the salt of the football earth, never asking for a ticket but travelling everywhere –

from Hartlepools to Plymouth to the Queen's Ground, Barnsley's nearby training pitch.

John Steele's Juniors played at 11 am, and the A team at 2 pm. Both teams used the old dressing-rooms at the corner of Oakwell when at home, trotting across to the Queen's Ground in twos and threes, threading their way through the crowd approaching Oakwell.

It was the Reserves who lived in luxury, even compared to the first team. The Reserves played mainly on First Division grounds. On 19th December they won at Blackpool, who were sixth in the Central League; Doug Kelly and Malcolm Graham scored against Scottish-international goalkeeper George Farm.

The Central League standard was high, and internationals occasionally turned out even in the Yorkshire League, starting back after injury. Any player could find himself in the A team. Take Ron Smillie, for instance. Late in October he was in the first team. On 19th December he was in the A team.

Smillie was a winger, and since the start of the season Tim Ward had signed four wingers. Two of these played on the right: Gavin Smith and Ron Riches, the only member of the 1950 Barnsley Boys team not to sign immediately for Barnsley. The other two played on the left: part-timer Les Stone and experienced Billy Wardle, whom Ward had bought for £1,000 from Birmingham City. In addition, Ward was making regular telephone calls to ensure the release of Arthur Kaye at week-ends, and he had tried both Bartlett and Pattison on the first-team left wing.

In all Barnsley had 42 professional and 40 amateurs signed on forms, and even allowing for players absent in the Forces or out through injury, each week there were some who had to stand down. The lower teams were unstable. Their composition varied and any youngster starting with Barnsley saw a forest of players between him and the first team. On 19th December the four teams looked like this:

First team: *Hough; Thomas, May; Smith (Norman), Spruce, Jackson; Kaye, Lumley, Chappell, Brown (Bobby), Bartlett.*

Reserves: *Walls; Betts, Hudson; Wood (Bob), Sharp, Dougall; Riches, Wood (Joe), Kelly, Graham, Stone.*

A team: *Leeson; Poole, Rowe (Arthur); Brown (Ted), McCullough, Archer (Trevor); Smillie, Lees, John, Gill, Gray.*

Juniors: *Guest; Summerfield, Rowe (Arthur); Handley, Hopkins, Barber; White, Rowe (Arthur), Breeze, Edgar, Markwell.*

With Ward's pattern modelled on Arthur Rowe's push-and-run Tottenham Hotspur team, it was perhaps not surprising to find Arthur Rowe named three times. In fact there were only two of them at Barnsley; one Arthur Rowe, a blacksmith's striker from Smithies, played twice because the A team left-back failed to show up. The other Arthur Rowe, known as "Chippie", was the son of the proprietor of Arthur Rowe's Buses, a firm from Cudworth.

With Barnsley's big staff there was a good chance of repeated surnames:

Smith, Brown, Wood, Archer and Rowe. Unlike registered racehorses, footballers enjoyed confusion unless they were called Ugolini, Delapenha, Quairney or Quested. In some cases, such as Arthur Rowe, the Christian names did not help. Gateshead had two players called Ken Smith so they called them Ken Smith no. 1 and Ken Smith no. 2. Later they found the ultimate solution by transferring one. Most people never knew which.

Barnsley had three players called Smith: captain Norman, winger Gavin and a mammoth centre-half from Liverpool called Brian, recommended by a director at a time when Tim Ward was willing to try out such recommendations. Brian Smith played few games for Barnsley. He was one who sat it out on this day.

Trevor and Ron Archer were no relation. Trevor Archer played left-half for Barnsley Boys in 1950, the year after Ron Archer had occupied the same position. Trevor had won schoolboy medals engraved with the name of his predecessor.

The high number of local players meant they kept their nicknames from school or even earlier: "Cabby" Swift, "Skinner" Normanton, "Chippie" Rowe, "Chuckie" Jackson and "Tich" Edgar. But that did not prevent some new names. Scots were usually "Jock" or "Haggis", Bobby Wood became "Stickie" for obvious reasons while Larratt Chappell had become "Lol" because reporters John Uprichard and Benny Hill decided that "Larratt" was no good as a headline. John Thomas had always been called "Joe" because Eddie Fleetwood heard his name wrongly before introducing him round.

Reciting four teams does not fully indicate the depth of Barnsley's playing staff. There were absentees due to injury, illness or the forces – Walters, Wardle, Normanton, Holmes, Anderson, Gavin Smith, Pattison, Jarman, Ron Archer, Roscoe, Swift, Gillott, Sidebottom – while amateur Jackie Pearson was playing for Oxford University against Cambridge University. It took all these players to constitute Barnsley FC on 19th December 1953.

The defeat by Port Vale looked like the end of the road to promotion, but 13 points from their next eight games started them thinking again. Both Bobby Brown and Lol Chappell scored eight goals in this successful period, but Tommy Lumley hadn't scored for four months, not since his late winner against Halifax. Port Vale, meanwhile, were dropping points and were liable to a fixture pile-up since they were still in the FA Cup. In the fourth round, while Norwich were winning 2–1 at Arsenal, Port Vale won at First Division Cardiff City.

1	Port Vale	28 – 44
2	Gateshead	31 – 40
3	Barnsley	30 – 40
4	Bradford City	30 – 36

On 20th February Port Vale won their fifth round FA Cup tie with holders Blackpool. But on the same day Barnsley lost at Bill Shankly's revived Workington Town. The following week Tommy Lumley returned to the scoresheet against Halifax. Ironically, Halifax won the game 2–1. This time they were without Jack Savage, who had been transferred to Manchester City.

Wednesday 17th March 1954

Harry Hough and Bobby Brown walked up the fairway while Norman Smith stood studiously on the tee. The weather was wet and the ground slightly muddy, almost too bad for golf. Smith took a long time to hit the ball, adjusting his balance before planting it straight down the fairway.

Three more wins, six more points, ten more goals and Bob Shotton, often superstitious about training, was happy to keep the players golfing one day a week. Walking was good exercise. At one point in Barnsley's history, director Horace Pickering had suggested that the players take long walks, noticing the way greyhound owners trained their dogs at Worsbrough Bridge. The walks led to a successful run so they stayed for a time. Likewise the golf.

For some younger players, such as Joe Thomas and Arthur Kaye, it was a question of learning golf or carrying somebody's clubs, but this foursome was more experienced. Harry May now took the tee. In the last Players' Union tournament May had returned a score of 101, an unusually high score for him, and his colleagues had not missed the chance to spread two football shirts over his place in the dressing-room before the next match. The no. 10 next to the no. 11, with the last digit covered, reproduced his score.

One of May's problems was that he was left-handed, so he had a mish-mash of clubs, a mashie missing and without a wood, their grips not very good. His improvisation with these clubs led to his drives taking a left detour halfway down the fairway. May compensated for this so cleverly that an entertainer once asked if he could learn the trick.

Harry May swung his club at the ball and then walked purposefully towards the clump of rushes. Norman Smith turned round and saw May scrambling. "Are you looking for your ball, Harry?" asked Smith.

"No, I'm looking for my club," replied May. The others fell about laughing even though it was a muddy day.

For 11 first-team players football was now fun. They could face the Barnsley public with their heads high. The previous season they were tempting fate to step into a coffee-bar because the late Angus Seed often suffered supporters' complaints. "That's why you get no results," he was told, "They're in Woolworth's when they should be training."

The players were ambassadors for the club and for various charities. They presented prizes, gave talks and displays, all free of charge. They met supporters to play snooker and table-tennis. They opened fetes, bazaars and garden parties (never knowing the difference), and they judged beauty queens and fancy dress. Tim Ward also attended such functions and he gave speeches at dinners. Bob Shotton held courses for local trainers.

Norman Smith and Harry May were well suited to entertaining people off the field. Angus Seed had once told May that he had only signed him to perform at the piano, and on away trips players found him one where they could. Places like the Greyhound on the East Lancashire Road always had a piano and drums in one corner, with a cloth tossed over them. Harry May would bring the keyboard to life, perhaps playing "It's Magic" while Norman Smith performed some tricks – cutting a rope or a pound note in half, then restoring it. An act where Smith once played second fiddle was the bending of 8 inch nails. He had gone up on stage with Tommy Lumley to assist strong-woman Joan Rhodes. Neither man could make any impression on the nails, whereas Miss Rhodes just placed a handkerchief on one and bent it with no apparent effort.

Norman Smith proved his worth on the drums at the Athersley Arms one night. He criticised the professional percussionist, who responded as any entertainer might, by saying that he doubted whether Smith could do any better. Smith promptly took over the sticks.

Comments from the crowd could be hurtful to a footballer whether they were true or not. Players at some clubs scoured the town to find a terrace wag at his own work so that they could stand there shouting "put your back into it", "go on, shift some earth", or "I could dig a hole quicker with an ice-cream spoon".

Tim Ward's first-choice team was altered only once in 12 matches, when Duncan Sharp deputised for the injured Spruce at Hartlepools. It gave the team a chance to form friendships away from the pitch. Arthur Kaye and Lol Chappell began to bear the brunt of each other's jokes. Bobby Brown and Harry May were regular companions, such that players sometimes ragged them "Mr and Mrs Brown" when they walked by them on the coach, perhaps heading for Harry Hough's card school – brag, poker, short pontoon.

Six of them were over 28, independent people who had seen war service. In fact Ward had known Billy Wardle when they played together for the British Army of the Rhine. Ward, at 36, had little seniority except for his position as "Boss". The manager mixed almost as an equal with wing-halves Walters and Smith and revelled in their wit. After the game at York, for instance, a young press agency reporter entered the dressing-room to ask who scored the game's only two goals. Henry Walters chipped in with "Harry Hough" instead of "Lol Chappell". For weeks goalkeeper Hough cropped up in away programmes with two goals to his credit and spectators would scratch their heads, wondering if he'd been injured and scored twice from the wing.

Such company helped Ward put his early difficulties at Barnsley behind him. On a personal level he no longer had the strain of playing every week and he had settled into the town and its activities, particularly Stainborough Cricket Club. As manager his first season was proving a good one, and his style and changes were on the whole accepted.

Although lapping was still the basis of Bob Shotton's training methods, there were now regular five-a-side games. Changes were encouraged by the hammerings suffered by the national team against Hungary. When players were given access to balls during the week, they started taking them everywhere and it became a joke that people could hear the sound of footballs pounding against the doors of the lavatories – with the players sitting inside. The style on the field became more adventurous, particularly at full-back, forcing Bob Shotton to shout for them to stay in their own half.

Tim Ward was determined that Barnsley should "play" their way out of the northern section. This season there was still just a chance. April was now beginning, and while Barnsley had nine games to play, the leaders Port Vale had to face the consequences of their marvellous FA Cup run, which had been halted just short of the final by West Brom.

1	Port Vale	34 – 53
2	Barnsley	37 – 50
3	Bradford City	37 – 48
4	Gateshead	37 – 46

Monday 29th March 1954

"I don't know why you take that lot, Raymond," said Tim Ward, sitting in his office chair, watching the secretary incredulously.

Raymond Vicary peered over the top of the bundle he was carrying.

"Someone might want to know something," he said, moving into the corridor. He walked to his car and opened the door with difficulty, dumping this new pile of papers with the rest. There were minutes of Barnsley meetings, books on company law, Football League handbooks, newspaper cuttings, rough notes, scouting reports, letters … if a director had once mentioned it then Vicary took it forevermore.

Raymond Vicary got into his car. There was an incident some years ago when it started but would not pull away, mainly because all the wheels had been removed and the axles supported with bricks. This time the car moved. "Dear God" Raymond Vicary thought to himself, "Let me not have undone the things I should have done." Tonight was the weekly board meeting.

In the Royal Hotel, Vicary staggered up three flights of stairs with his papers. Often he made two journeys. A small, bespectacled perfectionist, Vicary had never lost the image of office-boy, his position when he joined the club in 1930. He was meticulous, efficient and exceedingly hard-working, but his subservience was sometimes a fault. He would blame himself for everything. If it were foggy outside then Raymond Vicary considered it his responsibility.

After preliminary greetings, Joe Richards called the meeting to order. Ten people were present in the room – eight directors, manager and secretary. They looked at their agendas and the minutes of the previous meeting, which had been circulated in advance.

"Before we start, Mr Chairman," said Horace Pickering, diamond tie-pin catching the light as he shifted his small frame in the seat, "Could we make sure our envelopes are addressed correctly for the next meeting? My OBE was left off this week." Pickering, a director for nine years, had been honoured for his services as secretary of the Barnsley and District Co-operative Society. He was now retired and people often made the mistake with his letters. Within the football fraternity, honours and qualifications were rare, although recent exploits of right-back Joe Thomas led to jokes of permanently adding O.G. after his name.

"I'm sorry, Mr Chairman, I must have overlooked it," said Raymond Vicary meekly, without knowing who was to blame. He scrambled through his papers to make a note. The Barnsley secretary sat at a corner of the large table, keeping a separate, smaller table for his papers. Vicary was left-hand man to Joe Richards, who sat at the head.

The full composition of the board was nine, but it was depleted by the death in January of Richard Soper; the board had not used its power to temporarily co-opt another member. There was some casual discussion as to who should fill the vacancy. Names were mentioned and Joe Richards might make a comment such as "he's got no wool on his back". Not that money was the only important factor in becoming a director. There was an overdraft in five figures, and the board stood guarantee for it, but Joe Richards was the only one who went to the bank. As far as they were concerned, his standing in the town carried a lot of weight.

During the 1953–54 financial year some money had come in from the instalment arrangements of the Second Division transfers. With Ward's purchases amounting to a modest £6,306, the club could absorb the season's operating loss (about £10,000) and emerge with a profit of around £5,000. The overdraft usually reached its peak during the summer, when there were no gate receipts, but at least this year it was pegged back a little. However, the transfer revenue from the coming close season might be less than usual. Tim Ward wanted to keep his players.

Joe Richards was the dominant voice in financial matters, though other members of the board were Barnsley businessmen of various ages and experience. Former chairman George Tomlinson was beginning to take a back seat, but he could remember the 1912 FA Cup final, as could his fellow directors Horace Pickering and Billy Diggle, who were in their seventies. Pickering had been following the club since 1897, while Diggle still made a point of standing out in all weathers to watch the Juniors and the A team. A former pit deputy, grey-haired and retiring, Billy Diggle could occasionally become quite passionate about his two great loves, football and the church – a recitation on Glendinning, Bratley and Utley, or a recital on the organ.

Roy Lax was still in his fifties, yet he too could remember Barnsley's FA Cup win. He was at the Bramall Lane replay, standing on three Fry's chocolate crates, his arms held by fellow supporters. But Ernest Dennis and Arthur Raynor were too young to have seen that match.

They had both joined the board recently, after service with the supporters' Club. Raynor was soon considered a good director by players, because he took six dozen packets of chewing-gum to Oakwell every fortnight and carried a two pound bag of sweets for the return journey from away games. But the majority of the directors' work occurred behind closed doors, during quiet Oakwell afternoons or in the Royal Hotel.

The directors represented continuity for the club. Players and managers would come and go, but the experience of the directors was matched only by the most stalwart and informed supporters. Few of the public would recognise the state of the club and the reasons for sometimes difficult decisions taken in the Royal Hotel. Satisfying the shareholders and the supporters was a constant dilemma that was normally only aired in public once a year – at the AGM in August.

There was a month of the season to run. Barnsley might start next season in the Third or Second Division. This made a difference to finances and planning. The directors could only guess about future attendances, injuries and incidental ground necessities.

It was a hand-to-mouth existence, moving from month to month cautiously. The directors believed in balancing the books. No point, however small, would be overlooked.

"And what did we do last year?" asked one director. Raymond Vicary shuffled his papers and answered in detail.

"And the year before?"

Again the secretary shuffled. Again he answered in detail. Vicary was capable of filling a room with papers as fast as questions were fired. If he was defeated by a question, he would drop his head and appear very glum. "I'll bring it round to you tomorrow, Mr Chairman, I must have left it at the ground," he would say, but only very occasionally.

Tim Ward maintained the policy of picking his best 11 players and tried not to change the side unless absolutely necessary. He was aware that there were other players in the Reserves who thought they'd had a future under Angus Seed. As time went by some muttered that it would take double pneumonia and a broken leg before they got their chance. Others claimed that Ward would rather make six positional changes than drop one first teamer. As evidence they pointed to Henry Walters, who had played in three defensive positions before becoming established at left-half.

At right-half was Norman Smith, but only until 31st March, when the biggest Oakwell crowd of the season – 12,863 – gathered for the match against Gateshead. After 55 minutes Smith overbalanced in a tackle near the edge of the pitch. He tumbled across the cinders and smashed against the boundary wall. Despite breaking both his shoulder and collar bone, he returned to the pitch two minutes later, with his arm held loosely to his side. "I thought you played better after you got hurt," said one player after the 2–0 defeat, "You got shot of the ball quicker." Smith smiled cheerfully before going for the X-rays that finished his season. The Oakwell pitch was narrowed slightly to prevent other such injuries, despite an earlier FA ruling asking clubs to widen pitches.

The right-half spot went to Ron Archer, who many considered the outstanding prospect in the club. But after his third game back – a 6-0 walloping at Scunthorpe on Good Friday – Archer was dropped. With the "resting" of Harry May, left-back Morris Hudson was introduced for two Easter matches. In the second of these, the return against Scunthorpe, Barnsley were awarded a penalty in the 50th minute, a chance to draw level at 1–1. The penalty was taken by Hudson, who had scored seven this season for the Reserves. He shot wide and the game was lost. Bob Shotton reassured him afterwards, saying, "You had a fine game," but Hudson was dropped. When Hudson asked Tim Ward for the reason, he was told he should know. "Surely a player could not be dropped for missing a penalty," Hudson thought to himself. If so, Barnsley would find themselves a bit short of players. They had missed six of their eight penalties – all awarded at home. However, Tim Ward was unhappy with Morris Hudson's overall play, although he did not say so. Such small confusions might quickly accumulate in a player's mind to form frustration and resentment.

There were others who had played in the first team but had never had an extended opportunity – Walls, Betts, Jackson, Sharp, Kelly and Smillie. These players had all cost nothing. Of Tim Ward's first team, only Hough, Chappell and Kaye had not been bought. Yet the results encouraged a settled side. Had two clubs been promoted it would have been an exciting finish.

1	Port Vale	44					67
2	Scunthorpe	46	21	15	10	77–56	57
3	Barnsley	45	24	9	12	76–56	57
4	Gateshead	45					54

Wednesday 28th April 1954

Five crucial minutes of Barnsley's season remained. They were playing at Wrexham and losing 1–0. The prize for an equaliser was extra talent money – £220 for second place instead of £165 for third. The Football League instructed clubs to pay talent money on the basis of the players' appearances. The money meant a lot to the players.

Then came a right wing move. Joe Thomas passed to Arthur Kaye, who ran in and out of players until he had covered 40 yards. Kaye passed to Tommy Lumley who helped it through to Lol Chappell. The centre-forward was still running hard at the season's close. He took the ball through and shot past goalkeeper Egglestone for his 22nd goal of the season, second only to 24 from Brown. The Barnsley players congratulated Chappell. If they could hang on it could mean as much as £5 for Bobby Brown, Joe Thomas and Harry Hough, who were ever-present. They did so. The game finished 1–1.

It was a bunch of happy Barnsley players who gathered in the dressing-room. Tim Ward and the directors were also pleased. Ward remembered his conversation with director Ernest Dennis, who had been unable to travel to Wrexham but had arranged for Ward to buy the players a round of drinks, whatever the result. This was the limit of director generosity. Joseph Richards followed Football League rules closely. His club were known for not making illegal payments of any kind.

The season was over. Only the FA Cup final remained and a few of the Barnsley lads would go to Wembley on tickets provided by Jimmy Baxter, scorer of Preston's second goal in the semi-final win against Sheffield Wednesday.

The summer was easier for the staff but not easy. The players were absent – perhaps on building sites, in jobs found by directors or just resting. Some of them might have gone to Odsal Stadium, Bradford, where 102,569 watched Warrington play Halifax at rugby league on 5th May. At Oakwell, work on the ground was crucial. The "brewery stand" was being extended, the crush barriers were painted and Bob Shotton took stock of equipment. All participated in the slowest job – re-seeding the pitch. For the first time in the club's history there were no new signings from other clubs, although seven players left, five of them on free transfers.

On Thursday 5th August the club's Annual General Meeting took place at the Royal Hotel. There were five nominations for four places on the board, with a record – and almost complete – attendance of 173 shareholders. Each director served a three-year term of office and on this occasion it was the turn of Joe Richards, John Hirst and Ernest Dennis to offer themselves for re-election. The other two nominations were former club captain Gordon Pallister and Ralph Potter, a local builder. The voting produced a surprise:

Richards	99
Hirst	80
Potter	75
Pallister	68
Dennis	66

The exclusion of Ernest Dennis in favour of Ralph Potter was mildly ironic. The Supporters' Club, first formed in 1927, had been re-established in 1947 with Dennis as chairman. In the halcyon days of Baxter, Kelly and Robledo, membership rose steadily, reaching a peak of 3,000 almost overnight when the 1949 FA Cup draw paired Barnsley with Blackpool, and tickets were as rare as nylon stockings.

In 1951 Dennis was elected to the board, followed in 1953 by Arthur Raynor, who had in the meantime been Supporters' Club chairman. Now Ralph Potter, the current secretary of the Supporters' Club, was also elected, having been encouraged to stand by Ernest Dennis.

Ralph Potter would be able to take his seat on the board straight away whereas Gordon Pallister had to wait. As a former player he would have to receive clearance from the FA. Three ex-professionals were already board members – Stan Seymour (Newcastle), Tommy Glidden (West Bromwich) and George Edwards (Cardiff). Pallister also had to bring his shares up to the total of 50 needed to serve on the board. The extra shares were made available.

The extensions to the "brewery stand" were completed. The Supporters' Club provided £5,000 of the £6,000 cost, largely from donations. The first team met the Reserves in the public practice match, which was called Reds v Blues, although the Reserves wore white, as that was the only shirt colour available; 2,000 spectators saw Tommy Lumley score the only goal. Games against other League clubs were officially banned though they often took place in secret. Occasionally clubs were reported to the League.

It was an astonishing fact that the public practice match, a week before the beginning of the season, was the only time in the whole year that all the players came together. As such it was the sole opportunity for a general team talk and the full club photograph. Photographs of specific teams could be taken throughout the season with a bench hastily assembled for the five in the foreground – easy fodder for the traditional joke: "I see our forwards are on form today." If the *Barnsley Chronicle* took a team photograph during the season they would provide enough copies for each team member to have one, but it was a different matter with action shots, when more players might be involved than copies available.

Many Match-day Functions

Chapter Three

Tuesday 24th August 1954

A whistle went. "Stay where you are," called Tim Ward. Not all the players heard him, but the Queen's Ground evening practice match halted. "Right, Ted," continued Ward, "If you get the ball now what are you going to do?"

"Give it to Trevor," said Ted Brown, ready for the question though the ball was far away. Brown believed a wing-half both won the ball and gave it to a red shirt. Ward liked this quality and gave Brown special attention.

"Have you tried it this way, son?" asked John Steele of another young player, while demonstrating the use of the left foot. It was Steele who, along with Eddie Fleetwood, ran these Tuesday and Thursday evening training sessions for the part-time players and the amateurs. Steele moved with a top-heavy, well-balanced style, as though he had a weight on his shoulders, although in fact the job came very easily. He enjoyed being with the young lads and worked long hours.

The practice match restarted. It was near the end of the training session and the game was a reward for players persevering through the laps, half-laps, walks, sprints and pieces of ball work. The sprints were supervised by Fleetwood, an ex-sprinter himself and coach to Gloria Goldsborough, Jean Newboult and 14-year-old Dorothy Hyman. The ball work was encouraged by Steele, a former inside-forward with good close control and the ability to shield a ball cleverly. Players had turned up at different times and it was a long August evening for the early arrivals. But the advent of winter would shorten training and strain the facilities.

Since the war they seemed to have trained everywhere, even under the stand, where a player might stand on a chair holding a football for another to practise his heading. The really old balls wrapped themselves round heads like skullcaps.

The whistle went again. The last goal had been played for and the session was over. Players ran or limped back to Oakwell, although some stayed in a Queen's Ground goalmouth, playing with a ball until the trainers came to take it away. Volunteer helper George Jackson had already turned on the brass taps that set luxurious hot water in motion. Two hours of repressed conversation burst forth in the dressing-room.

"Hey, Gilly, you fancy your chance."

"Why's that?"

"That lad asked who was the fastest in the club and you said you were."

"Oh, fastest? I thought he said fattest." The others laughed as they often did at remarks made by Arthur Gill, who was in fact one of the fastest.

Players sang in the bath and talked of how much they had won at the dogs. Newcomers sat in corners, often too shy to use names, hoping to be invited to join in the gang.

"Let's take a look at your ankle. Get your sock off."

"It's off already."

"Then wash your feet."

"It's bruisin' that."

The players gathered their kit to take it home or back to the boiler-room. They talked about the last match and the next match while checking their money and valuables. Nothing ever went missing but the players played safe.

"Aren't you going to have a bath?"

"Waste of time. I'll only get mucky when I get into bed with our kid toneet."

"Are you goin' down t'Vimto shop?"

The dressing-rooms were crowded early in the season. Miners might arrive deep black from the pit, looking for any available kit. The resources of the club were stretched by sheer numbers.

When changed, some dashed to evening classes at the Technical College. Some sauntered to the town's coffee-bars or Gordon Pallister's temperance bar, and others stayed to play billiards or table-tennis, perhaps as late as 11 pm. The table-tennis table just fitted into the club's gymnasium.

The gymnasium? It was more like a dormer-bedroom, squeezed under the stand. It was so small that any games were limited to one-a-side, a post-war Friday morning tradition with almost sadistic overtones. Players then formed two lines, one group standing hunched where the slope of the stand prevented any other posture. Players in each group were numbered – one, two, three, etc. – and a number was called. Two players would step forward and do battle, attempting to wedge the ball against their opponent's goal (usually a medicine-ball) while inactive players occasionally stuck out a foot to interrupt the flow and relieve their boredom. Most entertaining were two players who in the claustrophobic atmosphere of the gymnasium would fight almost to the death.

The game was part of Oakwell history. The gymnasium still housed a dozen

Indian clubs – which might have been very useful, but no-one knew how to use them – and medicine-balls, which some claimed were stuffed with lead. The medicine-balls smelled more and more fusty as the wet winter took hold. Among them might also be an old football, which had been like gold in the days when ball work was restricted in training .

Now the gymnasium was the home of the club's two teams that played in the Barnsley table-tennis league. John Steele, a county-class tennis player, was one of the table-tennis players too. He stayed in the social scene, making a point of trying to talk to each lad and having a word with a newcomer before he left.

John Steele had a difficult job learning about all the youngsters in the region. They came and went from Oakwell, many returning to local teams. And most disappeared from the region for two years because of National Service.

Barnsley was not as badly disrupted as many towns. Coal-mining was still a reserved occupation, while apprenticeships allowed a deferment of National Service. There were miners who were part-time footballers and there were prospective full-timers who chose the pits, despite the longer commitment involved. John Stainsby spent six months in the pit and then joined the groundstaff knowing he would face National Service later. John Jarman spent six months in the pit and then joined the RAF. This was despite the sympathetic attitude to football held by managers and colleagues in the mines.

National Service could extend a player's experience. The 55th army regiment near Oswestry mustered 20 professional footballers, including Barnsley's Billy Anderson, and sport was highly regarded. On the other hand, Olly Hopkins rarely touched a football in his time with the Royal Artillery, and Tommy Holmes' lasting impression of football during three years in the RAF was of watching the 1954 World Cup on television, the crowd rushing from one end of the barrack hut to the other, hoping for a better picture from one of two tiny television sets. When Lol Chappell was in Suez they scooped mud from the canal bed and rolled it out. The sun dried it into a playing surface that was very satisfactory – until it rained again.

It was through National Service that many young men had their first taste of living away from home. Some went abroad, others to outposts, perhaps moving frequently and managing only occasional week-ends home. Before he reached 18, a young lad had a relatively stable football career, free from the pressure of points and bonuses that accompanied the first team. He was free from the frustration and disruption of the Reserves and A-team. And he was free from National Service.

Monday 13th September 1954

Joe Hooley and Barry Barber met in Barnsley bus station and took the bus to Doncaster, where they walked in the direction of Belle Vue, the venue for an England Youth trial. The organisation of the England Youth team had developed quickly. It was 18 months since Peter Gillott had become Barnsley's first youth international. Gillott had learned of his selection in a roundabout manner. When

Tim Ward congratulated him it could have meant good or ill given Ward's sometimes sarcastic sense of humour, but in fact it was just that Gillott had not received the letter promptly.

There had been changes since then. England Youth now had a team manager (George Smith). Professionals could be selected and players were notified personally by letter after regional trials. Barnsley sent four players to Doncaster – Barber, Hooley, Brian Summerfield and John Stainsby.

Barry Barber was nearly 18, enjoying football and life. He was flamboyant and friendly, a popular wing-half. Along with Brian Summerfield he towered above other Juniors. They were both growing lads who would eat anything.

When Barry Barber passed a butcher's shop he stopped. "Wait a minute," he said to Joe Hooley, "I've had nothing to eat. I'll just get something."

Barber left the butcher's shop carrying a bag of party pork-pies. He ate through several as they walked to the ground, where players had gathered from throughout Yorkshire. It was a pleasant Monday afternoon ideal for football, but when the players changed they found they were one short. Tim Ward stepped into the breach just before kick-off. He always kept his boots in the car for such emergencies.

None of the Barnsley contingent was selected for England Youth. Not Brian Summerfield, who was in the Northern Intermediate League representative team. Not John Stainsby, who would be eligible the following season. Not Joe Hooley who was still a 15-year-old. Not Barry Barber, who had to leave the field to be sick. And certainly not Tim Ward who was 37 that week.

Of these young players it was groundstaff boys who Tim Ward saw the most: John Edgar, Bryn Price, John Stainsby and Joe Hooley. Edgar had recently signed as a professional, just before entering the army, and just after Ward had signed Hooley.

Amidst much competition, Joe Hooley had joined the Bolton Wanderers groundstaff in December 1953, soon after his 15th birthday. Barnsley Boys were then out of the English Schools' Trophy and despite the likelihood of an England schoolboy cap, Hooley left school – unlike some players in trophy-hunting years. But by May his oldest brother was married and living away, the middle brother had broken his leg playing football and Joe Hooley's return was welcome for his mother, who brought up the boys alone.

Thursday 23rd September 1954

"Go over to the Co-op," said Joe Walker, "Ask Walt if you can borrow the spiker. The Queen's Ground needs spiking." He watched Bryn Price and Joe Hooley walk away. Joe Walker had been Oakwell's groundsman for 23 years, living across the road in Grove Street, where he had checked on generations of groundstaff lads from his bedroom window. Walker had two other assistants: Irishman Enoch Guy, who resembled Popeye's grandfather and frequently entertained with a clog dance and pipe; and Ernest Pyne, a grown-up groundstaff boy. A lad once provoked Pyne into running around the pitch against the clock, having flattered him that he must be the world's fittest and fastest for his age, which was substantial.

On a recent Friday morning, Bob Shotton had asked Arthur Kaye to practise a few penalties. Ernest Pyne, clearing up behind the goal, jumped over the wall and said, "Take one at me, Arthur." Kaye hit the penalty hard, as he always did, and Pyne's broken arm meant he was unable to help when Price and Hooley walked to the Co-op ground.

Bryn Price and Joe Hooley made a contrasting pair. Professional football had always appeared likely for Hooley. He oozed confidence and was not afraid to tell some senior professionals what to do. There was a time when he was called "Frewball" after his persistent advice during one practice match.

Bryn Price, on the other hand, had been raised in the rugby-playing Rhondda Valley, and his small, muscular body seemed suited to rugby. He had come to Barnsley through Emlyn Williams, a former BAOR colleague of Tim Ward's who ran a "bagwash" in Treorchi. Ward signed Price for the groundstaff at half-time in a trial early in 1954.

"Can we borrow the spiker?" asked the groundstaff boys when the reached the Co-op sports ground.

"I've got too much to do here." replied Walter Drewry the groundsman.

Drewry was a valuable man to know, not only for borrowing equipment but also for the use of the telephone in his house just opposite Oakwell. The trouble with borrowing the spiker was that Walt Drewry usually had to come with it, to drive the pre-war converted hearse which pulled the six-sided drum. Joe Walker, now 71 and failing in health, could not handle a vehicle himself.

"Can either of you drive?" asked Walter Drewry.

"Yes, I can," said Bryn Price. He was nearly 19, which was old for the groundstaff. He had failed his army medical because of perforated eardrums and flat feet. This was a big disappointment to him. It also meant that while Barnsley often signed players full-time when they enlisted, the club were under no pressure with Price. He stayed sweeping, cleaning, laying out kit and preparing boots. Groundstaff tasks had changed from the post-war period when roads and car-parks had to be built around Oakwell.

Bryn Price drove Drewry's car up and down the Queen's Ground, playing with the magneto that increased the speed.

"Let me have a go, Bryn," said Joe Hooley.

"No, no," said Price, enjoying himself.

Joe Hooley persuaded Price to let him drive. He drove the car alone and began to enjoy it. Price ran behind and Hooley used the magneto to increase speed. Price jumped on the running-board and Hooley accelerated again. Price fell onto the spiker. The hearse stopped, Price picked himself up; they looked around and laughed. When Bryn Price changed for the next A team game, a few players were surprised to see the marks on his back.

Tim Ward knew the names of all the club's youngsters – unlike some managers – but the time he could spend with them was limited. Like Bob Shotton, Ward was at Oakwell for most evening training sessions but not always in kit. John Steele gave undivided attention to the lads. He shared their training and the bath afterwards. He saw them developing as people. He watched them on match days, treated their injuries and shared their bus.

The man who drove the lower teams was Alma Bell. He rose at 3.30 am on Saturdays and made local trips before meeting the players at Oakwell. Bell was in his mid–40s and had once answered the classic question: "We're one short, Alma, do you fancy a game?" That was when a trialist failed to show up at Rawmarsh's "Hill 60" ground for an end-of-season A team match. Bell was warned to stay out of tackles to ensure the coach's safe return, but he still demonstrated skills learned with Yorkshire Traction, whom he had helped win the Sheffield Thursday League in 1929.

Driving the Juniors took Alma Bell to some unusual venues. When the Northern Intermediate League began in 1949, it was intended that games be played on first-team pitches on Saturday mornings, but this proved impractical. Barnsley, whose A team once played at Staincross, took a bulldozer to land adjoining Oakwell and fashioned the Queen's Ground, erecting a tin shelter for trainers. The first training sessions started with players collecting glass and avoiding dog dirt, until the ground could be roped off. Barnsley had been fortunate to own land so close by. Leeds played at Swillington, Newcastle at Wallsend and Huddersfield at Heckmondwike, all some distance from their main grounds.

Alma Bell drove to Heckmondwike three or four times a season. The route included one notorious stretch of road; a tight bend led to a railway bridge and the bus passed through the narrow tunnel with only six inches to spare on either side. The tunnel had flanges, too high to worry a car but just right for a bus. On one occasion Alma Bell took the necessary wide sweep and a man waved him through. Bell accelerated but the left-hand flange crunched two windows at the back. Glass shattered into small pieces and flew everywhere. The players roared with laughter. With exemplary drivers like Joe Thorpe and Alma Bell, such incidents were so rare that they were never forgotten.

John Steele had considerable freedom with the Juniors although he did lose players at short notice and he was often asked to include trialists. Tactics were therefore makeshift, and it was a case of "play your own game, son." Steele had recently included five 15-year-olds for a 7–0 win at Bradford Park Avenue. In 1951, Barnsley Juniors had won the Northern Intermediate League, but winning was not the main object. Steele certainly urged the players to win and would rave furiously if they slacked, but he recognised that his job was to produce players for the future, knowing that good players could come from poor teams. Other clubs had similar aims. The league secretary, Raymond Vicary, had a list of nearly 500 players registered by the 13 clubs, including 125 for Wolves.

The first team was another world. The Juniors took an interest in the senior matches because they were Barnsley supporters, not because they were likely to be picked. The bulk of the 1954 Juniors were from the previous year's Barnsley Boys – Brian "Bryn" Jones, Bryan Matthews, Billy Houghton, Jackie Lunn and Joe Hooley. By the time they played at Heckmondwike for the second time that season it was only late September. Barry Barber, nearly 18, was still at right-half although there was a wing-half injury crisis in the club: Norman Smith had a badly-sprained ankle; Maurice Jackson had suffered ankle trouble and concussion; Bob Wood had a dislocated shoulder; Ron Archer had undergone a cartilage operation; Henry Walters needed a fitness test before the Barrow game. The test worked out worse for Bob Shotton because Fred Semley's Alsatian jumped up and the trainer dislocated his elbow.

Tim Ward had so far been unable to field the settled side that he really wanted. Fortunately there was no outstanding team as Port Vale had been the previous season. Chesterfield, Scunthorpe and Accrington had all topped the table.

1	Scunthorpe	13 – 20
2	Gateshead	13 – 18
3	Chesterfield	13 – 18
4	Accrington	13 – 18
5	Barnsley	13 – 16

Wednesday 27th October 1954

Regent Street was lined with people. It was a welcome as grand as the homecoming of the 1912 FA Cup winners. It resembled the celebration of war victory. It was no less than when the 1949 Barnsley Boys rode through town on an open-top bus.

On Barnsley Road, Kendray, around 14,000 schoolchildren waited. They practised waving their Union Jacks and their sense of anticipation grew. Outside Exchange station there was a whisper of news. "She's here," people said. It was just before 10 o'clock.

The Queen was dressed in emerald green. Her Majesty and the Duke of Edinburgh were accompanied by the mayor and mayoress of Barnsley, Alderman and Mrs McVie, as they walked 300 yards to the town hall, where a special dais had been erected. Regent Street came alive with flags, streamers and football rattles.

On arrival at the town hall, 32 Barnsley people, including ordinary working folk, were presented to the Royal couple. The Duke of Edinburgh had a conversation with Alderman Charles Bentley.

"I used to keep a pub, Sir," said Bentley in reply to one of the Duke's questions. "Before that I worked down the pit for 32 years."

The Duke then asked him what he found to do now that he was retired.

"I'm just knocking about and watching Barnsley laik footy," replied Bentley, who had a season ticket in the centre stand and never missed an Oakwell match of any kind.

Football reached all levels of Barnsley society. The local MP, Roy Mason, an ex-miner, was a regular at home matches. There was never a shortage of volunteers for the position of club doctor. Season tickets were held by all sorts, and those who went never seemed to stop talking about football: about the last match until Wednesday and about the next match from then till Saturday. Attendances were now averaging over 12,000, but they only made Oakwell live on match days. It was an empty and eerie sight the rest of the time.

Thursday 28th October 1954

"But I don't like it at outside-left," said Frank Bartlett.

"You're doing alright. You're doing a good job, Frankie," replied Tim Ward.

"But the crowd will boo me."

"No they won't. If they do, you can blame me."

So Bob Shotton clipped another cross from the right wing. Strong in arm and leg, the former full-back had been a dead-ball king and penalty expert. He could reach the halfway-line with a goal-kick on the heaviest of grounds.

Shotton's cross arrived at the far post. Frank Bartlett ran in and swung his left foot, which was proving good for shooting but not for crossing. Meanwhile, Tim Ward rolled another ball under his foot and waited to provide the next cross.

This was special practice. It was not uncommon for players to be singled out. Bob Shotton, in particular, offered heading practice or the chance for a player to improve his weak foot – with a boot on the bad one and a plimsoll on the good one.

Frank Bartlett could run all day. Tim Ward was alarmed when he first saw him at inside-forward, thinking Bartlett would burn himself out. Bartlett wanted to be everywhere on the pitch. His stamina was endless. But the left wing really needed different skills. Bartlett hated playing in the position, yet he had put up with it for 13 games, always giving his best. He was the manager's dream.

People in Barnsley often used the phrase "black November" because it seemed to herald a decline in the team's performances. But this November proved an exception. Barnsley's four wins produced 14 goals, including three hat tricks. Two came from Lol Chappell, who was scoring so many hat tricks that the club stopped presenting him with the match balls. The other was scored by Frank Bartlett playing on the left wing against Gateshead.

November also included the two important goals from Tommy Lumley that saw Barnsley through the first round of the FA Cup – but not without a fright. They won 3–2 against Wigan Athletic of the Lancashire Combination, who had drawn at Newcastle the previous season. This was only Barnsley's seventh FA Cup win in nine years, and the first time they had been drawn against a non-League side since 1920, when Plymouth won 4–1 at Oakwell. Some supporters thought they were due for a run, but others said they were no longer an FA Cup side. However, there was no reason why they should not repeat the recent successes of Gateshead and Port Vale. But more important was the improvement in their League position.

Saturday 4th December 1954

2–2 at Carlisle. Harry Hough collected the ball and looked around. He usually kicked the ball, often reaching well past the halfway-line, an achievement always applauded at Oakwell. This time he saw Norman Smith, who like Tommy Lumley sometimes offered an alternative. Hough threw the ball to Smith and the ball plopped into the Brunton Park mud.

"No, no, Harry, get it kicked," shouted Bob Shotton, who had spent much of the afternoon taking mud out of players' eyes. Tim Ward was in a dilemma. He liked the ball thrown as part of the passing pattern but this was a real quagmire at Carlisle. The pitch was generally good and had drained well since Friday night when it was submerged in three feet of water.

Norman Smith dragged the ball to the left, away from the morass in the centre. He needed crow-bars on his feet, not just the built-up studs and high-ankled boots which at least kept some of the water out.

Frank Bartlett was free at outside-left so Norman Smith clouted the ball. Whack! Plop! Smith continued running. The ball had collected mud and grown in size. Whack! Plop! Smith tried four times before Bartlett ran to meet him. The ball was more like lead than usual. If anyone was to break this deadlock it would be from short range. The Barnsley build-up continued and Frank Bartlett finally shot, but the ball stuck in the mud, almost on the goal-line.

Tommy Lumley's passes were less than 10 yards range. As always, he concentrated on timing the ball correctly. In his wartime navy days, Lumley had played on a mudheap in an Indian monsoon and that was his nearest experience to what he found at Carlisle. Yet a foul on Smith led to a free-kick by Thomas, then a header from Chappell, and it was Tommy Lumley who tapped the ball into the net. Then Chappell left Doran lying flat in the mud and from his cross Bob Wood scored a fourth, again from close quarters.

When the game finished, at 4–2 to Barnsley, the players were tired and relieved. However, there was no immediate bath. The Carlisle United stand had been destroyed by fire and the players were taken by double-decker bus to the public baths. Some had to search for their bootlaces through thick layers of mud.

"Tell you who would have liked it out there – Eddie McMorran."

"Aye, Eddie liked a mudlark."

"I bet even Browny would have got his knickers dirty today."

"Hey, get away from me, Harry."

It was always the goalkeepers who came off worst. Hough was caked to the eyebrows in mud; when he discarded his green jersey it had doubled in weight.

"You need two teams, one for these grounds and one for proper pitches."

"Aye, we needed Woody's strength up front."

"We needed anybody's strength. Chuck some more soap."

"We nearly came unstuck though."

"I thought I was stuck all the second half."

"Are you going for a swim afterwards?"

"Who's got the shampoo?"

"Hey, Joe," said Norman Smith, seeing Thomas stripped for the bath, "You're the only bloke I know who can hula-hoop in a Polo mint."

"Rub my back down, Joe?"

"He's doing the boots."

Joe Thorpe looked up to see if he could be any help and then he continued washing the discarded boots, helped by reserve Geoff Lees. If left until Monday the sludge would be solid. Bob Shotton carried a butcher's wire brush for the job. After use in bad conditions boots were washed immediately, and then dried in the Oakwell boiler-room before being dubbined. The mud caused problems for everyone, but today the Barnsley contingent could afford to laugh at it.

As well as another defeat, Carlisle United were left with the problems of re-building the main stand and allowing the pitch to recover. The following week they shipped two loads of sea sand from Maryport for the pitch, and work finally began on the accommodation under the stand. Fire damage was not uncommon at Third Division (North) grounds – Rochdale had suffered a fire as recently as August. There was a famous story about the night another Third Division club lost their stand. The groundsman telephoned the news of the fire to the manager, who delayed calling help until a pair of boots and the club's only track suit had been rescued. The manager and the groundsman spent an hour creating diversions to prolong the fire. They moved cars in the way of fire-engines and pulled the heavy roller over the hoses. They worked until the stand was a bare skeleton and the insurance claim – which included a dozen track suits – put the club back on its feet, for a few months.

The following week the first team again visited a football outpost of limited resources. Their trip to Gateshead was for a second round FA Cup tie. The previous month they had won 4–0 in the corresponding League game, Gateshead's worst defeat for seven years. It was hard to think of two more different football officials than Bill Tulip, 78-year-old chairman/manager/secretary of Gateshead, and Matt Busby, manager of wealthy Manchester United. On Saturday 11th December both their clubs faced Cup ties against Barnsley.

Manchester United Juniors came to Oakwell in the third round of the FA Youth Cup. It was the third season of the competition and United had yet to lose a game, although Barnsley had given them a fright in the quarter-final at Old Trafford in April 1953, eventually going down 3–1 in front of a 12,400 crowd. Many of the United players, then and since, had played at League and representative level – Colman, Pegg, Lewis, McGuinness. When Duncan Edwards ran out at Oakwell on 11th December he was already an England B international.

Barnsley Juniors faced a match that would have tested the senior side. Yet at half-time they led 2–0. Duncan Edwards had had no success against Brian Summerfield so he moved from centre-forward to left-half. Manchester United scored twice by the 57th minute, then Edwards put them ahead when Barry Barber was off the field injured. They went on to win 4–2.

At Gateshead, Barnsley went 3–1 ahead after an hour. Then Lol Chappell dived for a cross as goalkeeper Gray came out feet first. Chappell had to leave the field for repairs. Bob Shotton held a naked bulb to his face as the loose pieces were stitched into place. During Chappell's 15 minute absence, Gateshead scored twice. 3–3. Replay on Thursday – early closing day.

At least Barnsley were still in the velvet bag when the "snooker balls" rattled for the third round draw. It gave Barnsley or Gateshead a home tie against Tottenham Hotspur. It was the chance to become a national name, with the certainty of bumper receipts. For Tim Ward it would be a good test of his team's style against the classic push-and-run of Arthur Rowe, who had just bought Danny Blanchflower from Aston Villa.

From Barnsley's first corner in the replay, goalkeeper Gray caught Chappell with a punched clearance. The cuts around the nose were so badly loosened that the normal temporary remedy of sterilised clips was useless. The 2 pm kick-off allowed for the possibility of extra-time, but it was not needed. A goal from Ken Smith meant that Spurs booked tickets for Tyneside rather than south Yorkshire.

Over Christmas Barnsley met lowly Grimsby twice. They made a typical nonsense of home advantage, each winning 3–1 on the other's ground. It left the division wide open.

1	Scunthorpe	24 – 33
2	Hartlepools	24 – 32
3	Gateshead	24 – 31
4	Accrington	24 – 30
5	Barnsley	24 – 29
6	Workington	24 – 29

There followed a period of bad weather. After home wins against Halifax and Wrexham, 15th January brought a journey to York, beaten only once in 19 games and 2–0 winners against Blackpool in the third round of the FA Cup.

A crucial moment came in the second half when Barnsley were leading 2–1. York's Arthur Bottom broke clear and ran over the snow towards Harry Hough. Hough narrowed the angle quickly and the shot went wide. Shortly afterwards, Bottom was cautioned by referee Jack Pickles, who was hit by a snowball as he noted the name. Barnsley won the game 3–1 and Pickles was pelted with cushions by the crowd.

Saturday 12th February 1955

The whistle went for half-time in the game against Workington. Tim Ward slipped out of the trainer's box and up the Oakwell tunnel before any of the players had crossed the cinders. He reached the home dressing-room just after the reserve, who had brought the tea. The tea was made by Sybil Parkinson, who had many match-day functions, including baby-sitting Harry May's daughter while his wife watched the match.

Most players drank tea at half-time. Some touched nothing while others plumped for Lucozade. The directors had once debated the cost of Lucozade. "It's just coloured water," one had said, but Arthur Raynor continued to provide it, footing the bill himself to save argument. He respected the opinions of Ward and Shotton, who stressed that if players believed it was doing them good, then it was doing the club good. "If they had a load of strychnine and played well, then they would want it every week," argued the officials, although this remained untested.

"What's in the 'brewery news'?" asked a spectator of his mate, thinking about the 10 minutes to kill. It seemed a long time on such a cold day. His mate turned to the front page of the programme as a small boy came out of the tunnel carrying a blackboard which displayed the lucky programme number. The winner received two free tickets for the next home game. Some wags considered it a penalty prize.

In the stands, the spectators stood up and stretched their legs. They reached for flasks of tea, tea and whisky or Bovril. The small crowd of 6,147 left the viewers feeling colder. Some shared fruit, which was less of a luxury now that rationing was removed.

Music crackled through the tannoy. After years of playing old favourites such as "Marching Through Georgia", the club now borrowed records from Joshua Marshall and Company. Raymond Vicary considered requests and collected the records on a Friday. His brother Leslie operated the gramophone.

Then the Butlin's PT girls put on a display for the spectators. Billy Butlin's recently-started holiday camps were canvassing for business. On big Oakwell occasions, a brass band would play at half-time, later carrying a blanket round for a collection; spectators threw loose coins. In 1950, during a collection for the Cresswell Colliery disaster fund, a policeman was dazed when a penny struck his head. "Copper bowled over by copper", the local newspaper was quick to note, and the policeman received treatment from the St John Ambulance Brigade. On duty for the Brigade that day, as always, was Fred Whittlestone, who sat in all weathers on a cushion or a stretcher near the trainer's box. There he could see the whole ground except the grandstand, where there was less call for his help.

Tim Ward knew that by the time the players had all had a wash and a drink there would be barely five minutes left for him. He followed them around, singling them out quietly to make one or two points. "Norman," he said, "We've got Johnny deep in defence. You've got more freedom. Take the ball up. Get it out to Arthur ... Joe, if you're in trouble just get it to Norman, easy ball ... Arthur, you're murdering this fellow. You're walking round him. If Walter Winterbottom were here you'd be in the England team ... Frankie, great goals, son. You're going to get about 28 crosses this half. Get in at the far post. If you can knock another two in ... Lol, stay away from the right wing. Keep the centre-half away from Arthur. Then go to the near post for his crosses. Frank's got the far post."

Tommy Lumley listened intently, memorising every move. Norman Smith thought of questions, details he wanted to know, but the buzzer went and it was time for the players to go back on the pitch.

"Hey, ref," shouted a spectator, "Are you going t'oppen both eyes this half?"

"Let's have another hat trick, Frank."

Bartlett stood close to spectators in the "brewery stand" as the teams lined up. Even two first-half goals couldn't make him like playing on the wing. It took him 13 more minutes to score his third of the game. That meant 14 in 19 games, plus two goals for the Reserves. But he had not really enjoyed his football.

The A team was a very competitive testing ground for the footballers who'd graduated from the 1949 and 1950 Barnsley Boys. They were in their early twenties, beyond the interference of National Service – Gill, Swift, Roscoe, McCullough, Ted Brown, Trevor Archer and Sidebottom. Unlike London and the north-east there were no top-class amateur leagues in the area and talented players were drawn into the Yorkshire League, where you could earn around £3 a week part-time. Some of the referees were local men on the full Football League list. When they had a free afternoon they were prepared to go out and earn a guinea, plus expenses, in the Yorkshire League. Not all the facilities were top class. They played in the middle of the dog-track at Owlerton and used good facilities at Stocksbridge, but there was a hill at Hallam, and after playing Sheffield Club players would sprint to reach the big round bath before the hockey and rugby teams.

There were five Football League clubs with A teams in the Second Division of the Yorkshire League. Barnsley A team were one of 18 teams in a First Division from which four were relegated. Barnsley were pushing hard at the top with easily the best goal average. The high-scoring forward line was led by Arthur Gill, who was approaching Ray John's total of 20 the previous season. But Barnsley still had to catch Stocksbridge Works, the steel-workers' team.

Alma Bell drove the A team to Farsley Celtic in March. The pitch was a sad reflection of the terrible weather that was disrupting everyone's fixture list. Geoff Lees went down in the area and the referee blew for a penalty. Lees stayed down. Johnny Steele, who was looking after the A team as well as the Juniors, ran onto the field with George Jackson, the volunteer sponge man. A piece of clinker had been driven deep into Lees' leg, making a deep cut. Steele was not a man to mollycoddle players but he had no hesitation in helping Lees from the pitch, turning just in time to see Phil Roscoe shoot wide from the spot. The game was drawn.

Lees needed 12 stitches in the cut; Raymond Vicary drove him home to Rotherham from the hospital. It was not Lees' only worry. He had joined the groundstaff in 1949 and now, six years later, he was uncertain about his future at the club. A lunch-time interview with Tim Ward had not cleared his mind.

Loser Buys the Biscuits

Chapter Four

Saturday 19th March 1955

Tim Ward knocked and walked in, hardly breaking his stride.

"Tim, you made it then, how are you?"

"Freddie, good to see you."

Fred Westgarth, the big Geordie who managed Hartlepools United, leaned back in his seat and spilled cigarette ash down the front of his suit. This office was one everyone liked to visit. It was the manager's office, the secretary' s office and even the boardroom. If Westgarth was not here, most people knew they could find him at the greyhound-track across the road, or at his bookmaker's business.

"Well, one of us is going up this year," said Westgarth. He knew the Third Division (North) intimately. It suited his toughness. Westgarth's managerial career with Stockport County and Hartlepools had meant scrimping, saving and surviving. In 1937 he had steered Stockport into the Second Division. They stayed one season and came down with Barnsley.

"I think it had better be us," said Ward, "You'd be losing your local derbies – Gateshead, Darlington ..."

"You might be losing Leeds, tha knows, and Rotherham could go up."

"Yes, Rotherham in the First Division." Ward shook his head, "Their ground'll shock a few."

"Aye, it makes ours look like Wembley."

Ward smiled. The Victoria Ground, West Hartlepool, was typical of the division. The fence was faulty and people could walk in freely except on match days when officials ensured that a turnstile was used. Dance-hall patrons next door found the grandstand accessible for late-night smooching sessions.

"A policeman 'phoned me at home the other week," said Westgarth, warming up as Bob Shotton and a few reporters formed an audience. "Friday night again. He'd caught a dozen courting couples in the stand and asked what to do with them."

"What did you tell him?" asked Ward, genuinely curious. He looked upon Westgarth as a mentor.

"I told him to fix t'bloody fence and board 'em in. Best gate of the season it would have been."

Ward laughed again. He could imagine Westgarth doing it. Ward felt privileged to know the man. Despite his unfashionable club he was well-respected inside football. Ward occasionally turned to him for blunt advice on other managers, getting replies such as "don't trust that bugger" or "he's straight".

"Now what about this John Charles at Leeds, would you have him in your team?"

"If I had him we'd win the First Division, the Grand National and the Boat Race." Westgarth paused. "Hey remember, Tim, if you do go up ... make as many friends as you can on the way, because you might need them coming down."

Then the telephone rang and Westgarth answered it. "What time do we kick off?" he asked himself, "Well, what time can you get here? No, no, three o'clock." He hung up.

"Now, I've got one problem," said Tim Ward, as the clock ticked by. "We've only got six complimentary tickets. Football League regulations say we should have twenty-five."

"Football League regulations never paid the wages for us."

"You can manage a few more, can't you?"

"Alright, we'll collect them at the gate and give them out again ... I'll go down and tell the gateman to let in anyone from Barnsley." As the door opened again he added, "I'll be down in a minute, Ned."

"That's your lad is it?"

"That's our Ned."

"Good trainer, is he?"

"Aye. None better. Our Ned stitches them up like sackbags. Look, I've something to show you." Proudly, Fred Westgarth led his audience to a table which had a towel drawn tightly over the top. Perched above it was an old-fashioned sun-ray lamp. "Our latest piece of equipment," Westgarth continued, "We're all up to date here."

The two managers left for a word with their teams. In the press-box, John Uprichard contemplated the preamble to his *Green 'Un* report. An Irishman, Uprichard was an experienced reporter who had covered Barnsley since July 1952. Employed by the *Sheffield Star*, he also wrote for the *Sheffield Telegraph* – under appropriate aliases such as Arthur Coleman – and for the Barnsley programme. His style was lively and adventurous. Once, when he described Bobby

Brown as an enigma, everyone was puzzled, including Brown.

There were now 10 minutes to kick-off and Uprichard began to worry about the lack of activity around him. There was usually a local correspondent to provide a telephone. Uprichard was looking for Mr Robinson.

"Do you know a Mr Robinson?" he asked a small boy.

"I'm Mr Robinson."

"Have you got a telephone for me?"

"Yes."

"Can I see it?"

"Have you got a bike?"

"A bike. Where is it?"

"Oh about a mile away."

Uprichard was used to inconvenient telephones. There was only one in the press-box at Hartlepools and eight reporters jammed into the confined space wanting to use it.

Yet it was worth the trouble to be first with the news in the *Green 'Un*. For Benny Hill at the *Barnsley Chronicle* the process was very different. Writing for a weekly paper that came out on a Friday he had to talk about the next game rather than the last one. He had extra time to prepare his report, and it had to be something of substance, something for the record. Hill certainly had more time to notice and absorb the finer points of the match. Uprichard was scribbling copy and telephoning every 15 minutes, and sometimes he had to rely on Hill for an account of an incident or the name of a Barnsley goalscorer. At away grounds there was little likelihood of any other reporter recognising the face in the red shirt.

Downstairs, in the dressing-room, Tommy Lumley removed his false teeth and Harry Hough still felt the effects from his usual cold shower, which at Hartlepools was taken with a bucket and string. Some players were still towelling their feet to keep them warm. At Oakwell they could run hot water over them first.

Two old footballs were thrown into the room. Some clubs only supplied one for kicking-in, but Barnsley had asked for more.

"Who's carrying this medicine-ball out?"

"This one'll change into Cinderella's coach."

Tim Ward looked at the shower system and made a mental note to close the bus windows as they left the ground. He then spoke his few words: "I don't know why I'm talking. You're the best team in this division. Let them worry about you. Now, there are eleven of you going out there today. Eight of you might have good games, but three of you might play badly. The rest have to help those three. It might be you next week." He paused briefly and looked for specific players. "Harry, remember what we said about 'Legs' Linacre. He's a bit quick." May did not mind speedy wingers. It was the ones that hung back that he hated, for they teased the full-back forward and then hit thoughtful long passes. "George, this Johnson's a good young lad. He should be playing in a higher class of football." Ward knew that Spruce always responded to such a challenge.

"Right, all the best, lads."

They left the token shelter to face worse conditions: a crowd of 8,231 and snow, which was swirling but not settling. It was here that footballers earned their living, in tense, difficult games that affected their future.

"They say Walter Winterbottom's here today," said one as they went down the passage. A few chuckled.

Today, one 15-minute period had more action than the others. It was the one just before half-time when all three goals were scored. They fell to Barnsley.

It was a working week-end at Oakwell. Sybil Parkinson started at nine in the morning on Sunday and often washed five sets of kit, perhaps staying as late as 10 pm. She boiled, washed, rinsed and ironed the kit, using an old tub and mangle until the club bought a Hotpoint. The socks were done separately, pounded with a plunger. She had joined the club in 1946 at £5 a week.

In the late 1940s, Barnsley's socks were red and white hoops, to balance the red shirts and white shorts. Unfortunately they had to keep the socks so long that they often turned pink in the wash. Another attempt, red with white tops, met the same fate and it was in October 1953 that the more practical all-red socks were introduced.

Also in the late 1940s, Barnsley had adopted a fashionable red stripe down each side of the shorts. Again this made extra work. Sybil Parkinson had to contend with repairs too. The cloth badges and numbers needed a lot of sewing, and for purposes of hygiene each player had his initials sewn on sweater, undershirt, socks and towel. At the height of rationing, kit had been thrown onto the dressing-room floor before training, and after a stampede for the best, the late-comers were left with the remnants. Nor did clubs have a range of colours to choose from. They often produced a change strip by dyeing old shirts or borrowing a set from a neighbouring club. However, Harold Wilson had announced the end of clothes rationing in April 1949.

The presentation of the Barnsley kit inspired pride, especially on match days. "If you look like footballers you'll play like footballers" was a favourite saying of Bob Shotton, himself always immaculate. Sybil Parkinson was responsible for the footballers' kit, working unseen on a Sunday. She was also responsible for providing the tea and biscuits, while Nellie Pape did the cleaning. Sybil Parkinson found herself collecting 2½d for a Blue Riband biscuit which was often the stake in a bet between players. "Loser buys the biscuits" was a common phrase around the billiards, table-tennis or even on the Queen's Ground.

A Monday was the calm after a Saturday storm. It was usually a rest day for players while the groundstaff swept up Saturday's rubbish for burning in the old Yorkshire boiler. Fred Semley prepared his injury report, Ernest Steele forked the pitch and replaced the divots, and the Customs and Excise men visited to check the mechanical counter at each turnstile, leaving their seal for future entertainment tax calculations. Tim Ward listened to accounts of other games from Eddie Fleetwood and John Steele.

Regular visitors to Oakwell realised that Mondays were quieter than Fridays.

One such visitor was Ralph Grimes, secretary of the Supporters' Club. Grimes was surprised when Ward told him how heavy socks became during 90 minutes. Ward explained that the weight of the socks and the threat of cramp was the reason players rolled them down.

This conversation led to another change in Barnsley's socks. Ralph Grimes discovered that red socks could be made by Barnsley Blind Welfare for 13/- a pair, using a nylon-based material instead of the traditional wool. They were half the weight of wool when wet, so blind ladies in York Street began to make the socks.

Grimes and his colleagues were having an active season in other respects: producing and selling 1,500 Supporters' Club handbooks, organising quizzes and meetings, arranging for the manufacture of "little tyke" lapel badges by Fattorini in Bradford. Support had improved since relegation, when membership dropped to seven hundred. The increasing number of branches helped provide transport to matches. The Supporters' Club liaised with the directors over tickets and facilities, and tried to raise money for the club. It was this last function that raised more problems than money.

Ralph Grimes received a warning about lotteries from Chief Constable George Parfitt, which was one of many issued throughout the country. For Supporters' Club officials who did not heed the warnings there were prosecutions. The officials were left with two possible defences. They could claim the competition was based on skill rather than chance, or they could appeal to Section 24 of the 1934 Betting and Lotteries Act. This proved controversial. Section 24 was designed to protect a club conducting a sweepstake among its members. But lotteries organised on this principle failed to satisfy some people. The police at Shrewsbury pointed out that attendances of only 2,000 hardly matched 30,000 lottery members.

Many clubs therefore closed down competitions. This was a staggering loss for some clubs. Colchester passed over £11,000 to the football club in a season, Burton Albion were making £1,000 a week at one time. Torquay United Supporters' Club became a test case. They were prosecuted, convicted and then they successfully appealed. A further prosecution was brought against them. During the legal process there was a campaign for a change in the Act, and eventually this happened. Barnsley meanwhile complied with the warning. The Supporters' Club did as much as they could with few facilities. They used a small office near the old dressing-rooms, but on match days only.

Saturday 9th April 1955

It was Easter Saturday. Match day. Oakwell started like any weekday. Around 8 am, new groundsman Ernest Steele made a security check, accompanied by his dog Bruce. On match days he also inspected the toilets and stands, cleaned by the groundstaff. He used the directors' box entrance to the stand and vaulted over a partition to dust the row of fixed seats at the top. On one such occasion he found a body stretched out asleep on the floor between two rows. Steele shouted for Bob Shotton and they quizzed the man. "Er, I've come for the match," said the intruder, thinking quickly. He was thrown out but Ernest Steele later learned from the CID that the man was wanted.

Lily Johnson walked to Oakwell from her home on Day Street. She had raised the status of the receptionist's job, duties which had been carried out by a winger on the groundstaff until she arrived in 1949–50. Although it paid much less than similar work at the Coal Board, it was far nicer than her previous invoicing jobs with Yorkshire Traction and the Co-op, especially considering she was a Barnsley supporter.

It was not yet nine o'clock, but the other Barnsley officials were all at Oakwell when Lily Johnson arrived. About once a week, when she was early, Lily Johnson used her key to let herself into the ground. When empty, the stadium could be a little alarming, though she knew Ernest Steele would be somewhere.

By mid-morning the scene was hectic. The telephone rang persistently. Lily Johnson created more stand tickets with a big rubber stamp which had changeable letters. Today they spelt "CHESTERFIELD". The lower teams congregated and left for their matches. Bob Shotton checked the two match balls for pressure and then left them in the referee's room to give him a choice. Ernest Steele climbed a ladder and walked along the gangplank to raise the main-stand flag, which had been presented by Ralph Grimes.

At noon Tim Ward escaped on an errand. He drove to three hospitals – Kendray, Beckett and St. Helen's – and delivered programmes for the patients who would listen to the hospitals' commentary on the game.

The gatemen arrived at one o'clock and the crowd thereafter. People pushed through the 40 turnstiles and sought their favourite positions. One boy walked up to the players' entrance as he usually did. He spoke to Bill Archer, the club commissionaire. "Could you give these sweets to Joe Thomas, please?" said the boy. Thomas was his hero.

By 3.10 the ground was far from eerie. It had an atmosphere. The Barnsley team ran out to a roar and peeled off to the Pontefract Road end. Behind that goal, close enough to feel they were saving shots, were a group of fans from Birdwell, who threw chewing-gum for Harry Hough. While other players spat out the gum at the start, Hough chewed through pieces as he awaited attacks.

Harry May sought the near goalpost. May always put on his right boot before his left, and now he held the goalpost and kicked with each foot until the boots felt comfortable. As he did so, he looked at the crowd behind the goal. He wondered who they were and why they came.

"Who's this Jarman?" asked a spectator enticed back by the recent good run.

"That's 'im. Number six. Can't use his left booit."

"He's alreet, Jarman, better than some of t'other lightweights."

"Aye, 'e gets stuck in."

"That Warrdy, couldn't pick his nose, ne'er mind a team."

"You won't say that if we go up."

The game started in breathtaking fashion. Hough saved from Marsden and Chesterfield's Stiffle hit a post. It took Barnsley a few minutes to settle.

"Give it to Danny Kaye," shouted a spectator, "Out 'ere." Instead, Norman Smith swung the ball across goal and it looked like being a goal-kick.

"Go on, Bartlett, you can get it." Both the Barnsley wingers were popular, Kaye for his obvious ability and aggression, Bartlett for his struggle out of position.

Frank Bartlett controlled the ball on the goal-line and banged in a shot from an angle. Goalkeeper Powell palmed the ball out, but Lol Chappell scored from a couple of yards. The crowd cheered.

"Chappell, it were Chappell."

"Aye, I could've scored yon goal. He can only score 'em from between posts."

Lol Chappell had subdued many barrackers this season, scoring three hat tricks at home, but some remained unmoved. Chappell suffered in the wake of international-class centre-forwards – McCormack, McMorran and Taylor. He missed goals every game, yet scored them often. Spectators varied in what they saw. When Chappell missed a chance the barrackers started again.

"Yer big tea-cake."

"Yer big nellie."

"I could have wafted it in wi' me cap."

"He couldn't knock skin off a rice puddin'."

"Come and stand wi' me, Chappell."

"Get off field, Chappell, let grass grow."

Lol Chappell had missed games at the start of the year and he still felt the lingering effects of a chipped bone in his foot. But still he ran … up and down the field, from side to side, along the wings.

"Oppen t'gates, let him run out."

While Tommy Lumley and Bobby Brown ran into position, waiting for the simple pass that usually came, Lol Chappell ran with no expectations. He harassed the goalkeeper and chased the full-backs. When the ball went back to the goalkeeper with the crowd shouting "windy", he ran again and stood covering the goalkeeper's good foot.

"Go on," Chappell baited, "Kick it with your bad foot."

Half-time arrived with just one goal scored, but the Barnsley players thought only of how many they would get. They started the second half confidently.

"Come on Arthur, we'll score here." There was a buzz of expectation when Arthur Kaye received the ball. Never losing balance or control, he looked up quickly and studiously, searching for Bartlett at the back, where the marking tended to be less tight. Bartlett was so quick, so fit, that if he wasn't at the far post he had to be injured. Over came the centre. In went Bartlett. He headed against the crossbar and Bob Wood hit the rebound into the net.

The fans threw up their arms. "Told you we'd score."

In the next minute, Lol Chappell raced through the Chesterfield rear-guard and scored with a cracking shot. He turned to receive a brief round of handshakes, the typical acclaim.

"There you are," said a Chappell fan, nudging his, mate, "What about that? That shook t'onion bag."

"I allus said he were a good 'un."

"Yer never."

Barnsley seemed safe with their 3–0 lead and some supporters grew restless.

"Come on, let's see more goals."

"They're saving themselves for Easter."

"Keep moving Chappell," shouted a barracker as the centre-forward lost one of his many fruitless chases. "I could 'ave bet you to that."

"The couldn't bet me," said his mate.

"You want to try?"

"Aye, race thee up the touch-line after."

"Yer on."

The noise of the players was drowned by the noise of the crowd.

"Man on."

"Square ball."

"Keep him there. That's it. He can't use his left foot."

"You wouldn't like me to kick you with it."

"Anything like your usual, you'd miss."

When the game finished, the score still 3–0, the crowd crushed out of the ground. When Bob Shotton walked onto Oakwell, 30 minutes after the end, he found three spectators leaning over the boundary wall, resembling hooligans about to be frisked. Drunk, they had argued all afternoon about who was the best runner, best footballer, so they raced about the track. Now they were being sick.

The crowd of 17,141 took less than an hour to disperse, and then police supervision ended. At the bus station, bus after bus left full, but the spectators waited in good spirits, talking to strangers about football or stopping for coffee.

"How did Lol Chappell miss that last one?" said a woman in a bus queue, "It was easier to put it in than over the top."

She turned round and went red. Behind her stood Lol Chappell, waiting for his bus to Gawber. He had moved into a club house on Limesway, finally able to afford the furniture. Players rarely escaped the crowd and the importance of football. When Jimmy Baxter was in Barnsley he found people persistently stopped him in the street to congratulate him on his chip over Huddersfield's Hesford in a 1947 FA Cup tie. A player caught laughing after defeat would be chastised by a supporter. To sit in a pub with a pint might be interpreted as "blind drunk". The players had to be careful. There was no high living.

Inside the manager's office at Oakwell, Lily Johnson continued to answer the telephone, which rang incessantly until 5.45. She had been at the ground all day, eating sandwiches at lunch-time to save the office being empty.

Ernest Steele's day ended only when everyone had dispersed. He would not go to bed until after 11.30, when the police had completed their first overnight check. The club enjoyed very cordial relations with the police, who had a key to the ground. Each night, tea and milk were left out for the local bobby so that he could help himself during his inspection of Oakwell.

The results on Easter Saturday threw the promotion race wide open. Hartlepools won 5–2 at Accrington, who had led the division since 15th January. York dropped a home point to Grimsby.

York City had taken Newcastle United to a semi-final replay in the FA Cup. This meant extra games and they were losing key players through injury. They had played most of the season without a manager. Jimmy McCormack had spent the summer signing players but he left soon after the start. He had paid a York record of £2,500 for Arthur Bottom of Sheffield United after the Football League Management Committee had reduced the fee. Bottom was scoring goals regularly – he eventually finished with 39 – and his opinion of himself rose. "Look at me now, 20,000 wouldn't buy me," he said at the height of the FA Cup run. A voice replied gently: "And I'm one of the 20,000."

1	Accrington	40 – 53
2	York	39 – 51
3	Barnsley	37 – 50
4	Hartlepools	40 – 50
5	Scunthorpe	39 – 49

On Easter Monday, Accrington drew with York – ideal for Barnsley, who beat Bradford City 1–0, which narrowed the gap to a point.

On Easter Tuesday, Barnsley played their game in hand at Bradford City. They produced a sparkling first-half performance, starring Maurice Jackson, who was in at left-half for the injured John Jarman. They led 2–0 at half-time and although Jackson pulled a muscle it did not affect the result. Barnsley moved to the top of the League on goal average and it was now 795 minutes since Harry Hough had conceded a goal. The unbeaten run was spectacular.

Feb	12	Workington	h	3–1	Bartlett 3
	19	Mansfield	a	1–1	Brown
Mar	5	Tranmere	a	1–0	Wood
	12	Stockport	h	2–0	Brown 2
	19	Hartlepools	a	3–0	Kaye, Wood, Bartlett
	26	Gateshead	h	3–0	Kaye 2, Wood
Apr	2	Darlington	a	1–0	Lumley
	4	Chesterfield	h	3–0	Chappell 2, Wood
	11	Bradford City	h	1–0	Chappell
	12	Bradford City	a	2–0	Kaye, Wood

Saturday 16th April 1955

Barnsley had recovered from Angus McLean's 5th minute goal to lead 2–1 at Crewe. The game entered its dying minutes. Bob Wood, playing at left-half with Jackson injured, challenged Williams inside the Barnsley penalty area. The referee, also named Wood, pointed towards the penalty spot. There was a moment's confusion. It was an indirect free-kick 12 yards from goal.

"Everybody back."

"Come on lads, a wall."

"Back, Lol."

"Stay up, Lol."
"Can you see, Harry?"
"Left, left."
"Right, right."

Harry Hough was the key man and Tommy Lumley, always thoughtful, always on his toes, organised the wall for him. Tim Ward and Bob Shotton wished they were on the field. Alongside them was Ted Brown, reserve at the last three away games. Since they had all been won he was now the mascot as well. Around the Crewe ground were coachloads of Barnsley supporters, ferried by Arthur Rowe's buses at 10/- a head.

As they waited for the indirect free-kick, the Barnsley players wondered where the ball would strike. The lace, most likely placed away from the kicker, might reach them first. Flying laces had been known to end a player's career.

"Oh no, have I got to head it?" players might think as the ball came, and they wondered where they would wake up. Ugly red welts might appear on their thighs, the pattern of the ball still there after the game. Faint-hearted players disappeared behind the wall or pushed players in front.

Harry Hough looked for a view through the long wall. During one of his rare appearances at a training session, Angus Seed had suggested a split wall, two players either side and the goalkeeper with the important clear view down the centre. But this was a nine-man wall. The usual was four.

McLean shot. Players turned their backs, players came forward. The ball was blocked and bounced loose. George Spruce, the silent, unsung hero of Barnsley's season, emerged with a solo run, reminiscent of his days at outside-left in the navy. Barnsley held onto their lead and their place at the top. When they left the field, both teams had to share the same bath.

The next three games produced only three points. The defeat at Chesterfield was Barnsley's first in 13 games. With Accrington winning again, the pressure was on.

1	Barnsley	43 – 59
2	Accrington	44 – 59
3	York	43 – 56
4	Scunthorpe	43 – 54
5	Hartlepools	44 – 54
6	Chesterfield	44 – 52

Ted Brown had missed the Chesterfield trip because it was mid-week, but Tim Ward named him as reserve for the match at Chester. This meant first-team money for Brown, who as an ex-Barnsley Boy was accustomed to travelling and eating at hotels. This hadn't always been the case. During the depression of the 1930s, when the manager signed players from poor areas, he had to feed them, buy them clothes and take them to the baths before bringing them to Oakwell. When one local lad went away for the first time, a hotel waitress asked what he wanted for a sweet. "A Nuttall's Mintoe," he replied.

Saturday 20th April 1955

1–0 to Barnsley. The second-half at Chester was lasting for ever. Barnsley were not at their best. Chester were desperate for points to avoid re-election and they did most of the attacking. Yet Barnsley still led through Tommy Lumley's first-half goal.

It was a trying time for those in the trainer's box. Tim Ward was quiet while watching the game, and he always preferred quiet around him. He did not like Eddie Fleetwood's frenetic behaviour on the bench. After five minutes of an FA Cup game against York he had to tell him to take a walk around the town.

Bob Shotton was more Ward's type. They talked only about necessities such as injuries and they shut their minds to crowd comments, building up a wall of concentration. They were as quiet as when they were scouting.

Alongside them sat Joe Thorpe, privileged since he kept the players' valuables and the dressing-room key. The reserve was Ted Brown, who was now so regular as a lucky mascot that he brought sweets to suit the others' tastes. Shotton was a man for mints while Ward liked anything that lasted.

The sweets went quickly as the second half dragged. Ward never looked at his watch. He got annoyed with people who kept saying how long there was left. Instead, Shotton held up fingers for the benefit of the players. Six minutes left. Five. Four. Three … three minutes to go and there was a goal. Tommy Lumley crossed from the left and Bobby Brown shot into the net from six yards. It looked as though Barnsley might weather the Chester storm. Now two minutes left. One. And then the final whistle.

The away-team dressing-room at Chester was so small that you had to leave the skip or two of the players outside, but Joseph Richards somehow brought elegance to the scene when he entered with the results of the important games. "Chesterfield 6," started Richards, and already the players were cheering, "Accrington 1." The nearest rivals had lost. "Tranmere 1 York 0." The players tried to work it out. "It seems to me," continued Richards, "that we are champions in everything except name." It was only some remarkable results that could stop them.

Joe Thorpe wouldn't have missed driving them back for anything. Virtually all the directors were on the bus, including Joseph Richards who normally travelled by car. Even Jack Clough the referee had accepted a lift on his way back to Bolton. This was most unusual.

"Have you heard all the scores?" started Tim Ward, who then began to fill in the details of an important Saturday. "Rotherham lost 1–0 at Port Vale. That's let Luton in. They won at Doncaster."

"Walsall, Boss?"

"They got a point at Northampton. 1–1. Re-election again though."

"Did Birmingham win?"

"Drew 2–2 at Liverpool. They have to win at Doncaster on Wednesday to go up. It's a good job they beat Liverpool 9–1 earlier in the season. And fancy Cardiff beating Wolves. They stay up. Leicester lost 3–1 at Huddersfield."

"Even Andy Graver couldn't save them."

"Yes, we'll be playing Leicester next season. And Sheffield Wednesday, even though they beat West Brom 5–0 today. And Preston won 4–0 at Charlton. I bet Jimmy Baxter got a few. Even I got one there once, Sam Bartram kicked it out ..."

"Did Arsenal win, Boss?"

"Lost 2–1 at Portsmouth. No surprise there."

"How about Stenhousemanure, and Patrick Thistle?"

Tim Ward continued to recall Scottish results with unfailing memory until Norman Smith asked his usual question: "How did Bishop's Stortford Reserves get on, Boss?"

"They lost 21-10, two last-minute tries."

There was no containing the players. They rehearsed their own version of the Goon Show; Norman Smith acted like Arthur Caiger, frequently starting the singing for the benefit of John Jarman, who always sang the same song: "She's got a hole in her sock, a hole in her shoe ..." And a bunch of Randolph Suttons would burst into action with the words of "Mother Kelly's Doorstep".

They celebrated at the Blue Cap, near Northwich, a hotel named after a racing dog. Cigars were brought out and the directors bought the players drinks, even though there were still two games to play in the next four days.

"Do you mind if we stop for a drink?" Joseph Richards had said to Joe Thomas, "You can have an orange-juice if you like." When Richards spoke to Tommy Lumley, he added, "I don't know how you manage to come out of all those tackles, being so small." Lumley looked back and noticed that Richards was the same height as him.

Joe Thorpe always advised a hotel about 25 miles from the ground to allow players time to wind down and recover their appetites. Three or four of the players now smoked and Norman Smith made a cigarette follow his finger across the table, fooling players for a long time before they realised he was blowing it.

During his career, Joe Thorpe had either arrived or left his home in Tower Street at every minute on the clock. He knew all the necessary places along any route – toilets, cafes and newspaper-sellers. Tim Ward always hopped off to buy a dozen copies of a sports paper, preferably the *Green 'Un* where they could read John Uprichard's report and the local news.

Thorpe was like a father to young players and made detours to drop them where they wanted – baths, dance-hall or dog-track. The first teamers took round a cap on the return journey, the minimum offering being a tanner, and the club supplemented this with a 10/- tip.

Making most of their return journeys in the dark, the players saw little of the countryside. Other people remembered places for golf-courses, cathedrals or pubs, but to these men it was the football ground and 90 minutes on the turf. The coach arrived at Oakwell late in the evening, sometimes too late for last buses. If Joe Thomas had wanted to catch a bus direct to Doncaster his last chance was the no. 14 at 9.05, so now he had bought a pre-war Vauxhall Velox for £115. This helped young goalkeeper Don Leeson, who could have a lift from Askern on training nights. Benny Hill of the *Barnsley Chronicle* frequently relied on a lift to Wombwell from Henry Walters, walking the remaining couple of miles to Darfield.

When the bus reached Oakwell, Ernest Steele heard it from his house and came across to open the gates. Raymond Vicary was also still there. He stayed until the last bit of business was finished, sometimes until midnight. The Northern Intermediate League kept him busy collecting results and producing tables. Rule 17 stated that results had to be notified to the secretary within six days on pain of a 10/- fine.

At the end of the final game, at home to Chester, a crowd gathered round the tunnel to applaud not only a 4–2 win but the fact that Barnsley had finished the season as clear champions. The players were ushered upstairs into the directors' box where it was arranged that Harold Shentall, chairman of Chesterfield and member of the Football League Management Committee, would present the Third Division (North) championship shield. The crowd showed some displeasure when Joe Richards stepped forward to accept the trophy, and he passed it on smartly to Norman Smith.

There followed the unusual scene of players relaxing in the boardroom with drinks in their hands. At the end of a heavy season and with nothing substantial to eat, Tommy Lumley found a couple of glasses of wine a little too much; Harry May made sure he got home safely.

Talent money of £275 was distributed according to appearances and the Football League issued 13 medals – 11 for the players, one each for manager and trainer. They allowed the club to buy a further two. Yet Barnsley had used 22 players and 14th on the list was Johnny Jarman, whose 12 games had brought 20 points. Tim Ward sacrificed his medal for Jarman but Ron Smillie, with nine appearances, was left without.

Bryn Price, meanwhile, was playing in the Central League for his future. Price doubted whether the club would keep him on the groundstaff after the end of the season. In the penultimate game he played his heart out against Huddersfield's Tommy Cavanagh. He felt his contract depended on this one and he might have been right. Ward offered him full-time terms after the game. It was the most wonderful event in Price's young life, though it was sobering to look at the other wing-halves available: Norman Smith, Jarman, Walters, Jackson, Wood, Holmes, Ron Archer, Trevor Archer, Ted Brown, Billy Anderson and the newly-signed Barry Barber. "I'll never get in the first team," Price told his friends.

When the directors gathered in the Royal Hotel for one of their monthly finance meetings there was still a loss of £7,000 to contend with. Attendances might not go up in the higher division if results were bad, as 1953 had proved. In any event it needed crowds of 14,000 to break even, let alone recover losses.

The directors agreed to increase admission charges by threepence, a return to their Second Division prices. Season tickets sold at £6/6/- (centre stand) and £4/11/- (wing stand). Holders had first option on renewing seats, and new buyers were allowed into the stand to test their choice before finally deciding. The only summer income was from season-ticket sales and the FA Cup pool. The club waited eagerly. Meanwhile, bills stacked up on Raymond Vicary' s desk.

Both Raymond Vicary and Tim Ward kept a petty-cash box for paying expenses, but any large bill required a cheque with signatures from two directors. It was very difficult to keep track of all the outgoings of a football club – quite unlike a small business. Joseph Richards was almost always one of the two signatories and he often decided the order of payment. "We're not paying him yet," Richards might say, while Raymond Vicary kept his eye on the pile. Sometimes the bills mysteriously arranged themselves into a different order.

While continuing their hand-to-mouth existence, the board took a rough look at the years ahead. Promotion to the First Division seemed a possibility with a settled team so they agreed not to sell important young players during the next five years. This meant that there would be no money to buy established players, but there were plenty of youngsters coming through and Tim Ward had every reason to feel content.

Two weeks before the start of the 1955–56 season, Tim Ward travelled to the BBC studio in Leeds for an appearance on Cliff Michelmore's radio show, linked to managers of other promoted clubs – Pat Beasley of Bristol City and Arthur Turner of Birmingham City. Tim Ward was on a wave of success and his club had faith in him. After Leicester City and Derby County had both made approaches for him in the summer, Ward was given a 50% pay rise by the Barnsley board, a decision confirmed when Joe Richards returned from an FA tour of the West Indies. There was talk of a Barnsley tour too, but tours were not easy to organise. Top-class amateur teams were as much in demand, there was no central organising body and it was not easy to get into certain countries.

Tim Ward was happy to stay put, although he still had a soft spot for Derby County, who had been relegated to Division Three (North). Promoted teams held the media interest. The newspapers were no exception and a story duly appeared – all was not well in the Barnsley camp.

After promotion, wages had been raised to £15 (winter) and £12 (summer), the Football League maximum. Harry May and Bobby Brown spotted a legal loophole – when should the winter wages start? The players were paid £15 from 22nd August and not 1st August. May and Brown consulted the other players and then acted as spokesmen.

On the Tuesday before the season's start, Tim Ward met the players in the billiard room. He explained that it was a moot point, but three weeks at £3 extra for all the professionals meant a lot of money to the club. They might have to release a member of the groundstaff. The players were disappointed but understood the argument. Nevertheless, a story appeared in the press. Brown and May were portrayed as being in dispute with the club. Bobby Brown was certainly upset at being picked at outside-left in the public practice match but now there was newspaper talk of transfer requests.

It was a club rule not to release stories without the board's approval and to do so was a sending-off offence in Joe Richards' book. Though the directors might be wrong, they should not be seen to be wrong. Richards thought the two players named in the article might have to leave the club. He and Tim Ward met them.

It was enough to persuade Harry May that it was time to go. He had always accepted the conflict between players and directors and three happy years at Barnsley was his longest spell with any club. He regarded his playing career as an interlude before going into business, for which he was well prepared, spending many hours studying economics. For Britain, consumption and investment were the watchwords and the consumer was beginning to prefer domestic luxuries on hire purchase to the outright pleasure of an afternoon on the terraces. The post-war football boom was over. Attendances had dropped slightly below the pre-war level. Joseph Richards was more concerned about the bank-rate, which was rumoured to rise to 4½%.

Harry May signed for Southend United, the first club that came, and Barrie Betts replaced him in the team against Leeds United, a home start to the season. Bobby Brown was selected at outside-left although a cloud still hung over him following the incidents of the week.

The beginning of Barnsley's 1955–56 season was most notable for the serious injuries. They started after 10 minutes. Norman Smith's thigh forced him off the pitch and then onto the left wing. That night, after dinner at Ralph Grimes' house, the injury stiffened so much that his host had to make arrangements for him to stay.

In the 29th minute of the second game, at Notts County, Joe Thomas injured a knee. Like Smith he stayed on the field at outside-left purely as "nuisance value". If possible, Ward would always move an injured man to centre-forward. So long as he was fit enough to stay onside and stick a boot out in the box the opposition would have to mark him, whereas out on the wing a player could be ignored until he got the ball.

Thomas aggravated his injury. When the bus reached Oakwell after the game the knee was swollen so badly that Thomas could not contemplate driving his car or working the next day. He stayed at Tim Ward's house, which was convenient for seeing the specialist. When the swelling subsided, the injury was diagnosed as cartilage rather than ligaments.

Bobby Brown played most of the first two games at inside-left despite being picked to play on the wing, and the injuries gave chances to two young players. Colin Swift, 20, reserve at Notts County, came in at right-back. Malcolm Graham, Ward's first signing, was introduced at inside-left. Graham scored seven goals in eight games, and this helped Barnsley to a respectable position, losing only once in the first nine games.

1	Bristol Rovers	8 – 13
2	Fulham	9 – 12
3	Stoke City	9 – 12
4	Sheffield Wed	9 – 11
5	Lincoln City	8 – 11
6	Barnsley	9 – 11
7	Port Vale	7 – 10

It was Graham who was next to go onto the side-lines. His left knee, the hinge for a dynamic shot, was giving him considerable trouble, as it had a year before.

By the end of September it was obvious that Barnsley would be missing the three players for some time. Thomas and Graham were both in Claremont Nursing Home in Sheffield for cartilage operations and Norman Smith was having injections after breaking down in training when simply pushing a penalty. The most celebrated casualty that month was BBC radio's Grace Archer, killed off on 22nd September. Her fictional death attracted a huge public response, taking attention away from ITA's first broadcast which also went out that Thursday night.

Without Floodlights

Chapter Five

Saturday 1st October 1955

The bus arrived soon after one o'clock. Out of the Great Northern Hotel came the Barnsley players, including Tommy Lumley, who looked even whiter than usual. He had contracted food poisoning on the Friday train journey.

At the best of times Lumley looked little like a footballer. He excelled through skill, courage and anticipation. Some of his colleagues dubbed him "Chopper" because it was the most unsuitable nickname that could be applied.

"Are you alright, Tommy?" asked Tim Ward.

"Yes, I'll be alright, Boss," replied Lumley, but when George Spruce, the new Barnsley captain, led the white-shirted "Reds" onto Upton Park, the effects of the sickness were still present.

Barnsley failed to reproduce their recent form. After 75 minutes they trailed 4–0. Tommy Lumley was having a dreadful game, Maurice Jackson had conceded an own-goal and felt a muscle injury, George Spruce had given away a penalty and Arthur Kaye was limping. Kaye was playing with a patched-up foot. The club's pleasure at Kaye's first England Under 23 cap the previous Wednesday was marred by him receiving an injury. He had had a tough time in recent weeks against Stonehouse of Middlesbrough and Thresher of Bristol City, who had eventually been booked. In fact three Barnsley opponents had been booked in the last four games, an unusually high number. John Bond of West Ham was the latest, for standing over the ball at a Barnsley free-kick.

George Spruce was at the peak of his career, subduing a string of Second Division centre-forwards – including debutant Brian Clough of Middlesbrough. But today things had begun to go wrong for Spruce. West Ham centre-forward Billy Dare had scored twice. With Kaye and Jackson injured and Lumley ill, there was pressure down the Barnsley right. Ken Tucker chased a through-ball and George Spruce moved across. He slid into the tackle and stretched for the ball.

There was a loud crack. Everyone stopped. The ball was forgotten as it ran loose on the edge of the penalty area. George Spruce lay with his left leg in the air and motioned away players who ran to help him. Ken Tucker signalled straightaway to the trainer's bench, but referee Reg Leafe had already called for a stretcher and Bob Shotton and Tim Ward were moving onto the field. When Shotton reached Spruce he knew it was a fracture. He could tell by the angle of the ankle. Even if in doubt he would have treated it as a fracture. The player's living was at stake. While Spruce received five minutes attention on the field under a doctor's supervision, Ambulance men were kept busy by the number of spectators who fainted nearby. Spruce was taken straight to hospital on a stretcher. Ken Tucker walked tearfully alongside as far as the dressing-room. Bob Wood moved to centre-half.

When the game ended Tim Ward left Bob Shotton in charge, handing over the money needed for tips on the return journey. When pressed for a few words by reporters he said that he was banning practice matches at Barnsley: "One more injury and we won't know where to turn." Finally Ward collected George Spruce's clothes before taking a taxi to the hospital. There was no way Shotton could accompany him. The 30 minutes after the game were the busiest time in the trainer's week.

George Spruce's broken left leg was X-rayed, set and put in plaster very quickly. West Ham supporters beat Tim Ward to the hospital, bringing fruit, condolences and kindness. Spruce could travel that night providing he put no weight on his leg. Ward telephoned Mrs Spruce, who was on a family visit in Chester.

Spruce and Ward took a later train to Doncaster. Spruce rejected crutches and hopped along the platform. The other passengers made room for him to stretch out his injured leg. Ward tried but failed to find him something to eat. Despite his immediate concerns, Ward was already thinking ahead. He had lost four dependable defenders – Thomas, May, Smith and Spruce. His stable Third Division team would not see him through this Second Division season.

When they reached Doncaster, a porter prevented another long-distance hop. "Hang on, I'll get a barrow," he said, then wheeled George Spruce to the goods-lift. Hours before, Joe Thorpe had collected the rest of the team in the coach. Now it was Arthur Raynor, who drove Spruce and Ward to Huddersfield Road, where George Spruce stayed at Ward's home. The back seat of Raynor's car was left with a white streak from the wet plaster.

George Spruce had eaten Saturday lunch as part of a successful side. Then it was a downhill day – a display below his usual standard, a penalty conceded, a fractured left leg, then hospital and a bizarre journey back to Barnsley. Lunch seemed a long time ago when Spruce entered a strange house in the middle of the night, yet to eat another meal.

The road back to fitness was one of isolation, but George Spruce was able to face it. It was hard to consider a man more popular throughout the club – for both his play and his manner. He always seemed surprised at his success. His father had regularly walked 7 miles to Ellesmere Port, done a 12 hour shift and then walked back. It made George Spruce feel fortunate to play football. So when a photographer came, Spruce appeared cheerful, which he was. Yet he received few visitors after his injury and he got a little bored. Someone gave him some bits of timber and he started making cabinets and tool boxes. His wife was glad of his company around the house.

When Joe Thomas returned to Askern, Fred Semley visited him with a big bunch of gorgeous, juicy grapes that Joseph Richards grew under glass at his home. But it was small compensation for Thomas, who had been on the verge of an England B trial.

While recovering, players were in the charge of Fred Semley and Bob Shotton. Semley in particular had the difficult job of a middleman. The club might want a player to play when not fully-fit. A player might want to play. He might be influenced by not wanting to let the team down and the danger of losing his own place.

Undoubtedly Semley was the pivot of a high-class medical system. Many of the town's doctors were interested in football. They watched the games and knew the players. Thomas Lawson was an outstanding orthopaedic surgeon, capable of conducting superb knee operations. George Spruce, for instance, could testify to a scar from a cartilage operation that was the smallest he had ever seen. And Mr Lawson was conveniently based in Sheffield, with consulting rooms in Barnsley. Before this, Barnsley had had to go to Mr Stewart in Newcastle.

Fred Semley insured the players and arranged the medical cover through the London Hospitals' scheme, a forerunner of BUPA. He had to stitch players frequently after training accidents and kept abreast of developments in the physiotherapy field. In the 1950s, when equipment at many clubs was Spartan, Semley ran a crowded room at Oakwell. Massage and electric heat treatment were continual functions. The latter replaced the traditional method where players sat all afternoon with towels over their legs, pouring boiling water over the towels. At the end they looked to see what was left of their leg.

The players were wary of anybody who had not had a career as a footballer and they were superstitious about their injuries. Bob Shotton found he could spray water on a player, tell him it was the "latest thing" and find the player reacted favourably.

Fred Semley tolerated the inevitable criticisms. His delicate methods suited some players but not others. Some of those who favoured the more physical approach of Bob Shotton were apt to think of anything less as skin polishing, and one player even took an injury outside the club, to Dodds of Cudworth. Fred

Semley suffered, as did all medical men, in that when players came to see him they were injured and were not in the best of moods.

Sunday morning was often the first time Fred Semley saw particular injuries. Injured players were required to report to Oakwell before 10.30. Serious cases might have to telephone to arrange visiting hours. Since not many players had telephones this could be an inconvenience and getting to the ground could cause problems. Half the first-team players lived more than four miles away.

Friday 14th October 1955

"Go..." yelped Eddie Fleetwood, as two more players reached the corner-flag, "Go ... go," he shouted. His voice was high and penetrating, and the players sprinted along the cinders. Friday was an easy day for full-time professionals. Training meant a few quick sprints, the final one for the wage packet.

While the players waited for their wages, reading newspapers or playing snooker, the trainers worked on the kit and Tim Ward took final stock of the various team-sheets he had carried in his head all week. He checked his injury list as late as possible, cautious about Friday training, brief as it was. This made life difficult for the *Barnsley Chronicle*, which went to press on the Thursday, but Ward tried to give Benny Hill as many indications as he could.

The players were encouraged to take it easy on a Friday. Every club had lost a key player in a needless Friday accident, and with almost a team injured, players' movements were watched anxiously. Fun-loving footballers could take advantage of this. If warned not to kick a ball – and they often were on Fridays – they might kit out a player, douse him with tomato ketchup, get him groaning and call the trainer with grim expressions. A favourite trick of Kaye and Chappell was to tour joke shops looking for the latest in plastic warts. Bob Shotton once tried to burst a particularly nasty boil on Chappell's leg only to find it fell on the floor. Norman Smith, member of the Magic Circle, set high standards.

Eddie Fleetwood lay in the bath after training.

"Aye up, lads," said one of the players, "Who's thrown that pair of braces in t'bath?" Eddie Fleetwood could take a joke. Slight and pale, he had played at inside-forward with Scunthorpe, Blackburn and Barnsley. He had always played part-time, working as a stores clerk for the Barnsley gas company until 1948, when he became assistant trainer at Oakwell. Fleetwood was popular with the players – except for 90 minutes each week. Then he would watch the Reserves and erupt into a shower of complaints. The team's reserve needed shinpads front and back as he lit the next cigarette in Eddie Fleetwood's chain. No player was ever out of range of his voice. In one game he had bounced too much in the trainer's box and knocked himself out on the roof. But soon after the game, Eddie Fleetwood was back to his warm-hearted self.

He donned his tank-top and collected a cup of tea before going to the boot-room for a cigarette. He handled the boots with Bob Shotton and John Steele, helped by the groundstaff. Shotton was a master at the cobbling craft. The groundstaff boys stood fascinated as the men nonchalantly dealt with studs and told stories that captured the passion and fun of football.

Cobbling was not an easy job. The size of the three-tiered leather studs could be varied with the state of the pitch. When the studs were taken out, they left three holes where the nails had been. These holes were plugged with broken matches. The boots were cleaned and the bottoms polished so mud would not stick. Players never saw their match boots from one Saturday to the next, unless they looked into the boot-room.

"The Boss isn't going to play you tomorrow, Tommy," said Bob Shotton when one player looked in.

"Fair enough," said Tommy Holmes, who had only played for the first team once.

"Any newspapers in there?" said another player.

"No time to read."

"Do you know where I can get a chair, Bob?"

"I'll go and see the chairman," said Tommy Holmes.

The hammering resumed. The boots were strong enough to stand it. Some players spent half a season breaking them in. They wore them in the bath and they wore them in the house without the studs. Fred Semley still had to drill some black toe-nails when the boots were new. They were often bought a size small and players would do anything to hang on to their old boots, even if they were patched like a quilt.

On the bottom of the boots were the owner's initials made from tiny brass sprigs knocked in by Bob Shotton. It was an unusual system, most clubs used numbers. The initials were not foolproof, as with Gavin Smith and George Spruce, but Bob Shotton could match boots and player without turning them over.

"Aye, he could get goals off a banana skin," continued Bob Shotton, taking the bait for another story, "On match days I could tell if he was going to score by how he walked in the dressing-room. If he'd been in the Mount, he'd sneak round the dressing-room. If he hadn't he'd walk straight up to me."

"What about that trainer, the one who wouldn't give you anything."

"If you wanted a spare bootlace he'd tell you the club wasn't made of money."

"Aye, you don't play with a lace."

"He'd glare at you if you wanted a ball and ask what you wanted it for."

"Then there was that cupboard on the wall he kept soap in. Billy always locked it and kept the key on him. He never realised that the cupboard had no back and the lads used to lift it off the wall and help themselves. He never understood where the soap went."

"Do you remember them blazers we had. No lining, not worth the badges they were sewn onto."

"I thought they were quite good."

"Wages have arrived, lads."

Raymond Vicary had returned from the National Provincial Bank. He always collected the wages in cash, accompanied by whoever was available. The players walked to the office where they poked their heads through the hatch.

"Oh, and could you sign this stencil for me, please?" said Lily Johnson, who dealt with autograph requests, so many that the master-copy soon grew tatty.

"Not already," teased the player, who had picked up the special pen.

Inside the office Tim Ward was coping with his worst day of the week. An hour on correspondence was followed by a word with the team and then the press. "Arthur is very happy with us," he told one reporter, word-perfect in his recitation, "All inquirers are being told he is not for sale ... no, no, that's the first I've heard of it. It's news to me."

Ward was suspicious of the national press and he chose his words carefully when talking to them. In fact he spoke carefully to anyone on the telephone. Soon after taking over as manager he had engineered an experiment with Sammy Crooks whereby the Shrewsbury manager telephoned to offer £10,000 for Norman Smith. The immediate interest of a reporter confirmed to Ward that there was a leak along the line.

There were two telephone lines into the makeshift office and extensions to the trainer's room and the directors' box. During the day Raymond Vicary moved through to the boardroom where he could spread out his papers.

Tim Ward's team for tomorrow's visit to Blackburn was now selected. Barnsley were going through captains like they were Smarties: Norman Smith, George Spruce and Tommy Lumley. But Lumley had been injured against Lincoln after scoring the game's only goal, so Ward's team for Blackburn would have Harry Hough as captain. They were eight players in their early twenties. One was Tommy Holmes, who was called back and told by Bob Shotton, just as he was about to leave for home.

Two weeks passed and another Friday came. Team selection was further complicated by two defeats, each time finishing with ten men. Despite Bobby Brown's early goal at Blackburn, they were beaten 5–1 – a brace from Briggs and a double by Douglas. At home to Plymouth they lost 2–1, Jack Rowley scoring his 200th League goal, just 12 minutes after his brother Arthur had reached the same landmark with Leicester. Onto the injury list went Barrie Betts and Maurice Jackson, who pulled yet another muscle. Ward decided that with no substitutes he hardly dare risk Jackson, in spite of his ability, and Billy Anderson was brought in at right-half.

Tim Ward had already moved Henry Walters to centre-half in an attempt to find a similar player to Spruce. To cope with the injury to Betts, Walters was moved to left-back. This was a disappointment to Phil Roscoe, who had received a hint from Bob Shotton that he would be in. Roscoe felt ready and expected to be partnering his former Barnsley Boys colleague, Colin Swift. Roscoe was more of a positional player than Barrie Betts, who concentrated hard and tackled even harder. Running with arch-back, Betts had learned the geometry of full-back play, closing angles, turning the winger where he wanted him. Henry Walters was not in Betts' style either but Ward now accepted that his push-and-run pattern was breaking up. This was demonstrated by the introduction of Duncan Sharp, a centre-half of complete contrast to George Spruce. In the last minute against Leeds, with Barnsley winning 2–1 and down to ten men, Spruce was up with his forwards. Sharp, however, was an ultimate stopper. He was big, dark and handsome, which made him a very conspicuous figure.

The accumulation of injuries made it difficult to maintain the rhythm. Kaye was seeing less of the ball and that in turn meant there was less point playing Bartlett on the left wing to connect with Kaye crosses. Since Billy Wardle had been released to take over a Lincolnshire pub, the left wing again became a priority for Ward. Then there was a need for goalscoring cover with Lol Chappell and Bobby Brown nursing knocks.

There were several ways Ward could find a centre-forward. Firstly, there were the youngsters. Both "Chippie" Rowe and Malcolm Hirst were promising but neither seemed destined for a lightning breakthrough. Secondly, Ward could convert a more experienced player. After seeing defenders burst through and try a shot, spectators often commented "They should play him at centre-forward," but the weekly hammering, back to goal, well-marked, was punishment that only an experienced man could handle. Ward tried Bartlett and A team centre-half Olly Hopkins at centre-forward, but the manager believed that both were better players when coming on to the ball.

Ward's third alternative was to buy an established centre-forward. He watched enviously when Roy Shiner scored two goals for Sheffield Wednesday at Oakwell, but £20,000 players were out of Barnsley's reach. Although hire purchase was becoming feasible for the working man, Barnsley had a big enough overdraft to worry about. Their informal rule was to nurture youngsters.

There were other ways of finding experience. Ward had enquired unsuccessfully about Jack Shaw of Sheffield Wednesday and then Joseph Richards sent a telegram to the Robledos, who were back in Chile. Another dead-end.

Tim Ward settled for the fourth alternative. He looked for a proven goalscorer in a lower class of football. The scouting skill lay in judging the pace of the game and the player's potential to adapt. The transfer fee would be less but the risks higher. It was through this channel that Ward made two signings in November 1955.

When the first team went to Doncaster on 12th November, Tim Ward travelled to Scotland in search of talent that had been Angus Seed's speciality. Since Seed's scouts were family and friends, many of them had died with him, but Harry Nattrass still patrolled the north-east and Jimmy Crapnell was still based in Glasgow.

John Steele and Eddie Fleetwood hunted local footballers by bus and on foot. Tim Ward covered 20,000 miles a year by car alone. Much of it was fruitless, apart from the enjoyment of watching football. The vital player might be missing or injured on the day. Most likely he was not good enough. A key function of scouts was to keep away the bad players.

Ward took train trips to Scotland once or twice a season. A galaxy of managers of English clubs would converge early in August when the Scottish season started. They were frequently keen on the same player, such as Third Lanark's Alistair McLeod, who signed for Blackburn in 1954.

A rail trip to Glasgow was awkward for Ward. It was almost better for it to be a "wasted journey" because then he would leave at half-time and catch the early train back to Leeds, where he left his car. But his November trip was a lengthy one. An attempt to sign a player meant tidying up loose ends while on the spot. This required an overnight stay followed by a late-night Saturday return.

Ward arranged to meet the Bridgeton Waverley team and travel with them to Lesmahagow. He found that their manager, John Rennie, had like him been in the 15th Scottish Division during the war.

Bridgeton Waverley were having a good season. They were still in the Scottish Junior Cup and wages, paid on a percentage of the gate, were up to 30/- a game. Ward was impressed with their win at Lesmahagow and asked for an option on three of their players: centre-forward Torrance, inside-left Quinn and outside-left McCann. The price was £500 per player.

In the end Barnsley only bought John McCann, a 20-year-old who was new to the left wing, a former wing-half who had been turned down by Stoke after a trial. Ward expected to wait until Bridgeton Waverley were out of the Cup but a thigh injury from the Lesmahagow game made McCann come down early.

With an overdraft of £20,000 Barnsley watched their cash carefully. Signing three players and paying their wages was a considerable outlay. Instead Ward signed a centre-forward, Gordon Duggins, from Gresley Rovers of the Birmingham Combination. The cost was £900 but Duggins would be part-time and did not need a club house. He was serving an engineering apprenticeship at the Coal Board and earning £3/15/- a week. Duggins would train on his own and travel at week-ends, staying Friday nights in the White Hart. It was a round trip of 140 miles. He was used to hotels, having been born at the Black Horse, Edingale, which his father kept.

The manager of Gresley Rovers was Sammy Crooks and the deal was completed at the Baseball Ground, Derby, where Ward and Crooks watched the first round FA Cup replay on the ground of both their First Division careers.

The first the Barnsley players saw of Gordon Duggins was at a Tuesday morning practice match. "Who's that bloke?" they asked when they saw the stranger standing with his hands in his pockets, singing "Robin Hood". For Duggins it was just another game of football to be enjoyed, but for the established professionals it raised questions: is he signed? what position does he play? does he make my position insecure? They were questions the manager wanted them to ask.

Towards the end of November the tide turned with a thrilling 4–3 victory over Bristol Rovers. Although he was barely fit to play, Bobby Brown scored five times in five games from centre-forward and the last of these brought a good point back from Liverpool. This left Barnsley halfway in the table and Tim Ward was free to make another important acquisition almost unnoticed.

Early December 1955

The Rimmingtons had recently moved into a bungalow. They had piled up furniture in the hall while they wallpapered and emulsioned the living-room. When they heard a knock at the front door they assumed it was carol-singers.

"Go away, you're too early," shouted Norman Rimmington.

"It's me, Bob Shotton, can you let me in?"

"Oh, I can't, Bob," said Rimmington, stumbling over furniture, "Can you come round the back?"

It was 12 years since Rimmington started a goalkeeping career that had taken him to both Barnsley and Hartlepools United for five years. Now it had ended. Rimmington had accumulated niggling injuries to his fingers and toes and finally a broken bone in his hand while playing for Denaby United. Although only 30 and deeply committed to the game, Rimmington decided to finish, and he was now an engineering foreman at the North Gawber pit.

Rimmington opened the back door and Shotton explained his purpose. "We'd like you to travel with the A team."

"What's happening at the moment?"

"Well, Jock Steele's doing it, but he has to take the Juniors as well." Arthur Glover had left the job some time ago. Glover worked Saturday mornings and then had to rush back after the game to tend his pigs and poultry.

"What's it entail, Bob?"

"Packing the skip, being with the team on Saturdays, arranging meals and writing a report of the game. Come down and have a word with the Boss."

"I'll do that."

Norman Rimmington had not visited Oakwell for years but he started on the right foot with Tim Ward since both men were interested in cricket. Rimmington was a well-known local fast bowler. He accepted the part-time coaching job and inherited George Jackson, the volunteer helper. Rimmington would start at the beginning of February.

Finding a backroom worker took as much scouting as signing a player. It was all done by word of mouth. In December 1954, the club had employed Ernest Steele as groundsman on Joe Walker's retirement. Steele was another cricketer, in fact a professional. For five years he had been Barnsley Cricket Club's groundsman at Shaw Lane.

Steele, who was also an ex-professional footballer, accepted the Oakwell job on the basis of more regular hours, especially in the summer. He required a house and the club bought one on Grove Street, opposite the ground. The job paid £10 a week with free house, coal, electricity and telephone.

Saturday 24th December 1955

On the morning of Christmas Eve Ernest Steele was confident the afternoon game with Fulham would be played. Two days previously Tim Ward and Peter Doherty had travelled to Derby through thick snow for the funeral of their playing colleague Leon Leuty. Only a remarkable Friday thaw unveiled the Oakwell grass.

Part of Steele's inheritance from Joe Walker was a rough map showing the location of the Oakwell drains. There were three. One ran directly across the pitch. Two ran from the centre-circle to the Co-op end, one finishing in the goal and the other near the old dressing-rooms. Steele thought of this area as "Lol Chappell's corner", for Chappell liked wandering towards that corner-flag to find space.

Ernest Steele walked from the tunnel to the far left-hand corner. He vaulted the wall and lifted the large man-hole cover behind. This corner was 15 inches lower than the other end of the same touch-line. This was where the drains needed to be working overtime. Steele noted with satisfaction that the nine inch pipe was gushing water and he went off to organise the forking of the goal areas. Then he could use his light roller, a six inch wooden one he had obtained from an old woollen mill in Huddersfield. It produced a nice smooth finish in the wet, where a heavier version would just skid.

At his home in Brampton Henry Walters had far less to do and he settled down to read the newspaper. Walters was a home-loving man with sedate interests such as classical music, but Saturday lunch-time was a different proposition. Walters found that he was gripping the newspaper tightly, his elbows pushing against the chair. He was thinking about the match. He might as well be at Oakwell.

When Walters had a bad spell he tried several remedies. He might step up his training and once he saw an optician about his eye strain. But the real answer was calming his nerves. It came to virtually all players at some stage of their career and the remedy was in their own hands. Both Walters and his father were more aware of any criticism now he was with his local club.

Henry Walters was always one of the first players to arrive at Oakwell. That was soon after one o'clock. There were no dress regulations but the players normally wore suits and ties. Norman Smith once appeared after a game wearing a suit and tie but no shirt. It had been thrown in the bath.

The Barnsley players were optimistic about the home game with Fulham but they had lost some of the conviction of the previous season. Lol Chappell had the pressure of playing for his place. It was his 10th game of the season and he had still to score. Even allowing for his unselfish running, his goal famine was crucial because the Second Division thrived on consistent centre-forwards. Duncan Sharp, at centre-half, had been coping well with them. In the last four games he had faced Andy Graver (now with Stoke), Stan Mortensen (Hull City), Billy Liddell (Liverpool) and John Charles (Leeds United). "If the centre-forward has a good game," Bob Shotton would tell him, "There's only one man to blame."

In the dressing-room the programmes were fanned out on the treatment table. The players picked them up and thumbed through.

"That Jezzard's down at centre-forward," said one, "He scored four at their place."

Duncan Sharp scowled. He pushed down his socks and pulled them up again. Before the game he was tense. In the Reserves, colleagues occasionally entertained themselves with lines like "I see Tom Finney's been dropped, he must be playing against us."

Tim Ward had done his best to resurrect his promotion team and there had been no changes in four games. Swift and Betts were at full-back, Sharp at centre-half, but otherwise there were familiar faces, with Bob Wood taking Norman Smith's important right-half position. The adrenaline still flowed for Arthur Kaye, who knew that he could face anyone in the Second Division.

It was a happy game for Barnsley. On a perfect pitch they won the battles of the big central men and registered a 3–0 win, their best of the season. Lol Chappell scored twice and the third was an own-goal by his marker, Fulham centre-half Ron Greenwood.

The bad news came after the game when John Steele returned from Beighton where he had accompanied the A team. At the last minute he had had to ask 21-year-old Ron Riches to play. Riches had completed his joinery apprenticeship and just happened to be home on leave from National Service at RAF Hednesford, near Wolverhampton.

Riches had not been on the field long when he accidentally kicked his own ankle, breaking it. Since it was near Christmas there were all kinds of complications and Riches had been married less than a month. Tim Ward rang the commanding officer at Hednesford who agreed to allow Riches to remain in Barnsley while the injury set. By the New Year Riches was at an RAF rehabilitation centre at Ely.

Saturday 21st January 1956

Spencer Hill walked along the back of the Barnsley press-box carrying a watch. He was dictating copy for the *Yorkshire Evening News*. Hill was "Rufus" in the evening's pink paper.

"… passed to Delapenha," continued Hill, "Who scores from close range in the … 78th minute."

"Er, excuse me, Mr Hill, I think it was Wayman. Number nine."

"Oh, was it? I can't see much from here." Visibility from the press-box was growing worse. It was a miserable day for the Middlesbrough match. Rain, mist and gloom swamped the ground. Referee Jack Swain was considering abandoning as Spencer Hill made a note of the goal along his copy of the *Guardian*. The free-lance reporter was somewhat of an oddity in the football world. Well-spoken and educated, he was smartly dressed but his bow-tie was slightly askew and his notes on the game even more so; jottings ran round the edge of his programme, over a cigarette packet and all round his newspaper. Rarely could he find what he wanted, but he was never at a loss for words. If anything he erred in the opposite direction, for newspaper requests of one hundred words might produce yards from Spencer Hill.

Oakwell was being overrun by darkness and Barnsley were being defeated by Middlesbrough. When the third Middlesbrough goal entered the net, the press-men established the goal rather than the name of the scorer.

Two Barnsley directors sat at the side of the press-box, commentating for the hospitals in the region. The Barnsley Hospitals' Commentaries Committee was the first of its kind in the country, commencing on Boxing Day 1952. Len Squires and Colin Wilkins were the organisers and the directors – although not every director – would take turns to commentate, usually two of them alternating every 15 minutes. Arthur Raynor always felt amateurish and exposed at the microphone, but the club's post-bag showed that the commentaries were appreciated. Players also visited the hospitals and displayed their championship shield. Commentating, however, was a thankless task, living by the moment without an overall picture. In the dark it was impossible.

Lily Johnson watched from the top step outside the press-box. After half-time she returned to this spot. When she first took her job as receptionist she understood that she would not see much of the game but she rarely missed more than 10 minutes. Against Middlesbrough, nobody could see very much.

Joe Richards watched from the back row of the directors' box, where he could stretch his legs comfortably into the gangway and knock in the odd imaginary goal with his bad leg. Raymond Vicary dashed all over Oakwell. He stood next to Lily Johnson for some of the game but also met head gateman Ernest Jepson to arrange for the money to reach the bank. They used a different procedure each week and policemen accompanied each gateman in turn.

Vicary was worried about the bad light. He kept meticulous records of each game, noting the attendance, kick-off time, weather, time of finish, state of the light and any changes over the course of the day. He kept details of everything and they proved useful for deciding the time of future kick-offs. The Middlesbrough game had started at 3 pm. Considering the current gloom, it looked a mistake. Vicary would pray hard before the next board meeting. He would take the blame.

Setting the kick-off time was always a problem. Barnsley favoured a late kick-off and at each end of the season they were able to start at 3.15. This allowed more time for pit-workers when they finished their shift. In the winter, with no floodlighting, kick-offs crept forward and attendances were liable to drop. In some towns there was not the same need for precision. At Swansea, for instance, favourable hours of sunset meant no kick-off earlier than 2.45.

"That's another goal." The press-box stirred.

"Well, there's 88 minutes gone."

"I don't know who scored."

"Middlesbrough, I think."

"I can see that. I don't know which player."

The spectators began to wander home. The result was assured and there was little to see. They could remember the game's first goal when Delapenha's centre struck Betts and they would have to learn the rest from the wireless. It transpired that Middlesbrough had won 4–0 and during the period of eclipse Charlie Wayman had scored a hat trick. It brought his Football League tally to 239 goals.

Spencer Hill finished his "Rufus" report and went to the telephone kiosk under the stand to convey a different report for a Sunday newspaper. The telephone booth was prominent in the main corridor, opposite the Visitors' dressing-room. Inside the kiosk, working under a solitary light, Hill sifted through his notes on the game. Thumbing through his mass of papers, he was a sitting duck for the post-match pranks of players. The light switch was across the corridor and players would flip it as they walked by. Spencer Hill would storm out with papers, programmes and packets flying around the corridor.

The timing of kick-offs was a topical point. The FA had decided to experiment with floodlights for FA Cup replays and then they allowed the use of lights in the third round on three conditions: both clubs must agree; emergency generators must be available; and there must be the fullest co-operation with the police and transport authorities. At the start of the 1955–56 season, 36 Football League clubs possessed floodlights.

Barnsley decided against floodlights for their third round tie at Aldershot. Joseph Richards had seen Aldershot's replay with Reading and considered that the lights would increase home advantage. The tie, which Barnsley won 2–1, proved frenzied and eventful anyway. First the referee spoke to Aldershot's trainer for coaching. Late in the game their centre-half Charlie Billington moved to centre-forward and then on to the dressing-room, sent off for challenges on Hough and Sharp. And a scuffle broke out around the press-box which stood in the middle of the crowd. When *Barnsley Chronicle* sports editor Benny Hill warned Aldershot supporters for picking on Ernie Jarvis, an ex-boxer reporting for the *Sunday People*, he was set on instead and clouted from the side. In the end referee Malcolm needed a police escort.

By the fourth round in late January, the FA believed the need for floodlights had disappeared and a 2.45 kick-off would be late enough to suit all clubs. Although Raymond Vicary might have had some cause for concern.

Barnsley's home tie with Blackburn brought Tim Ward two characteristic managerial problems. The first concerned Lol Chappell. He had trained hard for what was only the second all-ticket game in Barnsley's history, and then he read in a newspaper that he was dropped from the team. Tim Ward was not unused to newspapers jumping the gun over team selection but it never ceased to annoy him. It meant he had to explain his reasons to a player already upset and close to tears.

On the day of the game the team arrived back from the Majestic Hotel, Harrogate. They had enjoyed the break of a few days with fresh air, high spirits and regular doses of sherry and eggs. With its long straight landings the Majestic was big enough for training but the players spent their indoor hours playing snooker and table-tennis in the basement. But when the coach edged towards Oakwell it was a different atmosphere. People were already packed tightly down Oakwell Lane.

Just before the kick-off the second problem arose. Tim Ward had moved Bobby Brown to centre-forward and Lol Chappell's place had gone to Tommy Lumley, fit again after hurting an ankle on the Blackpool sea-front during a few days break just after Christmas. Lumley expected to resume the captaincy and was upset when, without a word of explanation, Ward handed the ball to Henry Walters, who although a part-timer had been captain for the last three games. Like Chappell, Lumley had trained hard for the game and his father had travelled from the north-east to watch.

The game brought a crowd of 38,163 with record receipts of £5,692. Tommy Lumley played below par. Barrie Betts held Bryan Douglas well but suffered a back injury and Barnsley went out of the FA Cup, beaten by Bill Smith's goal in the 66th minute. Lol Chappell handed in a transfer request that was turned down by the directors. It was ironic that less than a month later, when Barnsley played Blackburn in the League, Chappell scored twice in a 2–1 win.

Top: Tim Ward (left) is congratulated by Joseph Richards on his appointment as manager. On the right is Gordon Pallister.

Bottom: Tommy Lumley scores his dramatic injury-time winner at Halifax in October 1953.

Pre-season walks.
Top: (left to right) Bryn Price, Colin Swift, Bob Wood and Frank Bartlett.

Bottom: (left to right) Lol Chappell, Bobby Brown, Harry Hough, Harry May and Jack Walls.

Action at Gateshead in November 1954.
Top: Defence in depth from Maurice Jackson, Harry May, George Spruce and Norman Smith.
Bottom Left: Harry Hough.
Bottom Right: Bob Wood scoring.

Top: Third Division (North) Champions. Back row: Jackson, Smith, Thomas, Spruce, Hough, May, Jarman, Walters, Shotton (trainer). Front row: Kaye, Lumley, Chappell, Ward (manager), Wood, Brown, Bartlett.
Bottom: Ground unfit. Left to right: Fred Semley, Tim Ward, Bob Shotton and Joe Walker. The old dressing-rooms are in the background.

Top: White-shirted Reds at Middlesbrough in September 1955. Jarman and Betts cover as Hough saves.
Bottom: Ex-Barnsley All Stars, April 1956. Back row: Pat Gavin, Tim Ward, Sam Bartram, Mark Jones, Jimmy Baxter, Walter Bingley. Front row: Gavin Smith, Cec McCormack, Tommy Taylor, Eddie McMorran, Johnny Kelly.

Top: Syd Storey (right) in action against Stoke City.

Bottom: Gordon Duggins challenges Port Vale goalkeeper Ray King.

Top: Graham Vearncombe (Cardiff City) saves from John Edgar during the 1957 FA Cup tie.

Bottom: Arthur Kaye (left) on the attack against Hull City in January 1958.

Top: Duncan Sharp, Frank Bartlett and Colin Swift try to stop Blackburn's Tommy Briggs, January 1957.

Bottom: Raymond Vicary and Tim Ward in their office.

Taxed for Entertainment

Chapter Six

Saturday 11th February 1956

It was a freezing February. The first day of the month was the coldest English day since 1895 and by the second Saturday Barnsley people were accustomed to snow. Fred Whittlestone walked to Oakwell from his home in Wilthorpe. He had finished his shift at 1 pm and returned home from the pit for a quick bath. Now he wore his St John Ambulance Brigade uniform, which was heavy for walking, his overcoat and two haversacks adding to the weight. Inside all the pockets, Whittlestone carried a cargo of materials. He was an experienced man in first-aid.

The Ambulance men could not jump to the head of a bus queue like the police so Whittlestone walked to be sure of arriving in time. He crossed the Jumble Lane level-crossing, where he arranged for an ambulance to stand by for a big match. Otherwise if the gates were closed the ambulance might be stranded on the bus-station side.

Whittlestone warmed up walking but he knew that on cold days few volunteers braved the Spartan conditions at Oakwell. Although they had requested their own cubby-hole, there was still no cover and they sat on the touch-line. They treated patients under the stand or in Fred Semley's room if it were a serious case. Space was in short supply on match days.

Early arrivals in the Oakwell crowd were surprised to see West Ham United warming up 15 minutes before kick-off. Not only that, but they were dressed in track suits and lightweight boots, fresh from FA Cup success against two First

Division teams, Preston and Cardiff.

Fashions had arrived from the Continent. Wolves had made floodlit games more acceptable and Manchester United had brought new style to kit, their players wearing brief shorts and V-neck shirts for a Central League game at Oakwell. "Don't they look fit and muscular?" spectators said, "They're a big team."

Before the war Banbury Spencer had experimented with silk shorts and technicoloured socks provided by a nearby textile business, but new trends had reached few teams. Individual players tried ripping off long sleeves in hot weather (to the disgust of trainers), or folding over tops of shorts to make them more comfortable. Lol Chappell did the latter, following the example of Sheffield Wednesday's Albert Quixall, one of the first in short shorts.

The game started and Freddie Whittlestone was soon soaked. It was snowing and hailing and blowing. He sat by the tunnel with a clear view when handkerchiefs waved from immediately opposite. Unlike the trainer, Whittlestone had to run around the perimeter of the pitch.

If a spectator had fainted he would ask the crowd to pass the patient over their heads, but with epilepsy or heart attack, Whittlestone needed to work his way through the crowd. Getting back was the problem. The patient could not be thrown about and pushing would cause a swaying effect. Besides, some of the crowd would not move, worried about losing their view.

Fred Whittlestone treated two boys and then ran to join Bob Shotton when a player was injured in the Co-op end goalmouth. The handkerchiefs waved again. He ran back to the two boys.

"Are you the father?" Whittlestone asked a nearby man.

"Aye."

"You should take him home. He's too cold."

No sooner had Whittlestone finished than there was a signal from the Pontefract Road end. He ran and reached the corner short of breath.

"Get a move on," came a voice, "Tha's running like an old man."

Whittlestone stopped and looked up, but the crowd was too dense to spot one spectator. Those nearer turned to the heckler.

"He'll have another case if tha says owt like that agen."

"Aye, he's doing more running than the players."

The home win against Blackburn ended two months without a win in the League, but the problems started again at Plymouth, now accepted as a Barnsley bogey. The 3–0 defeat was to a Plymouth team fighting against relegation. It left Barnsley with just four wins from 28 meetings with Plymouth in the FA Cup and League. Plymouth's dark green shirts, unique in the Football League, seemed to produce strange effects on Barnsley. Harry Hough, for instance, looked unusual in a blue jersey. In fact Plymouth loaned out more goalkeeping jerseys than any other club. Norman Rimmington had once borrowed a white one that finished halfway down his back.

The 650-mile round trip was the longest possible for Barnsley, but the strangest journey was one that occurred on the Home Park pitch. Malcolm

Graham, back in the team since New Year, was playing at outside-left, a position he disliked because of periods of inactivity. At one point in the game he received the ball on the Plymouth goal-line. Coming up against a defender he turned inside and then back towards his own half. Challenged again, he kept the ball on his left foot and repeated the process. He dribbled back still further and took the ball over the halfway-line, towards his own penalty area. Tim Ward and Bob Shotton wondered what he was doing. It appeared that he might score at the wrong end and even his own players were worried. "If I'd brought him down, would it have been a penalty?" Duncan Sharp asked afterwards. No-one knew.

But even bogey towns had their good points. While in Plymouth a couple of the players got a tip on a very good greyhound, which romped home. The players talked the owner into bringing the dog to Sheffield, where as an outsider it won again.

Saturday 10th March 1956

Ernest Knowles walked at a carefully measured pace around the Oakwell pitch. "Never look as though you're in a hurry," they had taught him at police college. "Don't stand still," they were told at the ground, because it was important not to block a spectator's view. Not that Ernest Knowles needed telling. It was his 10th season of duty at Oakwell – inside, outside, guarding the cash office, escorting the takings. He was a familiar and popular figure with the Barnsley crowd, who tended to regard their policemen as personal property. Some of them were not pleased with their team's efforts today. Three early goals from Liverpool had killed the game.

"You should get out on field, Ernest, lock 'em up."

"No, you should be locked up for coming," Knowles replied, "I'm getting paid."

There was a ripple of laughter and he moved on. The Liverpool forward line mounted another attack. As Knowles walked down the spion kop end towards the terraced stand he saw the ball come off Barnsley's full-back, onto Billy Liddell's leg and across the goal-line. The referee gave a corner. The crowd were furious and Ernest Knowles threw his helmet and cape into the air for the first time since the championship win. Next moment he found himself on the sacred turf remonstrating with the referee. The crowd howled.

The corner came across and was cleared. Knowles looked up to see a stick waving at him from the mouth of the tunnel. He walked down and was met by Superintendent Harrison.

"It's your job to control the crowd," Harrison told him.

"Oh, I thought it was my job to see justice done," he replied.

It was the last time Ernest Knowles saw anything at Oakwell in an official capacity for two years. He was relegated to outside duties. There were some at the Liverpool match who might have envied him. Barnsley lost 5–0. In fact, five games in March brought only one point and two goals, while 17 went past Harry Hough. It meant 5 points from 13 games and the risk of relegation.

18	Rotherham	33 – 29
19	Barnsley	37 – 29
20	Notts County	38 – 28
21	Plymouth	38 – 25
22	Hull	35 – 19

Monday 2nd April 1956

"Now remember," said Tim Ward, leaning back against the radiator in the Oakwell dressing-room, "Play it simple. Football's an easy game, just do the easy thing. Keep it on the carpet." Tim Ward had done most of his talking the day before the game. He never said much in his pre-match talk. It was difficult to relax all the players with the same phrase or the same sort of humour, and Ward had to give 42 talks a season. "What would you be doing if you weren't here?" he asked his players, "You'd be playing anyway, out on Locke Park. Go out and enjoy yourselves today."

Ward looked around the dressing-room. The players sat in order, from Harry Hough behind the door round to Frank Bartlett next to the bathroom. "Remember, Tommy," continued Ward, "Let's stop this Allchurch from having a kick." Tommy Holmes nodded. He knew he was in the team to mark closely.

But the game started disastrously. Only 12 minutes had gone when Welsh-international Ivor Allchurch scored his second goal and it was virtually identical to his first. He received the ball from a short corner on the right and worked his way to the corner of the Pontefract Road penalty area. Then following one of the bodyswerves for which he was famous he produced a left-foot shot that deflected past Harry Hough.

Tommy Holmes looked towards the trainer's box. Short corners were becoming more fashionable. They were a way of slipping a marker. Two goals down, Allchurch on song, it would have been easy for Holmes to give in, but he stuck to his task. He followed Allchurch and kept him quiet. He saw the goals pulled back and slowly overtaken – Wood, Chappell and then Chappell again, with just two minutes to play. Two vital points and Barnsley were almost safe.

The last weeks of the season were the only time that games could be organised to bring in money for players' benefits. There was just enough light in the evenings and less to lose from injuries, though there might still be important fixtures to play in the April pile-up. Both Arthur Kaye and Lol Chappell had more than five years' service with the club and qualified for the full £750 benefit. This was the maximum sum laid down by the Football League, payable on the basis of £150 a year at the discretion of the club. This was a lot of money, equivalent to a 20% bonus, yet the player had no right to it. Boards of directors were justified in any decision on benefits. The wording of the rule was that after five years a club *may* enter into agreement with a player.

Big clubs had the reputation of paying the full amount as a matter of course and in the old Second Division days Barnsley did the same. Now there were many grey areas, principally the question of whether National Service, periods of injury and reserve team football should count towards the benefit.

In the last week of the 1955–56 season, Barnsley played an ex-Barnsley team which included internationals Taylor, McMorran, Kelly and Ward, as well as former Charlton goalkeeper Sam Bartram, now manager of York. A crowd of 8,416 paid £918 to watch. When expenses were deducted there was enough for one benefit and only one. Arthur Kaye was in no doubt who would get it. Kaye was the star, while Chappell had had an indifferent season with only six goals. Chappell would have to wait.

Tommy Lumley suffered a similar fate. Lumley had not played in the first team since the Blackburn FA Cup tie. He asked Tim Ward whether he would receive a full benefit if he stayed for his fifth season, but the answer was no. Lumley asked for a transfer and later went to Darlington for £800, of which he received half as an accrued share of his benefit.

Payment of an accrued share – and often it was a crude share – was easier to secure when a player was transferred. Having received a full benefit in 1953, Syd "Skinner" Normanton conducted his own negotiations with Gerry Henry when he signed for Halifax a year later, obtaining an extra year's accrued share.

Morris Hudson thought he was working on the same basis when Bradford City agreed to pay £500 for his signature. Hudson had been part-time for two years and full-time for a further five, making 30 first-team appearances in all. When the money was paid by Bradford City he received a £50 share. The Players' Union, which was affiliated to the TUC in December 1954, said they could not help Hudson unless there had been an agreement in writing, and a meeting with the Barnsley board got the player nowhere. It was hard to convince businessmen that they should sell a player and then give him the fee, especially as he would never play for their club again.

Moving to another club often involved the substantial expense of a car. When Doug Kelly moved to Bradford City he received a £600 accrued share (minus tax, as they all were) but he found it necessary to sell his old Austin Eight for £320 and put up another £400 to purchase an A50. Phil Roscoe also bought a car for his journeys to Halifax. But Syd Normanton had not and he was suspended by new manager Willie Watson for being late – albeit through no fault of his own. The difficulties of Arthur Gill, who commuted by train to Rochdale, can be imagined. For him every game was away. Eventually he was suspended for six weeks by Harry Catterick after misjudging the series of connections.

The problems of players released by their local club were not helped by a Barnsley ruling. Players of others clubs were not allowed to train at Oakwell. The directors believed that training sessions were crowded enough anyway. So the transferred players resorted to training on their own, as most found it impractical to move from Barnsley. Occasionally, Oakwell offered temporary training for players such as Joe Wade (Arsenal) and Lewis Clayton (Bournemouth) but only if they respected Bob Shotton's authority. And there were others who joined training sessions more permanently, like referees Arthur Holland and Harold Hackney.

Friday 27th April 1956

A day from the end of the season, Syd Storey sat in the front room of his home in Ardsley and looked out of the window. He recognised John Steele and Eddie Fleetwood walking past. Storey thought it strange because his house was at the end of a cul-de-sac. There was a knock on his door.

"Hello," said Storey, face to face with the Barnsley officials, "What are you two doing here?" They knew each other because Storey was a Barnsley miner and a York City footballer for nine seasons.

"We want to sign you."

Storey looked puzzled. "You know I'm a York City player?" he queried.

"Oh, don't you know? They're going to release you."

"No, I've not heard anything yet." It was not a surprise to Storey since he had been out of the team for most of the season and he was always worried about being retained, though at least he had a job at Houghton Main Colliery. New manager Sam Bartram had decided the York "Cup team" had had its day. Now Storey was being given a free transfer, in recognition of his services rather than his value, and it meant he would soon find another club.

"How did you find out?"

"There was a game last night. The Boss had a chat with Sam Bartram."

"We want you to play in the Reserves, Syd. Help the youngsters on. We've got some good young lads."

It was an ideal offer for Storey, who was 33-years-old. It meant he could play for his local professional club who had rejected him just before the war after Charlie Baines had invited him for a trial. Now Barnsley had come for him, offering a rise in his part-time wages to £11 (winter) and £9 (summer), plus an extra £2 for playing in the first team. The most he had earned at York was £10 after a £1 rise following the great FA Cup run. Their biggest bonus that year was £7/10/- for drawing the first semi-final against Newcastle. And they received £5 between the team when Arthur Bottom was interviewed.

Just as Arthur Kaye was given an immediate benefit, so he also enjoyed a secure position in the team. A queue of right wingers from Barnsley Boys formed behind but none could dislodge him. Ron Smillie had been in the lower teams until near the end of the season when he was introduced in games that earnt vital points. Like Joe Hooley he was slight in stature and not afraid of speaking out. Arguing with the manager was an ordeal, if not unthinkable, for most players, yet Smillie took it in his stride. He was a part-timer and there was a feeling in the club that you had a better chance of finding favour if football was your only work. Ronnie Smillie's emotional involvement with the club was complete, and that was the way he wanted it, but when he was offered terms for the next season he found that they included a drop in wages to £9. Henry Walters' wages went up by a pound. An interview with Joseph Richards persuaded Smillie that his future lay elsewhere and he signed for Lincoln City.

Compared to the national average weekly wage in the pits, the full-time footballers were no better off. Tommy Lumley, for instance earned an average of £14, below the maximum because of the close-season rate and a few weeks out injured. It was the part-timers who were in a more favourable position, but they missed some of their working days in the mines.

The club were watching every penny. They faced a summer without income and a further loss to announce to the shareholders. There was also the question of entertainment tax, which had been introduced during the First World War. Amateur sports were understandably exempt from the tax, but so was first-class cricket, for reasons unclear to most people. The tax was levied as a proportion of total receipts. Butler's budget of 1954 had at least reduced the tax by a halfpenny on each person through the turnstiles, but recent payments made to the Inland Revenue were enough to pay several benefits a season.

Entertainment Tax Payments

Source: Barnsley Football Club Balance Sheets

1952–53	£5,607
1953–54	£4,145
1954–55	£5,210
1955–56	£8,252

The question of transfers lingered on, allowing interest in football to intermingle with more traditional summer pursuits like nipsy, cricket and athletics. Already, Michael Parkinson had scored the first century of the Yorkshire League cricket season and Arthur Rowe was selected for the county as a shot-putter.

John Jarman's wife had not settled in Yorkshire and the player made preliminary arrangements to join Walsall. Barnsley, however, held out for their asking price. When Jarman received a second offer, from non-League Peterborough, he saw his way clear to forcing the issue and went to see Joseph Richards, who was in a Coal Board meeting at the Queen's Hotel.

Richards was displeased at the interruption of his business affairs. He told Jarman that it was not the place for such a discussion, but he became more concerned when Jarman told him he could go to Peterborough and Barnsley might lose on the fee. The two men reached a compromise and Jarman signed for Walsall.

Offers from non-League sides were a very real attraction. There was no accrued share of benefit and still a transfer fee to be paid if they returned to the League, but higher wages and substantial fringe benefits were usually a good compensation. The contracts offered had to be checked carefully, sometimes containing a clause which tied the player for a further season on less favourable terms. Ron Archer was warned about this when he moved to non-League Worcester City. No League club would pay Archer's £3,000 fee, which would then drop £1,000 a season by Football League rules.

Wigan Athletic wrote to Tommy Lumley to ask what wages he would require to be their player/manager. When Lumley suggested £16 a week he heard no more, so Tim Ward advised him to write to six League clubs. If all rejected him he could apply to the League for a reduction in his transfer fee.

After eight years in which he impressed with both his goalkeeping and immaculate grooming, Jack Walls moved to Peterborough. Although non-League, it was a growing town, well-connected by road and rail. Manager George Swindin was forceful and forward-looking, and there was no maximum wage. Walls was flattered to receive a telegram from such a famous ex-goalkeeper, and when he and his wife visited the town one sunny Thursday to look over club accommodation they were convinced. This left Don Leeson clearly second in line to Harry Hough, who was in his early thirties.

May 1956

"I can't accept these terms," said Joe Hooley, who was signing professional four months after his 17th birthday. His home situation still made him worry about money.

"Why not?" asked Tim Ward, taken aback and increasingly reticent with the youngster. Hooley was not a domineering figure. He weighed little more than nine stone and did not dwarf Ward's medium build as did Duncan Sharp and Olly Hopkins, but Ward sat back as if threatened.

A year ago Ward had arranged with Joe Richards for Hooley to work on a farm and build up his weight in the outdoors with good food and physical work. Richards knew a Barnsley supporter who readily accepted Hooley onto his farm, but the youngster only stayed a week before his mother visited Oakwell to complain that Hooley was working for nothing. In fact the club were still paying his wages, but Ward preferred to end the project rather than argue it out.

"£5/10/- in the summer," read Hooley from his contract, "£7 in the Reserves and £9 in the first team, plus bonuses." He looked up. "I'm only 30 bob better off than on the groundstaff."

"There's the £10 signing-on fee."

"Yes, but I'll be in the Reserves with players earning much more than that." The offer to Storey confirmed this.

"Joe, you're only seventeen. There's only so much we can pay you." Until players reached 21 they were subject to other maximum rates laid down by the League. This was a good economic reason for the club releasing a few older players in favour of products from the Juniors.

"They're as good as anybody else's terms, Joe," Ward continued.

"But I've played in the first team."

"Joe, Joe, those were friendlies ... and I was playing against you the other night. It was for experience."

"There's Jeffrey at Doncaster, he's in the first team. Edwards at Manchester United. When am I going to be in the first team?"

"Be patient, Joe, you'll be in the first team eventually."

"What's wrong with now? All I need is an opportunity."

"It'll come. When we get 35 points and we're safe I'll play you, no matter how many games are left."

Hooley left the room. He had often said to John Steele that he saw no way through the forest of players in front. Steele would tell him that they were only moderate players.

Schoolboy stars stood out, like Joe Hooley in 1953. The only problem was signing them. Many top clubs had scouts around Barnsley who tried to break the pressure for the boys to join the local club. The 1949 Barnsley Boys team had all received offers from other clubs, especially Wolves, for it was Mark Crook who scouted the hardest. Crook was a former Wolves player who came from Brampton. He ran a nursery team called Wath Wanderers and was a major reason for so many Wolves players in the Northern Intermediate League.

Some youngsters joined Wolves and then returned to Barnsley later. Joe Thomas and John Stainsby had stayed short periods at Molineux, but it had taken Henry Walters 10 years to join his local club. Wolves had won the Football League in 1954 and finished second in 1955, and they had several of Crook's Yorkshire discoveries on their staff: Ron Flowers, Dick Neal, Roy Swinbourne, John Short, Joe Bonson, Geoff Sidebottom and Cyril Beavon.

The football "fathers" of Barnsley Boys, Harold Rushforth and Ted Davies, were loyal to Barnsley. If the boy were set on becoming a professional footballer then they recommended staying in the close-knit community with the local club. But if a boy worshipped Sheffield United and lived that side of Barnsley then they would see the sense in an alternative choice. However, they were careful about recommending Wolves, as a boy would be based at Wath, away from the club itself. "You'll only get to Wolverhampton once or twice a season," they would warn.

Barnsley Schools FA was not a football nursery. The major purpose was to encourage a lifelong leisure interest. It was impractical to try to produce a team of professionals every year. Harold Rushforth told hopeful fathers that only a very good Barnsley Boys team resulted in more than one or two professionals. Even then there was the risk of accident, injury or falling away. After Ron Smillie signed for Lincoln, Colin Swift was the only 1949 Barnsley Boy left at Oakwell.

In 1955 Barnsley Boys had produced another star. David Wright played in all the England schoolboy games and captained the team against Scotland. His mother was approached by many clubs, including Manchester United, and she sought advice from the teachers. She was told that her son was a brilliant scholar and stood a chance of Oxford or Cambridge entrance.

David Wright's education came first. Tim Ward admired Wright's character and his full-back play. Ward believed in encouraging a boy's education. He accepted Wright's decision but still welcomed him to training anytime, hoping that he might sign professional one day. At Easter 1956 the youngster played three times for Barnsley Reserves but he was never really tempted, and groundstaff wages of £3/10/- were little incentive. Nevertheless he was glad to sign amateur forms for Barnsley. It kept the other clubs away.

Increased competition from other clubs was making it more difficult to sign local boys in the summer rush. Ward had missed Kevin McHale (Huddersfield), Edwin Holliday (Middlesbrough) and Mark Pearson (Manchester United). In the

1940s, with Barnsley an established Second Division club and local loyalties more apparent, this chase had been less of a problem. But two years in the northern section had lowered the club's status.

In 1955 Tim Ward had taken on David Barber and Frank Beaumont, Don and Dearne Valley Boys contemporaries of McHale. He signed Barber without seeing him play. John Steele, Arthur Raynor and Gordon Pallister had given good reports on the outside-left. Ward made a point of going to sign the boy in person and was impressed with the spotless, orderly house in Wombwell. It reflected favourably on the lad.

When he saw him play, Ward was unsure whether David Barber would make the grade, until the day that John Steele took the Juniors to play Wolverhampton with a scratch side that won 4–1. Steele returned with a big smile. He had moved David Barber to wing-half and liked what he saw.

Saturday 25th August 1956

"Get you boot down, Joe."

"Put heater on."

"Turn heater off."

"Drop her down a gear, Joe, you'll be changing on the roundabout."

"It's quicker down there, Joe."

"Yes, fork off, Joe."

"It's not an easy ground to get to, is it, Joe?"

"No, I don't like coming here. There's so many intricate ways to the ground," said Joe Thorpe, not that any ground gave him much trouble. In his first season his wife bought him a Michelin Road Guide as a birthday present, and he had since been able to use tram-lines as landmarks.

It was almost a tradition that the opening day of the season should be sunny and sleeveless for spectators, but today was cold, wet and windy. Barnsley were travelling to the Midlands to play Port Vale and Joe Thorpe was starting his 30th season driving the team. Port Vale had been the start of it all.

In the mid–1920s Joe Thorpe drove a choir party every summer to Trentham Park and Wedgwood Potteries. As the 1927–28 season drew near, Thorpe was called into his manager's office. Barnsley and District Traction Company – soon to become Yorkshire Traction – had been chartered to take Barnsley FC to Port Vale. "It's somewhere in the Potteries," the manager told him, "You go down there every summer. Do you think you could find it?" Joe Thorpe thought he could, although the name gave him no assistance. "If you make a good job of it," the manager continued, "It could become regular." Thorpe had made a good job. Borrowing a map book from Frank Caffrey, who kept a cycle shop in Doncaster Road, he had headed for Vale Road, Burslem, and by chance had landed outside the Etruria Road entrance to the old Port Vale ground.

"It's better coming here than the old ground," mused Joe Thorpe, "The players had to walk through a ginnell, along the back of some houses and they stripped over some stables."

"Aye, I played there," said Henry Walters, "I played there with Walsall. We needed a map to get from the dressing-room to the ground."

The new stadium, Vale Park, had been built to First Division standard in 1950, a complete contrast to the Recreation Ground, Hanley, their previous ground. So far, Port Vale's iron defence had seen them to an FA Cup semi-final and a safe spot in Division Two, although their ground had brought complaints from West Ham, who were knocked out of the FA Cup on a muddy day in 1955.

"They're a team of cloggers," said one player as Joe Thorpe weaved the bus through the narrow streets of the town. "But they did well enough last year."

"I thought I'd broken my leg here last year," said Walters, "Turner caught me on the shin when I pushed the ball too far forward."

"I can remember you moaning over the moors on the way back."

"Aye, he did me again the next day. Same thing. I pushed it too far ahead and went for it. I never felt a thing but it was draughty when I ran back. I looked down and there was a big tear in my knickers. He done me twice and I didn't feel the second one."

"Do you know how Port Vale got its name?" asked Joe Thorpe, when players' sympathy and smiles had died down.

"No, tell us, Joe."

"Well, I keep asking people and nobody knows. I think it's because there was a canal at the top of Etruria Road and barges could reach the Potteries. The Vale must have been a port of call for the barges."

"That 's interesting, Joe."

"Aye, but it doesn't explain why they're a bunch of cloggers."

A point gained in the goalless draw at Port Vale was followed by two home defeats – Swansea (2–3) and Middlesbrough (1–3) – that added to the continuing saga of penalties. Middlesbrough goalkeeper Peter Taylor punched clear the latest, taken by Malcolm Graham. It was the fifth successive miss by a Barnsley player.

Since Tim Ward took over as manager, Barnsley had been awarded 14 penalties and only four had been scored, although Bobby Brown got a goal in an FA Cup game when he followed up a penalty blocked by Aldershot goalkeeper Jackman. In three years, seven players had missed penalties.

Curiously, Bob Shotton had been a penalty-king in his playing career. In seven years he had missed only three for Barnsley. His strategy was to use a little direction, either side of the goalkeeper, and then hit the ball so hard that the goalkeeper certainly knew if he got a hand to it. Shotton had always worried in case another player had wanted to take penalties, but now it was the reverse. The Barnsley players worried about taking them. The only exception was Arthur Kaye. Shotton knew that Kaye's temperament was ideal because even if he missed it never affected his game. Yet Kaye had missed four penalties in two years, and he had shared the duty with Lumley, Brown, Wardle, Hudson, Bartlett and Graham.

It had reached the stage where, after Tim Ward's Friday discussion, Shotton would ask who was taking the next penalty. The trainer would often take players out for a practice of 10 attempts. But in a match it was a different proposition, more tense, with a history of failures in your mind.

Not that Barnsley would be any less firm in their appeals for a penalty. In the last few moments of the defeat by Swansea, Malcolm Graham's ferocious shot had cannoned off a defender. Arms went up. There were cries of "penalty".

The Barnsley players were still talking about it when they left the field. The referee explained why he had refused the penalty, pointing to his chest. "It couldn't have hit him there," said Malcolm Graham, "He'd be in the chest clinic by now." One point from three games was a worrying start, especially with a return at Swansea to follow, although there would be no Allchurch brothers this time. They had asked not to be selected because of the death of their father.

Thursday 30th August 1956

It had already been a strange day for Henry Walters. George Spruce had talked him into a cup of tea before the game and this broke a 20-year habit. As a boy Walters had once drunk a glass of water before an important game in the *Daily Dispatch* competition. His mouth had felt so dry and uncomfortable after 10 minutes that he had refrained from pre-match drinks since.

Henry Walters was modest, considering himself an ordinary 90-minute man. He was a "bread-and-butter player" who often went unnoticed despite his hard work and strange running style – head back and chest out. He was perhaps a little clumsy and largely right-footed. His recovery wasn't fast, which was why he tackled thoughtfully and tried to remain on his feet, unlike George Spruce.

There were nine minutes gone. Henry Walters received the ball with oceans of room. He ran a little and then shot, wondering why. It felt as though he were 40 yards from goal. Yet as he looked up he saw the ball disappearing into the distance and on the right course. He watched as the ball sped off the wet turf, past goalkeeper King and into the net. The wing-half turned round, chuckled and received the congratulations. It was his third goal for Barnsley in exactly 100 games, but the others were less spectacular: one from centre-forward when injured and the other late in a rampant Third Division win.

Henry Walters' major task was not to score goals, or even to make them, but to mark Mel Charles. Swansea Town struck back. By half-time, goals by McIntosh and Griffiths had given them the lead.

After an hour's play Henry Walters again found himself in a strange position, lurking on the edge of the Swansea penalty area. He shot, but this time he topped the ball horribly, and he was prepared to disown his attempt as the ball bobbed towards the crowded goal area. He watched, half in shame, as somehow the ball avoided all the legs and squeezed in at the post with the goalkeeper unsighted. Walters chuckled again. Two goals from wing-half. It meant he would be presented with the match ball.

It seemed that two goals had earned a point – until the last minute. Then came the treat. Arthur Kaye, cautioned earlier in the game, collected a pass from Smith near the halfway-line and proceeded to do it all himself. He went past a few forwards, defender after defender, dribbling and tackling and bouncing off players, before arriving close enough for the finishing shot. And Barnsley had won 3–2 .

As ever, there were mixed fortunes from the match. On the Friday coach trip back from Swansea it was a happy Barnsley contingent except for full-back Barrie Betts, whose back was so painful that he had to stand. Betts had slipped a vertebra in the January FA Cup game against Blackburn, and despite hospital treatment during the summer the injury was still present.

A Thursday evening game meant less than two days to recover before Sheffield United visited Oakwell. Betts thought he could run the injury off as he had on other occasions. Unfortunately leaders Sheffield United won 6–1 and left-winger Colin Grainger scored three. With the back injury showing so early in the season, Tim Ward and one or two others hung a question-mark over Barrie Betts.

For the next mid-week game, at home to Lincoln, Tim Ward made three changes. Colin Swift replaced Barrie Betts and there was a new left-wing pair of Syd Storey and John McCann. When Fred Semley saw Syd Storey in the summer he had commented, "I'll give you six games and you'll be in the first team." And Storey was, despite thinking he had come to play in the Central League.

Short, Swift and Sharp

Chapter Seven

Wednesday 5th September 1956

The man ran when he heard the noise from the crowd. He knew the teams had kicked off. He showed his season ticket but was too late for a cushion or a programme. He took the steps two at a time. When he reached the top he looked down at Oakwell and gathered his breath and his bearings. Which way were they kicking? Who's playing for Barnsley?

The spectator walked up the wing-stand steps during a lull in the play. There were 2,000 seats in the main stand, including these long benches divided by slats. When he reached his row there hardly looked room. People pushed together to create space. It was cosy in winter but cramped in September.

"Hello, I didn't think you were coming."

"Just missed it, lad, one-nowt, just scored."

"They haven't, have they? I nivver heard nowt."

"Come on, get sat down."

"Don't you believe it. They've only just started."

"Who's playing on the left wing?"

"McCann. Him from Scotland. Here, have a look at team changes. Storey's in."

Syd Storey was another Barnsley inside-forward capable of defeating a "What's My Line?" panel. Like Baxter and Lumley before him, he was wiry and wily. He liked the ball on his left foot for simple, accurate passes, working an alternative rather than passing to a colleague in trouble. He wriggled in and out of players, falling over a lot, scrambling up again. He was elusive. If an opponent kicked him he felt he'd had a good day to get that close.

Storey was never a goalgetter, although he scored more often than Henry Walters. Storey worked with a winger. At York he had supported two contrasting types. There was Jimmy Rudd, an Irishman who wanted the ball played to his feet so he could tease a full-back. And there was Billy Fenton, a flyer who revelled in Storey's chips into space.

While captaining the Reserves, Storey had decided that John McCann needed the ball at his feet. McCann sized up opponents carefully. If they were thick in the hip they were likely to be slow on the turn. McCann was a winger who hugged the left touch-line, coming deeper and deeper if the service was unsatisfactory. He did not especially like through-balls that led to sliding tackles or physical contact.

No sooner had the spectator sat down in his wing-stand seat than there was evidence of all this. With just five minutes of the game gone, John McCann jinked to the goalline and crossed the ball. It fell to Syd Storey who smashed it into the net with his left foot. It was a beautiful start and a few spectators in the wing stand felt knees in their backs from excited supporters behind. After another 12 minutes, McCann himself scored. Barnsley went on to win the game 5–2.

John McCann was an immediate success at outside-left. With one problem solved, Ward spent two months concentrating on two defensive positions. First he dropped Norman Smith. "One or two players in the first team are still going strong at the end of the game and they create a good impression," he told his captain. Ward knew that a bad game for a 32-year-old player such as Smith was not necessarily a matter of being "over the hill". A similar bad game for a younger player was simply a bad game. But Smith's groin injury had left him less mobile, and stamina had never been his strongest asset. He was a player who used a lot of energy with the ball at his feet, beating players, creating space. Into Smith's right-half position came Frank Bartlett, who was no longer needed at outside-left. It was a very welcome reward for him.

The second position Ward considered was right-back. Two years before there had been a glut of seven full-backs, but Hudson, May and Roscoe had been allowed to leave and the specialists were showing no sign of progress with Barrie Betts' back injury. Peter Gillott had played once in the first team but he was a left-back.

Ward's first-choice full-backs were now Joe Thomas and Colin Swift, but at Doncaster late in October, Thomas was given a torrid time by Ron Walker and Barnsley lost 5–2. Players recovering from a bad injury were liable to the same close scrutiny that Smith suffered, and they ran the risk of being written-off for sub-standard performances. The club could not afford to carry passengers. They had played the first 13 games of the season for just 9 points, and with a shortage of experienced full-backs, Ward decided to buy.

The directors looked at the kitty. It was still deep in overdraft though slightly healthier due to summer sales, a smaller staff and the £1,500 Rotherham had recently paid for Bobby Brown. The directors' responsibility was to decide whether the money was available. The choice of player was the manager's responsibility. Tim Ward opened negotiations with Stoke City for John Short. When he told Joe Richards that the fee was substantial, the chairman supported him, but added, "Try and get him a little cheaper if you can."

On Wednesday 24th October Tim Ward met Short and Stoke manager Frank Taylor in a Manchester hotel. Ward was the only one who did not come from the Barnsley area. Short was from Great Houghton and like Walters and Storey a local lad coming home. Ward had first tried to sign him in 1954 when Short played 26 times for Wolves' Championship side.

When Barnsley played Liverpool, three days later, the Short and Swift full-back partnership was on show to the Oakwell public. Kaye and McCann were becoming established on the wings and Barnsley won 4–1. It was only their second home win in eight attempts.

But where did that leave Barrie Betts? He was 24 and the father of newly-born twin boys. His back injury was still painful and tremendously restrictive. His career had been a patient apprenticeship until he had played his way into the first team. For a season he had been established as first-choice. Now he knew that when he was fit he would have to do it all again.

Yet it was the forwards who expected more punishment. They could argue that defenders had nice steady jobs, facing the right way, knocking the ball back down the field. The full-timers in the first team were all earning the maximum £15 a week, but there would always be a debate over importance. Wing-halves thought they were running for the full-backs. Inside-forwards believed they were grafting for wingers. There were creators and destroyers, architects and demolition men. There was also an unequal distribution of glory.

Not that much glory was coming Lol Chappell's way. He had missed games through injury and had scored 3 goals in 10 games. Then on 10th November Chappell sank in pain after a collision with the Huddersfield goalkeeper. He was carried from Oakwell on a stretcher and rushed for a cartilage operation. Worse followed. In his absence Barnsley were beaten 5–0. "And they were lucky to get nil," said Bill Shankly, Huddersfield's new manager. Shankly had visited Oakwell on two successive Saturdays, the first with Huddersfield Reserves, who lost to two goals from Gordon Duggins.

Life as a Barnsley centre-forward was up and down. In September, Gordon Duggins was under a cloud, losing his temper at Eddie Fleetwood after suffering incessant criticism during a Central League game at Sheffield United. This cost Duggins his place. Then the first team needed a centre-forward, and it was Malcolm Hirst who slipped in for a solitary appearance at West Ham.

With Chappell injured and Brown transferred, Duggins was back in the first team for Barnsley's game at Bury on 17th November. Memory man Leslie Welch forecast a home win for Bury, who had never been out of the top two divisions since their election to the League in 1894.

18	Rotherham	15 – 12
19	Barnsley	16 – 11
20	Port Vale	16 – 9
21	Bury	17 – 8
22	Notts County	16 – 8

Injury struck again at Bury, strengthening the view that forwards suffered most. Like any job there were things that had to be done. Malcolm Graham hated following the ball to the corner-flag, hearing the heavy tread of defenders' footsteps behind. The forward needed to be a magician to get anything except a hammering.

Graham did not relish pulling back a cross with a defender sliding in, and it was this that caused the trouble at Gigg Lane. When crossing the ball from the left wing, Graham was tackled and he went down thinking he had broken his left ankle. After treatment behind the goal, he was carried off on a stretcher. The injury proved to be a bad sprain.

Barnsley played with 10 men for most of the Bury game but they won 2–1, Gordon Duggins scoring both the goals. As he came off, Duggins gave thought to his return train journey to Lichfield. One of five part-timers in the team, but the only one not in the Barnsley area, Duggins only travelled in the bus if it was convenient, so this time he fixed up a lift to Manchester with a couple of Bury players. There he bought a copy of the *Pink 'Un* and read the headlines. *Duggins is Dynamite to Bury.* It gave him a shock. He had never seen anything like it.

With forwards falling all around him, Gordon Duggins could expect an extended run. Opportunities filtered through to the Reserves, where there was competition for centre-forward between Arthur "Chippie" Rowe and Malcolm Hirst, both former Darfield Road Juniors.

When Manchester United Reserves visited Oakwell on 1st December, Arthur Rowe scored twice in a 2–2 draw. He might have had a hat trick. John Edgar's late cross was tempting but Rowe had had stitches inserted in a head wound and Eddie Fleetwood had warned him not to head the ball. Alex Dawson and Bobby Charlton scored for United in that game and Duncan Edwards rattled Don Leeson's crossbar from a mammoth distance. It was characteristic of Edwards' reputation that Leeson said afterwards that the bar was still vibrating at half-time.

All players settled into a match-day routine with which they felt comfortable. Arthur Rowe always took a walk for 10 or 20 minutes before settling down to a light late breakfast. He usually wore the shoes and check lumberjack shirt that convinced him he would score. Gordon Duggins always started the kick-in by hitting two practice shots straight into the net. This surprised some goalkeepers, who expected balls chipped into their arms. Malcolm Graham was on the injury list, vowing to tape his ankles securely for the rest of his career.

Beginning with the game at Bury, Barnsley scored two goals in each of six games and won 9 points. That brought them to Christmas Day, when they drew 0–0 on a bumpy Rotherham pitch. Harry Hough injured his left ankle, which ruled him out of the Boxing Day return.

Hough was injured on his 161st consecutive appearance. Such a run was a particular achievement for a goalkeeper since the job attracted so much physical contact. The heavy ball alone produced regular bruising and finger dislocations, and there was minimal protection from the robust challenge of opposing forwards. Hough had already broken an arm in 1952 following a challenge by Derek Dooley, and Hough's predecessor, Pat Kelly, had suffered a similar injury in collision with Roy Swinbourne. Knees and ankles had additional pressure imposed by continual kicking of a stationary heavy ball. The weight of the ball also meant you had to settle for deflections rather than catches.

Punching was another essential art. Bodies and ball were bundled into the net from centres and it was dangerous to catch. Crosses from the right wing were more crucial. Players swung them away with their right foot and the goalkeeper's best hand for punching was usually trapped on the outside; crosses from the left wing could be helped on with the right hand. While jumping with arms outstretched, leg muscles were slack and "dead legs" were common, clots forming under the skin causing painful haematoma. Harry Hough was adept at taking and nursing these knocks, but 24 hours was not enough for him to recover this time.

Wednesday 26th December 1956

Two inches of snow fell overnight and there was not a blade of grass to be seen. Don Leeson might miss his chance. Linesman Kenny Tuck arrived in the morning and thought the pitch was unfit. The referee, Jack Clough of Bolton, was stranded by the weather at Penistone. That meant that Tuck was in charge, but after some discussion with Tim Ward he agreed to wait for the referee. Arthur Raynor went to fetch Clough.

When Jack Clough arrived he asked about the pitch. It was common for referees to check with the groundsman and manager for expert local advice.

"It'll be alright," said Tim Ward, "I've played on worse. We're having some blue lines put down."

Clough walked down the tunnel and satisfied himself. Ernest Steele was painting the lines. He had borrowed a stick of Reckitt's "Dolly Blue" (price a penny) from Sybil Parkinson, who used it regularly to keep shorts white. It was a small cloth bag containing blue dye, which could turn whitewash blue. As usual, Steele used a three inch Turk's head brush. Alone it took him two or three hours. If there was just a sprinkling of snow the lines were simply swept, but today there was too much.

So Don Leeson made his debut after all. On Christmas Day he had received a telegram, which had simply said, "Phone Barnsley 5042 at eight tonight." There was no point asking him to report to Oakwell in case he did not receive the telegram. Poor communications at Christmas were a reason why the club took all the players away on Christmas Eve; this year they had watched "The Way of a Gaucho" together.

In the dressing-room, preparing to face Rotherham, Don Leeson rubbed himself with wintergreen and pulled on the heavy polo-neck jumper. The players warmed their feet and savoured the radiator. On the sound of the buzzer they went down the tunnel and turned right.

The right turn was an important tradition. It would cause great consternation if an opposing team went there first, and usually someone was there to prevent it. The previous day, at Millmoor, the Barnsley players had left the visitor's dressing-room with its central boiler and had been forced up the slope. The Rotherham tunnel was at the corner of the ground. The home side usually went out first and took the near end. Rotherham always kicked uphill if they won the toss and the second half could be like a cavalry charge.

Don Leeson was beaten once on his debut, but Gordon Duggins scored from 25 yards and the game ended 1–1. The teams retired to the baths and Ernest Steele took tea and biscuits to the match officials. Soon afterwards, Raymond Vicary handed them their respective fees and expenses – five guineas for the referee and half that for each linesman. One linesman put in for overnight expenses even though he lived less than 30 miles away. Vicary went to the boardroom for guidance.

"Overnight." said Joe Richards, "He'll get no 'overnight' from us."

Referees like Harry Husband took a different line. They even left a tip for the groundstaff boys.

Lol Chappell would walk through a wall to play for Barnsley. He was happy to be back in action and pleased with his first performance, a Central League game at Derby on 5th January 1957. Other people were astounded. It was just 55 days since his knee had locked against Huddersfield. His appearance that day had a background of conflicting opinions from specialists. Cartilage or ligaments? It was a recurrent question. A cartilage injury would mean an operation but a strained lateral or cruciate ligament could be even worse. It was also argued that the surgery itself was not necessarily the cure; the spell of rest might have done the trick on its own. Chappell's operation cost the club £50, plus £50 for 14 days in Claremont Nursing Home in Sheffield.

Lol Chappell was considered a credit to the profession. He was always smart, always fighting-fit or fighting to be fit. The quicker, fiercer tackling of the Second Division meant he incurred more injuries. He was still barracked by some spectators and was always glad to see his name on the next team-sheet. It would be difficult now. Gordon Duggins had scored 5 goals in 10 games during his absence. Chappell's return had been accelerated by having no pot on his injured leg, enabling him to exercise his thigh daily before running up and down the terrace steps to regain fitness.

Back in Barnsley, supporters started on their teas, not knowing whether they should feel downcast or relieved. Barnsley had recovered from an early 2–0 deficit to lead 3–2 against Port Vale in the third round of the FA Cup. Supporters had seen Arthur Kaye score his fourth successive penalty and follow it with a second goal after Frank Bartlett had equalised. All this with players injured: Syd Storey had hobbled from soon after the start; George Spruce limped later; Bob

Wood got a lasting lump on his right thigh from goalkeeper King's raised knee.

In the last minute Harry Hough became the villain of the piece, drifting across to collect a long, hopeful upfield ball. It hit a divot on the muddy ground, hit Hough and bounced out of his grasp. Port Vale's Poole had followed up, as Lol Chappell would, still running for a certain goalkeeper's ball. This time Poole popped it into the net and it was this incident which stayed in supporters' minds as they picked at their teas.

The ball, pitches and physical pressure from forwards ensured that all goalkeepers periodically let through a sloppy goal, and Harry Hough's "costly" blunder did help the club's finances. On Monday afternoon, knowing the winners were away to First Division Cardiff City in the next round, Barnsley played at Port Vale and earned extra revenue from the replay. Confusion surrounded the choice of team. They took 14 players, including a handful of part-timers. They all needed the day off and were lucky to have sympathetic employers.

One goal settled the replay. It came from the head of Port Vale centre-half Basil Hayward, but it went in his own net as he tried to divert a centre from Lol Chappell on the left wing. The game also saw the birth of a defensive back line that reeled off the tongue: Short, Sharp and Swift.

Wednesday 9th January 1957

Sheffield Wednesday were playing Preston North End in an FA Cup third round replay. A posse of Barnsley players went to watch Jimmy Baxter. Like all Football League professionals, they had free passes which permitted entry to grounds until their 35th birthday. There were other perks although free cinema passes were disappearing.

At Hillsborough, Henry Walters stood in a queue that stretched across the pavement and along the main road. A full house seemed certain. A man walked up the inside of the queue and those at the front looked over their shoulders and spotted him. There was a rush and the man was squashed against the wall. He peeled himself off and inspected the damage. The custard-pie he was carrying was all down his clothes.

"Well, it was a bit stupid," said Henry Walters, "Pushing in like that."

"But I'm not going to the match," he replied, tears starting to form, "I'm trying to get home. I only live up the road. This was for our dinner."

Barnsley prepared for their fourth round FA Cup game at Cardiff by taking the players to the Marine Hotel, Porthcawl, on the Wednesday before the match. Their training started at 10.30 with a run along the promenade to Coney Beach. Then Bob Shotton started them on exercises. "Remember," Shotton told them, "You're here today and some poor bloke in Beckett's Hospital would give anything to be here." The players stretched and jumped like Eileen Fowler, thinking it was nice to be paid to keep fit. After 20 minutes they started a seven-a-side game on the hard, desolate sands. There were few holidaymakers in January.

The howling wind and spray gave way to a heavy shower at noon and the players returned to the hotel for a steak dinner. This was the time for interviews and pre-match clichés. "Cardiff are obviously favourites," Tim Ward told the *South Wales Echo*, "On the other hand there would be no football pools if position and form counted for everything."

Cardiff were 20th in Division One, the same position as in January 1927, the year they had won the FA Cup. They had won their last three games, including a 2–1 win at Leeds in the third round, an exact repeat of last season's third round game, even the scorer of the winning goal, John McSeveney.

"Obviously Cardiff must start favourites," Ward repeated for Benny Hill's benefit, "They are a First Division side playing on their own ground but they must be more worried about the game than we are. We shall go out on the field and give everything we've got and, naturally, we hope to be able to pull it off."

It was the usual message: "the pressure's on them", "let them worry about us" and "there's only eleven of them and eleven of us". Or as Brough Fletcher might have said: "There's eleven of us and there's only going to be ten of them." When the players were asked for a quote, one was original . "We don't see much of the sea at Barnsley," he said, "It's just what we need."

Newspaper coverage was a chance for a club to cultivate its public image. FA Cup games often brought a series of staged photographs. Barnsley had a dummy radio that they resurrected for an FA Cup draw photograph, posed with a cloth over the billiard table. When Syd Normanton injured his knee at Arsenal, the photographer arrived at the physiotherapy room and took the picture with Fred Semley treating the wrong knee, in order to get both men in shot. And when a picture was taken of a player signing forms, a blow-up might reveal that his signature was really going on the back of an old team-sheet.

Since the players were rarely out of the public eye in Barnsley, any high living was likely to occur on away trips, but the players were generally well-disciplined. Early in his management career, Tim Ward had learned the value of keeping players together on a Friday night, to prevent the problem of some looking for a good time. Nevertheless, there were odd incidents, such as the player who crept down to eat ice-cream in the early hours before a game, or the time that Shotton and Ward walked into a dance-hall and spotted players hiding behind pillars. "We're just listening to the band, Boss," said one innocently.

Then there were the pranks between the players. To move furniture out of a player's room and replace it with chickens was an extreme move which took a lot of planning, but shuffling the shoes to be shined overnight was more commonplace. Angus Seed, of all people, went one further on a train trip back from London. He was teasing Johnny Kelly by holding one of Kelly's new shoes out of reach, but then he slipped and dropped it out of the window. The players loved it. "Never mind, Johnny," one said, "You might injure that leg next week." Seed had to buy a new pair.

Plymouth was Angus Seed's real bogey town. On one occasion the players hired taxis and charged them to the club, and another time Seed was presented with the bill for a standard lamp that had been demolished by a footballer's crash tackle on a rugby-player in the lounge – just to prove that rugby was an easy game.

The night before the Cardiff game there was revenge for a player who discovered his own bedclothes ruffled. He borrowed the hotel's passkey and entered the suspect's room, simply dumping all the bedclothes in the wash-basin and turning on the taps.

Due to recurrent injuries to Storey and Wood, Tim Ward selected John Edgar and Tommy Holmes at inside-forward for the game. It was a simple trip along to Ninian Park, although two players were nearly late for the coach.

For Barnsley supporters it was a difficult journey. Although they might have preferred to travel by bus, which went directly to the ground and left soon after the finish, they were forced to use the train. The Suez crisis had reached its climax the previous November. Harold Macmillan had taken over as Prime Minister from Anthony Eden but petrol rationing remained. Any Barnsley fans taking their cars sacrificed a month's petrol coupons, while the trains left Court House station soon after 6 am on Saturday morning and the journey was six hours. It would be almost 24 hours before the supporters saw their town again.

In line with FA regulations, Barnsley received 25% of tickets for each section of the ground and a third of directors' box complimentary tickets The cost of 5,000 grandstand tickets was raised from eight to ten shillings.

Outside Ninian Park, street-sellers sold red-and-white berets, ideal for committed Barnsley supporters. They were selling well until one supporter turned one inside out. The name "Wales" was painted in bold white lettering. They were left-overs from a recent rugby international.

Early February 1957

The Barnsley players sat in the Ritz cinema. A cockerel crowed. Cardiff City v Barnsley. Pathe News. A distant picture of footballers waiting for the kick-off. Movement. The ball went from Chappell to Edgar and out to McCann. The players laughed as they saw themselves, their legs moving so quickly. John McCann watched with surprise at his skilful work down the left touch-line. Was that really him? For the first time he realised that he ran with arms out, hands at right angles to the arms. Some of the Oakwell crowd had christened him "Twinkletoes" or "Ballet-dancer". It made a change from the wiggles of Marilyn Monroe, who had been showing at the Ritz in "Bus Stop". There were one or two typical shots of staged crowd reaction and a characteristic sequence of Lol Chappell dispossessing a defender after a head-on confrontation. It was not a classic match but hard-fought. Some called it drab and dour as it progressed without goals into its last moments.

Arthur Kaye won a corner and took it himself. A crowd of grey shirts jumped together. Cardiff's Ron Stockin headed the ball out to Frank Bartlett on the edge of the penalty area. Bartlett chested it down and shot left-footed on the volley. It went through the players and past Graham Vearncombe, slithering down the back of the net before players could consider the consequences. Henry Walters, the proud captain, saw it again, not from the film but from his original position, four yards from Bartlett the hero. Walters was first to reach him, the first of nine. Barnsley supporters among the 31,919 crowd were elated dots amidst the expressionless Cardiff faces. Their sacrifice was worthwhile. Cardiff City 0 Barnsley 1.

To see it again was like a second win, and some of the players, remembering a remark of Tim Ward's, expected a double bonus although there was never any possibility of Joseph Richards agreeing. Roll on Nottingham Forest in the fifth round and the chance for more glory.

Monday 4th February 1957

"Well, this is all-ticket, gentlemen," said Joe Richards, conducting the board meeting. They had read the minutes and heard matters arising. "It's certain to be a sell-out. It will help pay summer wages and will please the bank manager. I spent a morning in that sweat shop today." Raymond Vicary scribbled and shuffled as Richards continued. "I'm sure Mr Secretary will be grateful for help." Vicary nodded nervously. He was a little scared by the forthcoming big game, Nottingham Forest at home in the FA Cup.

"The manager will give you all the help he can. Then there's Mrs Thompson, she's very efficient, and perhaps some members of the Supporters' Club." Joseph Richards had called Lily Johnson by the wrong name since her marriage and she had never corrected him.

The office would be the headquarters of sale, vendors locked inside, serving through the counter window.

"Have we had further word from the police?"

"Yes, we'll have the tickets locked away."

"Now we directors should be allowed to buy tickets, Mr Chairman."

"Yes, we'll be pestered by everyone. We'll have to find our real supporters." The directors settled for 16 grandstand tickets each, paid for at the full price.

"I think the chairman should have more than 16 since he's chairman."

"No, no. I'll have the same as everyone else."

They moved on. Tim Ward outlined his next team. He would rest a couple of players and Joe Hooley and Jackie Lunn would play their first games. Curiously this League game was away to Nottingham Forest.

Joseph Richards went round the table in order of seniority to decide on directors' box tickets at Nottingham.

"Er, two, Mr Chairman."

"Yes, two."

"Two, please."

"Four."

"Oh, then I'll have four."

"Four for me too." Sometimes it was almost an auction. Tim Ward listened. He had been annoyed with his chairman at Cardiff, needing tickets himself when none remained, the left-overs having been taken by Richards.

Certainly there would be some disappointment in the rush for 40,000 Oakwell FA Cup tickets. There was no pleasing the whole town and all the players' long-lost cousins. There were nine local lads in the team at Cardiff. Only Bartlett and McCann spoke with accents from further north. The crowd were proud. "Ours are home-grown," they would say to visiting supporters. This was

Yorkshire, where county cricket meant Yorkshiremen only.

"There's the question of taking the players away."

"Yes, it gives them a break. Gets them away from the ticket-hunters."

"It cost more than we thought at Cardiff. Those biscuits weren't in the estimate." In three evenings at Porthcawl the bill for biscuits had mounted to a sum noticed by an eagle-eyed director.

"I suggest the Majestic."

"Or there's the Crown at Bawtry, where we go at Christmas."

"The Majestic has a bigger games room." This was settled. Outwardly there was no indication that the club were penny-watching. The Majestic Hotel, Harrogate, was above the Second Division in the northern hotel league.

Joseph Richards ran his finger down the agenda typed by Lily Johnson. Tomorrow the receptionist would rapidly type Raymond Vicary's precision minutes, most likely working late. "Report on the Central League team," said Joe Richards, "Mr Hirst."

The appropriate "directors in company" gave reports of the upper two teams, including the playing side, although Tim Ward had already heard Eddie Fleetwood's opinions on the Reserves. Some directors had their pet Central League trips. Billy Diggle clamoured for Leeds and Horace Pickering enjoyed Lancashire, where he was well-known and well-liked from Co-op contacts.

"Well, we set off at nine and it was a lovely day for this time of year," started John Hirst, "We passed a lovely golf-course on the right, short 13th by the roadside. Ran into a bit of traffic, passed a wedding, stopped at Leeming Bar for a meal. Really good meal, service was excellent." By Hirst's left hand, Ward stared at the table. He was never sure about John Hirst's reports, suspecting they were mostly tongue-in-cheek, Hirst knowing his inadequacy to judge football although he had played for Barnsley Amateurs and YMCA. But Ward dare not turn his eyes. Board meetings were not a time for laughter. They were for financial wizardry and Vicary's defensive meticulousness. "We arrived in good time," continued Hirst, "And then there was the game, that wasn't bad, then on the way back..."

"Yes, thank you Mr Hirst. Now we're still to decide on the referee's mark for the last Saturday. Thank you, Mr Secretary."

Each club was responsible for marking the referee from zero (bad, incompetent) to four (very good).

"Well, he wasn't worth three, but if we give him two he'll go off the list." Referees received a warning at Christmas if they were below average.

"Yes, he's quite highly thought of on the League."

"Perhaps we should give him four then."

It was complex reasoning. No referee was ever awarded nought. If he looked like a referee he scored one to start. Less than two led to a report. If your team had lost and the referee was bad then a low mark might look like sour grapes, so you gave him three anyway.

"Let's give him three." Three was the norm.

"I think there's just time to mention our latest representative honour – John

McCann is in the shadow squad for Scotland B." Tim Ward was especially pleased with his signing. Moreover, Bill Houghton and David Wright were awarded England Youth caps.

Tim Ward, wondered, however, about Arthur Kaye, who was now too old for England Under 23s but not in the England B team to play Scotland. Ward was disappointed, but stayed quiet, not knowing what part Joseph Richards might have played in selection. Richards had his fingers in so many football pies that it was easy to forget their effect on Barnsley.

"Have we had any more offers for McCann since Cardiff came?"

"No, there's been nothing this week, and you know our policy is to keep him, although it's nice to have this Cup run ... now then gentlemen, what'll it be? Whisky, whisky, beer for Mr Lax."

Tim Ward and Raymond Vicary each collected a bundle of papers and slipped away. They were quiet. They were always careful what they said as they walked down the steps of the Royal Hotel and through the crowded bar.

Thursday 14th February 1957

"Yes, Mr Chairman," said Raymond Vicary, a cigarette burning in his ash-tray. He seemed to smoke more than all the players combined, "I'll get two to him straight away."

When Vicary replaced the receiver the telephone rang again immediately.

"Barnsley Football Club," said Lily Johnson, who had worked every day for a fortnight, "No, I'm sorry there isn't a ticket left. Yes, completely sold out. Yes, I'm very sorry. Goodbye." She hadn't let go before it rang again. "Barnsley Football Club ... yes ... yes, he is, just a moment Mr Morris."

Tim Ward took the telephone deciding it would be his last call before leaving. It was only Thursday but he looked forward to tomorrow's peace when they left for Harrogate. "Hello, Trevor," Ward said to the Cardiff City manager. The two men had been talking a lot recently, about their FA Cup game and Cardiff's offers for Kaye and McCann.

"You must have some keen supporters at Barnsley," said Morris.

"Why's that?"

"We've had hundreds of requests for programmes. We've been sending them off every day."

"Ah ... oh... I know why that is."

Barnsley's plan was to guarantee tickets to people producing a programme of the fourth round tie, expecting only true Barnsley supporters to have one. But ticket schemes often misfired. When they introduced cheaper tickets for old-age pensioners, a youthful Raymond Vicary unsuccessfully chased one man who looked a little young.

Tim Ward was tired; remembering the promise to himself, he left the office as the telephone rang again. Ward was spending his mornings thinking about the team and training, especially necessary after the League game against Nottingham Forest. With a side including two debutants, Hooley and Lunn, Barnsley lost 7–1, and when John McCann made a wry comment about surroundings not fitting for a Scotland B international, the others threw him in the bath. McCann had been a late selection for Scotland B at Birmingham the previous Wednesday.

Tim Ward walked through the swing-doors and almost tripped over Saturday Sam, one of Barnsley's keenest supporters. Rigged out in red-and-white, Saturday Sam sat against the wall, crying his eyes out.

"What's the matter?" asked Ward.

"I haven't got a ticket," said the other, normally a very quiet man.

"Why didn't you write in to us?"

"I did."

Ward was puzzled. "What is this man's name?" he thought. He did not know. Here was a man who watched all four Barnsley teams as often as possible, who saw the team training, who travelled the country, but who was simply one of the crowd. Now he had no ticket for the biggest game in years. Ward felt compelled to find him one. Some tickets were kept for emergencies and Raymond Vicary dealt with priorities. Tim Ward returned indoors, hoping he would not be detained by other things. Then he could go home, where reporters would have been telephoning, wanting his team. Nancy Ward was honest with the reporters. She wouldn't go as far as to say, "He's at Port Vale watching a player," but she would tell them when he was expected home. Otherwise it was a waste of everybody's time.

Saturday 16th February 1957

Two years before, an ageing Syd Storey might have been excused for thinking that York City's semi-final defeat had ended his dreams of Wembley. But now he covered Oakwell with short, wispy strides, searching to pin-point his passes, hoping to change the 1–1 score. Storey tumbled and picked himself up. "It's a bit muddy out there," said Henry Walters before one game, "You might need longer studs in your knickers, Syd." Storey always laughed at Walters, but on the field in the fifth round of the FA Cup it was a different world. Both men did their urgent shouting … "Come on, ref," "Never, ref," "Come on, lads" … they gritted their teeth and clenched their fists.

They knew how far they could go, but the referee was working overtime. Syd Storey had received a severe warning after Jack Burkitt had been badly winded. Then Storey was bowled over by Hutchinson. John Short and Tommy Wilson were lectured. Kaye and McCann shuffled and swerved; they stood in front of players taking throw-ins, but they didn't jump up and down like Bournemouth's Olly Norris was doing against Spurs. Arthur Kaye's headed equaliser had given Barnsley heart. A place in the sixth round was for the taking. The adrenaline buzzed all over Oakwell. There were 20 minutes to play.

In the directors' box, England team manager Walter Winterbottom sat calm and unemotional on a rare visit to Barnsley. There were again nine local lads in the Barnsley team and they wore the current England kit of white shirts, black shorts and red socks. Forest wore blue shirts. A colour clash in the FA Cup meant both sides had to change. Tim Ward had made sure his side wore their usual socks. He believed they were more important than the shirts, although he always said that dark blue was the most difficult colour to spot, especially on a gloomy day. Not that it was gloomy today. Barnsley had the sun at their backs as they attacked the kop with 20 minutes to play.

The crowd of 40,626 and the receipts of £5,966 were both club records. Mounted police had come from Barnsley, Wakefield and Doncaster, and the police's major preoccupation was pickpockets. Lavatories were blocked by discarded wallets in the cisterns. It seemed as though it was only the pickpockets who reached them, the spectators were wedged like sardines. In order to urinate, some men could only use rolled-up newspapers or someone else's pocket.

The whole spectacle was all over 20 minutes later. The Barnsley dressing-room was very quiet. All the trainer could see was the top of players' heads. A few hands picked at laces. A white shirt was peeled off and hammered onto the floor. A boot went down with a bang.

"He was from here to Worsbrough Bridge offside," muttered one. No-one listened. Stuart Imlach's 75th minute goal had won the game for Nottingham Forest.

President of the League

Chapter Eight

Saturday 2nd March 1957

Three weeks went by. George Spruce was back at centre-half and Malcolm Graham had returned to inside-left. Graham was easy to spot with his ginger hair and characteristic style. He could infuriate the crowd, a man to win a game or fluff an easy chance, never good at keeping his feet in the penalty area. Some loved him, some hated him. Some talked of his Puskas-like left foot, his left bias. He shot with his left, he headed with his left side, if he could he even sat on the left side of a bus. Others talked only of his poor right foot and Graham was considering a transfer request. The crowd could be cruel.

"It must be nearly half-time," said a supporter. The local derby against Doncaster Rovers had yet to produce a goal for the Oakwell crowd.

"Look at that Graham," demanded his mate, "Can't use his right foot for toffee. Can't even stand on it." He turned to the pitch. "Come and sit up 'ere, Graham," he shouted, and then added, more quietly, "Couldn't use his right to kick out the cat."

"One day Mal'll get a bag full."

"Tha what? He's wood from right hip down. Might as well chop his leg off … Foul, foul … did tha see that? The dirty …"

"We've got t'free-kick, any road."

Gavin had fouled Edgar over 30 yards from the Doncaster goal and now John Short stood watch over the ball. He seemed set to clip the ball to the far post.

Defenders were milling haphazardly. For free-kicks outside the penalty area, goalkeepers never organised large walls. Rarely was the heavy ball hit with power or swing – unless it was losing shape. Some players believed you could swerve the ball by placing the lace one side and hitting the other.

John Short was still standing near the ball when Malcolm Graham appeared in front of him. Impulsively, Graham ran at the ball. Wham! It was nestling in the net behind goalkeeper Harry Gregg.

"My God," said the Graham fan, too startled to brag to his mate. "Did you see that?"

"There were a few tins of spinach behind that one, Albert."

Malcolm Graham had provided a treasured memory in the time it took the ball to travel 30 yards. It was the type of goal that had the press-box remembering the date rather than the time.

Graham scored again after half-time, and when Doncaster pulled back a goal Arthur Kaye stayed cool to score his fifth penalty of the season. Two games later, Kaye scored another penalty in the 3–0 home win against Leyton Orient and Barnsley were now in a respectable position in the table.

16	Barnsley	34 – 31
17	Fulham	35 – 30
18	Bristol City	33 – 29
19	Lincoln	34 – 29
20	Bury	36 – 20
21	Port Vale	32 – 18
22	Notts County	33 – 18

For the first time since becoming a manager, Tim Ward had a team free from interest in promotion or relegation. Eight matches remained. Youngsters like Joe Hooley waited for their chance.

It was just over three years since Bryn Price had arrived at Sheffield station and had been driven through the pouring rain into Barnsley by Tim Ward. Price had moved through the wing-half queue. Soon he might have to worry about those behind him. The regular right-half in the first team was Frank Bartlett, a man with unlimited energy, but Norman Smith and Henry Walters were in their early thirties. Bob Wood was capable of playing wing-half but for much of the season he had suffered from a leg-nerve operation. Then, for the Easter Monday match with Fulham, with Bartlett and Wood injured, Bryn Price got his chance and Peter Gillott came in at left-back.

Price, who was marking Johnny Haynes, linked well with Arthur Kaye and had a couple of shots at the Fulham goal. His standard had improved as the season progressed and when he came off Oakwell he felt satisfied with his performance in the 1–1 draw.

Tim Ward missed the match. He went with the Reserves to Bolton, but arrived back in time to watch the A team evening game at Oakwell. The coach returned from Bolton without stopping for a meal. Players received tea money of about 6/- instead. It had been raised from 5/- after lengthy discussion at board meetings.

Ward heard good reports of Bryn Price's debut but the youngster was immediately returned to the Reserves, who had to win at Chesterfield to avoid seeking re-election to the Central League. They did win, and finished 20th in the table. Price was disappointed to lose his first-team place but he accepted the explanation. He looked forward to the next season optimistically.

On the first Saturday in May, with the Football League season over, Barnsley people were able to watch local-boy Tommy Taylor playing in the Manchester United team that lost 2–1 to Aston Villa in the televised FA Cup final. Ownership of television sets had escalated after the birth of ITA in 1955 and the majority of British homes were now equipped with screens of up to 14 inches.

On the evening of the FA Cup final Oakwell staged an important amateur occasion. Harold Rushforth and Ted Davies had again led Barnsley Boys to the English Schools' Trophy final. They faced the second leg against Southampton 1–0 down. The attendance of 19,429 was the highest of the whole season apart from the Nottingham Forest FA Cup game and the Sheffield United derby.

The boys looked like professionals in their "lucky" white shirts, retained after an earlier colour clash. Their boots gleamed. The lace knot was made on the outside to prevent interference with kicking, while the tie-ups were turned inside the calf so that they rested against the fleshy part of the leg.

The team undoubtedly had a star performer at outside-left in Colin Brookes. Scouts had begun their interest at his Yorkshire trials. If his parents watched they were soon identified and approached. Colin Brookes found that people in the street sometimes discouraged him from joining Barnsley and he accepted several trips to meet top managers – Stan Cullis (Wolves), Alan Brown (Burnley), Bill Riddings (Bolton), Bill Shankly (Huddersfield) and Jimmy Milne (Preston). But by the beginning of May, Brookes knew his destination – Manchester United.

Tim Ward missed the Barnsley Boys game. He was in London for the hectic FA Cup final week-end. Thursday night was the sportswriters' dinner, Friday lunch was the Internationals' Club dinner and Friday evening was when England Under 23s played England Select. It was only the second occasion that Ward had used a FA Cup final ticket issued to Barnsley. He did so out of admiration for Tommy Taylor and was disappointed when Manchester United lost. Colin Brookes was of course unable to use the two tickets he was given by Manchester United.

Peter Mulligan scored for Barnsley Boys and then Max Bristowe added a penalty to give them a 2–1 aggregate lead, but Roger Carrington soon replied for Southampton. There was no further scoring and the trophy was shared. Each side was allocated six months.

In the same summer that John Charles left Leeds for Italy, there was competition to sign Barnsley schoolboys. Clem Wood joined the Barnsley groundstaff, but Hurd and Harvey followed Brookes' example, signing for Huddersfield and Leeds respectively.

Full-back David Wright had proved an exception in signing for no-one. Already an England Youth international, he was the only boy in the England side without a League club. Wright stayed at the grammar school, where his major interest was chemistry. Tim Ward still allowed him use of the Oakwell facilities whenever he wished.

It was seven years since Ron Riches had been selected for England Boys and 16 months since he had broken his ankle in an innocuous A team incident. Riches stayed in the RAF for only 10 months. At first his ligaments set badly and Wing-Commander Keirs, the Queen's orthopaedist, advised a tricky operation, which was successfully performed. It wasn't until he started physiotherapy exercises that Riches could move off straight.

After his demob in August 1956 Riches got a built-up shoe and Tim Ward signed him full-time. Most of the season went by before he could kick a ball and then he only played two games, the second in the Reserves at Blackburn. Now he was given a free transfer. Although Accrington Stanley showed interest it meant moving house, so 22-year-old Ron Riches signed for Worsbrough Bridge and went down the pit, attending electrical courses at Barnsley Technical and Mining College.

Barrie Betts' playing career was now closed. For nearly as long as Riches had lived with his injured ankle, 24-year-old Betts had nursed his back. "Funny things these backs," people in football would say, knowingly. The nature of the problem was difficult to diagnose. Betts' training was restricted and he played under the handicap before being sent to two specialists by the club. The injury remained although one specialist even had two of Betts' teeth extracted in an effort to find the source. The specialists were very pessimistic, as were Fred Semley and Tim Ward. It was difficult to overrule a specialist, whatever you thought of his pronouncement. Very occasionally a second opinion was sought, but any action taken as a result would necessarily be extremely sensitive.

Barrie Betts was in very low spirits. He had lived and played with pain and been in and out of hospital. He had been encased in a plaster jacket and had undergone traction. His twin boys were seven months old and the back injury had persisted in flaring up and calming down, enough to reduce the strongest of men to tears. Only Betts' determination had pitched him into Football League games during the emergence of the pain when he was a first-team newcomer. He had overcome injury before, a broken leg at 16, but in January 1957 a specialist had given him the advice all footballers dreaded. His playing career was over. The club had found replacements and the cancellation of his registration was mutual, although Betts considered the decision premature. They could have frozen the situation for an agreed period. Barnsley collected insurance and Betts, like most players, had made similar private arrangements. Barrie Betts was able to start a credit drapery business although Joseph Richards had also arranged a clerical position in a colliery for him. But the worst was leaving football.

Gordon Duggins had no reason to contemplate injuries at the start of the close-season. He had played 14 first-team games and was moving up. The next season he hoped for 20 or 30, especially as Barnsley had released Arthur Rowe after a two-year spell as a part-time player. Both Rowe and Duggins had stayed part-time, wishing to keep their jobs and football separate. It was still a disappointment for Rowe when his local club rejected him, even though Gainsborough Trinity signed him part-time for £12 a week plus expenses, an improvement on the rates at Barnsley (£7, £5 and £3 plus bonuses). The other part -timers released, Ted Brown and Harold Sidebottom, had each spent four years with the club.

Living in a small village, Gordon Duggins bought a motor-bike out of necessity. A bicycle had been sufficient for the early years of his local career but, unable to afford a car, Duggins now travelled by motor-bike, for which he should have had the club's permission. It was the end of May when Gordon Duggins rode his 350cc BSA back from a cricket match at Ashby. He collided with a motor car and went through its windscreen, receiving cuts across his face and a badly broken nose. He was taken to Burton-on-Trent General Hospital, where he stayed for two weeks.

Saturday 1st June 1957

Joseph Richards walked out of the bright sunlight and into London's Cafe Royal. It was an important day for him but he took it in his stride and moved to the head table, which was reserved for the Football League Management Committee. This AGM would have Richards in the chair. Despite news that he was tipped for high FA office, Richards had accepted the nomination for League president. As the only candidate he was certain to succeed Arthur Oakley of Wolverhampton Wanderers, who was forced to give up the job through ill-health after two years in office.

Richards was confident. Although 69, he sustained his working schedule, studying stocks and shares, keeping track of his Barnsley businesses. He continued to deal in coal, bargaining as hard as ever, particularly with blast furnaces. He was familiar with every rule and regulation and he was determined to uphold them in football. This was how Barnsley FC was run, which could place them at a disadvantage. Richards disliked seeing young players disappear from his area. He even called it "babysnatching" and once blamed Harold Rushforth and Ted Davies, although of course it was beyond their control. Richards had a vested interest in youth. He took the credit for introducing the Northern Intermediate League, the FA Youth Cup and the England Under 23 team.

The delegates and observers gathered in the Cafe Royal. They talked about the hot weather, but they mainly talked football. Joe Richards looked round at the delegates, flipping through his notes. He always wrote his own speeches, often using reams of paper. If anything he overprepared and spoke nervously, fidgeting with cutlery or other odd items. Tim Ward had never forgotten the time in Canada when Richards had plonked down a salt-pot with the force of a successful draughts player. "Crown that one," Nat Lofthouse had said to his neighbours.

Seven years had passed since the Canada tour and now Tim Ward sat at the back of the hall with Raymond Vicary. Secretaries were needed for an afternoon meeting, when there was a brief trading of fixtures. Around Vicary and Ward sat other officials: a glut of directors from successful clubs; a few managers and secretaries with hangovers from their association's dinner the previous evening.

"Here we go again, same old stuff."

"Are you backing Crepello for the Derby?"

"I might win on these new Premium Bonds today."

They peered down past the 48 club representatives, one of whom was Arthur Raynor. Each First and Second Division club sent one man and the remaining four represented the two lower divisions, whose views would have been established at a previous meeting.

Joe Richards spoke of taking the first steps towards a complete overhaul of the League's rules, indicating that there would be big changes within 12 months. With entertainment tax finally abolished, there was some extra money available to clubs. The maximum wage was increased to £17 (£14 summer). Bonuses went to £4 (win) and £2 (draw). Talent money was doubled and the benefit limit extended to £1,000 after 10 years service, although on the same arbitrary basis.

Players would now earn £2 for playing in televised games, although live coverage was rejected. Since September 1955 the League had agreed to five-minute tele-recordings being shown after 10 pm. Walley Barnes had joined the BBC as advisor and "Sports Special" had been born. The possibility of a League-sponsored floodlit competition was broached and the League would re-organise after 1957–58, when the top halves of the Third Divisions would merge and the bottom halves would form the Fourth Division. It would then be four up and four down between the bottom two divisions. But no door was yet opened to a non-League club. Midland League champions Peterborough United gained only seven votes. The other 11 non-League clubs polled just three between them. By the end of the morning Joe Richards felt satisfied, but he was already working out how the changes would affect his own club.

Joseph Richards was put in a paradoxical position. The new agreements were ideal for wealthy clubs but not for Barnsley, who increased players wages to £17 anyway. Despite their FA Cup run, Barnsley had added a loss of £1,489 to their overdraft. The bank were pacified periodically by Richards but were no more generous than was commercially realistic. The overdraft entailed interest payments and the directors established collateral – financial security in case of bankruptcy. The Barnsley board were still reluctant to sell their best players. The younger directors in particular had seen supporters' reactions to post-war sales when attendances were better. These directors were learning that it wasn't easy to hold on.

Each year the sheaf of unpaid bills stayed longer on Raymond Vicary's desk. Admittedly Barnsley's playing staff had been reduced to 34 – including recent part-time signings of Cade, Houghton, Jones and Matthews – but perennial problems such as benefits needed answering. Barnsley had again played a late friendly to raise money but interest had dwindled and the game attracted only 2,816 people, raising a mere £266. The Supporters' Club organised a £520 payment to Lol Chappell – eight years after Chappell had signed professional. Cricketers' testimonials were free of tax but footballers had to pay it, though clubs were experimenting with ways of overcoming the anomaly. Barnsley were making a second appeal to the public in the summer of 1957, starting a floodlight fund. Joe Richards had opened it with a donation of 100 guineas.

The players would start the next season earning better wages than the local coal-miners. But what of the risks? There were 318 NCB fatalities in 1956, the lowest figure in history, but Ron Riches and Barrie Betts could testify to the hazards of football.

Norman Smith recommended Barrie Betts to an osteopath in Leeds. A good one could be very good, but many football clubs thought that there were also poor practitioners and they were reluctant to take the risk. On a rainy night, Colin Swift, first-choice Barnsley full-back, drove Barrie Betts to Leeds in an old Thames van. The Stow brothers had two practices in osteopathy, one in Hull and this one in Leeds. Swift and Betts sat in the waiting-room next to a couple from London. Here there looked to be hope. Stow was encouraging. He was astonished that Betts had been advised to finish his career. "I think you'll play again," he said confidently.

Betts progressed very quickly. After three or four visits to Leeds the pain started to disappear. His determination was revitalised. "Here's me wallowing in self-pity," he said after one visit, "Yet look at some of the cases they have." He had been given an automatic free transfer by Barnsley but now he felt he could recover.

The club came out of the incident in a poor light. Joseph Richards was a distant, powerful figure. Some footballers saw a saga: Short bought perhaps too hurriedly to replace Betts; specialists who could not agree; a player's career abruptly ended. "There but for the grace of God go I," thought some of the other players.

The club, however, had a well-organised medical side which stretched through the West Riding. Excellent specialist treatment was available. It left them thinking that you could never really tell with back injuries. The club looked on Barrie Betts' quick recovery with a hint of suspicion. But by the end of the summer, Betts was wanting to play football again. He would have to wait until the Football League dealt with his case, and the new president was Joe Richards.

Tuesday 23rd July 1957

It was the first day back. The summer was long, hot and dry. Stand-pipes were erected and fire-engines were needed to pump water from the River Dearne to Oakwell. Somehow, Ernest Steele had protected the bowling-green appearance.

Not all the players were present. Tommy Holmes and Olly Hopkins had no cars and the Yorkshire Traction bus strike had stranded them at Hemsworth and South Kirkby respectively. Eric Anderson was allowed to continue living in Manchester and travel twice a week during the season. Anderson, 25, was the club's only signing, a £4,000 buy from Liverpool. He had helped Liverpool win 5–0 at Oakwell two seasons previously.

Cars were becoming more common among players. A down payment of £4/8/5 could now buy a Ford Popular on hire purchase. Bachelor Norman Smith had owned a car since arriving in Barnsley. Duncan Sharp had a lilac Morris Million with a registration (HHE 678) that closely followed that of Tim Ward's 1955 Ford Prefect (HHE 567). Arthur Kaye had bought a car in 1956, when the initial enjoyment of being recognised on buses became too much. Gordon Duggins had to buy a car during his recovery. He had a friend who would teach him to drive on journeys to Barnsley. Lol Chappell had taken lessons from Norman Smith. He'd had trouble finding the gear-stick until Smith advised him to keep one hand on it all the time. Chappell had failed his first test for not having both hands on the wheel.

"Do you want to see my car?" asked Lol Chappell, as the players started to congregate. A few of them wandered out to the car-park. With his benefit money, Chappell had bought a Triumph "Razor-Edge" Mayflower. It was a splendid sight in the sun, built like a tank, real leather seats, blue with a white top.

"Ay up, that's snazzy, Lol."

Henry Walters walked round the car and went to the driver's door.

"I'll have three cornets, two choc-ices and an ice-lolly," he said through an open window.

The players laughed heartily. They went inside to tell the story and taunt Ernest Steele about the sacred Oakwell turf. "It's not as good as last year," one of them said. Steele smiled. He knew that all through the season he would receive accolades from visiting players. Some of them clamoured for a game in the Reserves simply for the privilege and pleasure of playing on Oakwell.

The players were welcomed back by the chairman, manager and trainer. "Remember," said Tim Ward, "You only get out of football what you put in. If you cheat in training, the only people you cheat are yourself, your family and your team-mates. You won't be cheating me because you won't be in the first team. Can you tell me a better job than being a sportsman? Getting paid for something you love doing."

The players were weighed and measured. Some had put on weight and would have to sweat it off. Bob Wood bought army vests and long johns from the market and was pleased at losing three pounds. After Joe Hooley's first summer as a professional he had put on all the weight Tim Ward had wanted him to – by watching televised cricket and doing little else. He had lost the weight so quickly that it took him until November to adjust.

The club hardly ever updated their rough list of measurements for the programme. Lol Stafford was 5ft 6in and 9st 2lb, though the club always listed him at 9st 7lb. Before Phil Roscoe went to Halifax Town, where he was now established in the first team, he was listed for four years as two inches shorter than his 6ft 1½in.

Despite being nearly 33, there was no player fitter than Harry Hough, who had played golf during the summer, winning the Barnsley and District Golf Club championship for the second successive year. Hough had recently been elected to the Players' Union executive committee, and today he led the pack of players who walked through Stairfoot, Ward Green and Worsbrough. People occasionally leaned out of an upstairs window to deliver a comment.

"You'll have to go quicker than that this season."

The walks were designed to strengthen muscles. The pre-season training moved slowly from strength to stamina to speed to skill. Many trainers believed that there was a danger of pulled muscles if a ball was kicked too soon. Their opinions were reinforced when players started to drive to the ground.

The road from the town centre to Oakwell went over the level-crossing at Jumble Lane, which had an appropriate name. It became a club joke that the signalman made a hobby of trying to trap cars as he shut the gates. This happened a lot due to trains shunting and frequent traffic hold-ups occurred. Henry Walters always said that he left a day in advance to be sure of getting over the crossing in time for a home game.

Tim Ward usually avoided Jumble Lane, especially after the gates had hit his car and caused £5 damage. After a series of letters, British Railways paid the repairs, although they did not accept responsibility. Harry Hough was another at loggerheads with the signalman. If he got through, Hough would wind down his car window and shout, "You missed me that time." It was hilarious – if you weren't in a hurry.

The part-time players and amateurs started training with three evening sessions a week in July. A five-mile walk was followed by laps until the players had to check their legs were still there. Bob Shotton pushed them hard. Tim Ward rarely showed sympathy for minor ailments. "The best way to cure stiffness," Ward would tell players the next day, "is by doing the same thing that got you stiff."

The groundstaff boys trained with the full-timers except for the rare occasion when there were too many players, or when a friendly was arranged. It was during a pre-season friendly that George Spruce broke his arm.

Groundstaff member Frank Beaumont was on the touch-line and able to substitute at inside-left, with Wood and Bartlett dropping back. Beaumont scored a goal in that game and he played in the return friendly, then again for the Reds against the Blues.

Although he had never played for the Reserves, 17-year-old Frank Beaumont was kept in the first team for the opening League match, at home to Bristol Rovers. He scored after 35 minutes and became big news. When he came off at half-time his walk to the dressing-room was interrupted by a reporter, who hastily arranged a broom and a camera. Tim Ward was furious when he found out and he led Beaumont away. Monday's *Sheffield Telegraph* reported on the 2–2 draw and included a picture captioned "Sweeper-up gets a goal". Frank Beaumont was shown holding a broom in a completely impractical manner.

On the Tuesday the team travelled to Bury St Edmunds, Suffolk, and Frank Beaumont caught influenza. He played in the 3–0 defeat at Ipswich but felt awful and he was too ill to continue in the first team. This caused Tim Ward some concern because Syd Storey was ill, convalescing at Skegness, and Tommy Holmes had broken a bone in his hand.

Before the third game of the season, Ward spoke to 33-year-old Norman Smith, who was still club captain although he had played most of the last two seasons in the Reserves. He asked Smith if he was interested in playing inside-forward. "I'll play anywhere to be in the first team," Smith replied, so he took Beaumont's inside-left spot for the away game at Derby.

Saturday 31st August 1957

This was Barnsley's first game at the Baseball Ground since 1925. The clubs had missed each other with their recent two-year stays in Division Three (North), but the gap was mainly caused by Derby County's many First Division seasons. Tim Ward had played during their most successful period and was full of enthusiasm about the Baseball Ground.

Ward showed his players the home-team dressing-room. "This is where Raich used to change," he said, "And Peter Doherty was here, and Jack Stamps there."

"Norman'll be playing like Raich Carter today."

"The clown's hat's vacant now, Norman. Len Shackleton looks like he's finished."

"You always were an adventurous wing-half, Norman."

"That's right," agreed the normally quiet Arthur Kaye, "You're the best wing-half I've ever played behind."

The mood was good and Tim Ward was happy, giving no indication that he was suffering from a headache until after half-time. Then Ward returned to the directors' box and inhaled ammonia from a capsule that Bob Shotton had given him. They were designed to clear the head and Shotton often gave them to injured players during a game. They sometimes confused spectators because they could look like discarded cigarettes when players threw them away.

Ward was still sniffing his capsule when in the 51st minute Arthur Kaye crossed for Lol Chappell to score his second goal of the game. With a Kaye penalty sandwiched in-between, Barnsley had a comfortable 3–0 lead. Tim Ward sat apparently unmoved.

"I'm surprised you're sniffing that, Tim," said a voice from behind. "I reckon it's Harry Storer who's got the headache."

As another wave of red shirts attacked the Derby goal, Tim Ward turned round and tried to hold back his smile, but no game was over until the end. Anderson, Wood and Bartlett all hit the woodwork in the second half, and when the final whistle came, Barnsley led 4–1. Lol Chappell had registered his first Second Division hat trick. He could settle back with his place secure for the next game, while Tim Ward showed his elation as he went to congratulate his players, walking along the Derby County corridors that were once his second home.

Barnsley won their next two games, beating Ipswich 5–1 and Swansea 1–0. Arthur Kaye scored four more goals, including three penalties. With 7 points from 5 games, Barnsley under Tim Ward had never had it so good, especially with so many youngsters yet to be given a chance.

In December 1953, there were 42 professionals. Less than four years later only 15 of these 42 remained. However, the club still had 35 professionals and four groundstaff members. With Frank Beaumont having a run in the first team, it implied that 39 players were competing for the 11 first-team positions. Only John Stainsby was on National Service.

There was little to encourage the lower-team players. Six of the first team had figured in Tim Ward's plans from the start and three had been signed specially from other clubs. Only two provided models for hope. Colin Swift was the 1949 Barnsley Boys player who had stayed to settle at left-back. Duncan Sharp had played his way into the A team and then slowly through the other teams. Only now, at 24, could Sharp think of himself as the first-team centre-half, although his contemporary Olly Hopkins and the injured George Spruce were still in competition.

Tim Ward watched the lower teams when he could and a Monday evening A team game at Hull gave him one such opportunity. Barnsley had taken their A team out of the Yorkshire League and into the newly-formed North Midlands Combination, of which Joseph Richards was president. Barnsley now competed in four leagues exclusive to Football League clubs.

The A team at Hull included seven part-timers, two amateurs and two trialists. The amateurs were right-half Barry Hines and outside-right Bobby Smith. It was a patient wait to see whether they would develop as players. More pressing were the trialists – Melville Neil, recommended from Preston North End by Jimmy Baxter, and Denis Coughlin, a Harry Nattrass discovery from the north-east.

Ward looked for the qualities needed by a professional footballer – some could be learned, some not. Ward thought that balance was the hardest thing to be without. He signed Coughlin, who would continue to travel down on Saturdays.

The back-bone of the A team defence at Hull were former Barnsley Boys – Brian Summerfield, Bryn Jones and Bryan Matthews. Jones and Matthews had been playing together since Burton Road Juniors, where Joe Hooley, Peter Whyke and Jack Lunn had also been in the team.

Barry Barber was now at inside-right in the A team, scoring a few goals and enjoying his football, although sometimes in trouble with referees. In one game, against Chesterfield, Bryan Matthews was cautioned. The referee noted the name "Matthews" and then asked for his Christian name. "Stanley," said Barry Barber, from over Matthews' shoulder. Matthews was sent off.

That incident had been cleared up later. In the Football League, a referee would immediately inform the home-club secretary of the players cautioned or sent off, no reason given, then in due course a full report was written and a pink or white form would arrive at the club. A referee might be tempted to go into the office and withdraw a caution in the hope of getting a better mark, but the League soon put a stop to this.

To be spoken to by the referee was generally considered embarrassing. To be sent off was a disgrace. One player wrote to a well-known League referee apologising for the trouble he'd caused the previous Saturday. On the other hand, Joe Richards once asked for a special hearing when Jarman was sent off, and the appeal was successful.

It was unusual for a referee's decision to be overturned. Referees and linesmen might understandably confer prior to a League commission to make sure there weren't any basic contradictions in the factual evidence. The enquiry took care over such details, even as far as reconstructing the incident with Subutteo figures. Commissions were expensive and difficult to organise. It meant a committee, referee and linesmen synchronising time off work and travelling to Birmingham, Manchester or London.

Saturday 28th September 1957

Just after half-time at Oakwell. No goals. West Ham right-back John Bond had cleared off the line, while their left-back, Noel Cantwell, was trying to master the man of the moment, Barnsley's Arthur Kaye.

Kaye was on the ball again. The crowd buzzed, Cantwell backed and the winger boiled. Other Barnsley players swore they could hear Kaye grating his teeth over the noise of the crowd. He saw his chance. Confidently, he pushed the ball between Cantwell's legs. He ran by and looked up. His cross was deliberately shallow. Norman Smith ran into the penalty area and hurled himself full-length, back-arched, like the deputy goalkeeper he sometimes became. Smith met the ball with his head and glanced it further forward. His arms were outstretched for the landing and his eyes followed the ball as it looped over Ernie Gregory's right hand and into the top of the net. Smith's acrobatic header was the only goal of the game. The next day he would buy all the Sunday newspapers he could find.

Oakwell spectators had talked about wingers for years – Eric Brook, "Tubby" Ashton, Gavin Smith, Johnny Kelly and now Arthur Kaye and John McCann. Many people considered that wingers were among the more feeble of footballers. "Kick them down the passage and they're finished for the game" was an old saying. But no full-back worried Arthur Kaye. When he played against some full-backs he started the match by pushing the ball down the wing and running full pelt into them, willingly conceding a free-kick. Kaye was surprised that so few wingers got their retaliation in first. Even when awarding a free-kick in his favour a referee might have to speak to Kaye.

While Arthur Kaye was the acknowledged idol of the crowd, John McCann was still very popular. McCann was a left-wing fixture with his peculiarly Scottish skills – swerving past defenders, flicking the ball over sliding legs, driving the ball hard as a pioneer of low crosses, pulling it back, chipping it forward. He was slick and stylish, his Brylcreemed hair bouncing up and down as his elegant left foot caressed the ball.

Kaye and McCann worked unusually close together. They found each other with long, accurate crossfield balls that switched the direction of attack. Kaye might dart through a ruck of players at a McCann corner, enticing two defenders out of position, accepting a short pass before turning it square to the incoming McCann. Both used the procedure of running up the wing and then turning back sharply to receive the ball, making space to turn on the full-back. Their share of the ball was balanced, although Arthur Kaye occasionally complained that the lack of left-footed players worked against him.

Wingers were also responsible for another important function. Because they were constantly on the touch-line, they would be used by managers to pass on messages to the rest of the team. The practice remained illegal but was too subtle to prevent.

Tim Ward had moved Norman Smith to inside-right and had brought in Malcolm Graham at inside-left, with Billy Houghton at left-half in place of the injured Wood. Houghton was young enough to have played for England Youth that month, news of which had caused some excitement. His mother, a regular centre-stand spectator, had rushed to the builders where Houghton worked with the letter. Then Tim Ward had taken him to the town hall for a duplicate birth certificate, which the opponents could demand to see. Finally, Houghton had been sent to the *Barnsley Chronicle*, where he had a passport photograph taken, still in his overalls.

Thinking about Promotion

Chapter Nine

Thursday 10th October 1957

"Syd, Syd, there's someone to see you, Syd."

Syd Storey looked up from his lapping. He stopped running. "Who is it?" he asked.

"It's Wattie Galbraith."

Syd Storey thought it might be. With Barnsley's permission, Accrington Stanley manager Walter Galbraith had approached him two days before.

"I've got a contract here, Syd," said Galbraith, when Storey walked over, "There are a few gaps because we want you on loan, just for a month. We'll pay you what you're getting here."

"Are you sure you want me?" asked Storey, who was an honest, dedicated professional, "I've been quite poorly. I've only just started playing again."

"Oh, yes. You'll do us a bit of good, Syd. We 're bottom of the table with a lot of injuries."

"Well, alright then," said Storey, and he signed for Accrington.

"Right," said Galbraith, "First team on Saturday."

"I can't play in the Third Division," pleaded Storey, "I've only had one A team game this season."

"Well, we really need you on Saturday. We're playing Scunthorpe. They're top of the division."

Walter Galbraith was a persuasive Scot. Accrington Stanley had finished in the top three in each of the last three seasons and their success owed a lot to Galbraith's ability to motivate players – mainly Scots.

"Where's the game?" Storey asked.

"At Accrington."

"How am I going to get there?"

Syd Storey had no car. His part-time football career had been conducted by bus and train. When returning from matches at York he had to make hectic dashes in both Wakefield and Barnsley in order to arrive home for his Saturday evening dancing.

"I know," said Galbraith. He had been thinking with all the enterprise needed by football managers. "Scunthorpe will have to come through Barnsley. We'll arrange for them to pick you up."

The following Saturday Syd Storey stood at the end of his road where he was collected by Scunthorpe United, taken for lunch and delivered to Peel Park. Storey worked as hard as his health permitted and Accrington surprisingly won 2–1. After the game Scunthorpe drove Storey back, took him for another meal and dropped him at the end of his road. "Well, Syd," said Scunthorpe manager Ron Suart, "We take you for a day out and you take two points off us."

Barnsley had put memories of the Third Division well behind them. The next few weeks saw Tim Ward discover his new settled side. The first indication was a 4–1 victory against promotion-contenders Charlton Athletic. Nine days later Barnsley drew 1–1 at Doncaster. Because of a Saturday race meeting, the Doncaster game was played on a Monday evening and supporters' cars stretched back in a jam from a blocked right turn onto the A1 at the Sun Inn. Crossing the A1 was always a patient business and the Barnsley team arrived only 30 minutes before kick-off. Benny Hill of the *Barnsley Chronicle* got caught in the jam and for the only time in his career missed the kick-off. Arriving 10 minutes from half-time he hastily arranged for a free-lance, Leo White, to cover the game for his paper.

The evening kick-off was possible because the low-lying Belle Vue floodlights were permitted for League matches. The Barnsley players chased the white ball wearing white shirts, white shorts and white socks. They changed because Doncaster wore red, appearing like rugby players with a white U-shaped sash on their shirts. As is typical when many spectators arrive late, both goals came in the opening minutes; 18,971 was the official attendance.

The next game produced an impressive 3–0 home win against Rotherham United, but it was the 5–0 win away to Huddersfield Town on 9th November that set Barnsley people debating whether this was the best Barnsley team since the war. They couldn't have picked a better fixture for the display as the 21,667 crowd included many Barnsley fans.

The stadium at Leeds Road contributed to the sense of occasion. It had a large capacity, shelter and good vision, although a stand had burned down in 1950. Huddersfield's 1920s team won the FA Cup and clinched their third successive Championship in the season that Herbert Chapman left for the Arsenal.

Huddersfield Town were really a First Division club, with third place in that division as recently as 1953–54. But now Bill Shankly was bringing in some young players. Outside-left Vic Metcalfe was almost twice the age of outside-right Kevin McHale.

The Barnsley team was generally more experienced. In goal was Harry Hough, a brave 'keeper who narrowed the angle superbly. Although he was apt to perform the odd entertaining piece of heading or dribbling, his concentration and consistency gave the whole side confidence. (Referee Harold Hackney once consulted Hough about players in an offside position "interfering with play". Hackney was impressed with Hough's definition, that if he could see a player out of the corner of his eye, even if he was out on the wing and lying injured, it was bound to affect his concentration.) Hough's full-backs, Short and Swift, knew that when Hough called for the ball they had better step back or pick themselves up.

The full-backs pivoted around centre-half Duncan Sharp, now a well-known figure throughout the division. Sharp always stuck to his task. He played with teeth out, chest out, continually pulling up his socks. Some of his tackles made Tim Ward wince. He was not Ward's ideal footballer but he was picked because he was the best for the job.

No centre-forward relished a duel with Duncan Sharp. "Do you feed him on raw meat ?" asked Tommy Briggs, who was hardly a powder-puff himself. "Do you keep him in a cage?" asked another. Sharp rarely inspected the pitch before the game so the other Barnsley players sometimes received shy enquiries about whether Sharp was playing. A centre-forward's face would fall if they said that he was. Tim Ward preferred to be on Sharp's side in five-a-sides and practice matches.

Barnsley spectators loved Duncan Sharp's mannerisms and his straightforward style. After a tackle they might turn to each other and say "What's the verdict, murder or manslaughter?" He was "Our Duncan" and on Saturday afternoons the crowd took him to their hearts.

Opponents also disliked playing against left-half Bob Wood. It was like facing a windmill on a conveyor-belt. Wood was persevering, strong and steady, all elbows and legs, crowding and hindering opponents. Now 29, he was playing better than ever. His leg felt tight after the operation, but at wing-half he was coming on to the ball and he was pleased that Tim Ward was allowing him to settle in this position. Here he could feed John McCann and race to reach positions for his favourite left foot shot when McCann pulled crosses back.

At right-half was Frank Bartlett, a man with the stamina of Gordon Pirie. Both Bartlett and Wood had the energy and inclination to stop inside-forwards and turn their attention to attack. Both had played up front and knew the effects of being clattered by defenders. And since both had been clobbered from behind by Duncan Sharp they kept an eye in the back of their heads, for Sharp regarded the middle of the defence as his preserve.

Huddersfield left-back Ramon Wilson was Arthur Kaye's most difficult opponent. Kaye struggled to upset Wilson's balance enough to beat him and, besides, the man could recover so quickly. Kaye still tried to beat Wilson, to keep variety in his play, but he laid the ball off more often. The Barnsley pattern was to keep the ball on the ground, a necessity with a small forward line.

No matter who the opponents, there were times when Arthur Kaye took over a game. He might spend 15 minutes at inside-forward, bouncing off players, onto the floor, up again, grinding his teeth, shaking his fist. He wanted the ball. He needed the ball.

At inside-right Norman Smith was enjoying himself. He challenged bravely, saw a lot of the ball, shielded it and worked it out to Arthur Kaye. Smith hardly seemed an injury risk now because he'd suffered almost everything once.

Barnsley moved up a table that had no outstanding teams.

1	Liverpool	16 – 22
2	Blackburn	16 – 22
3	Stoke	18 – 20
4	Charlton	16 – 20
5	Middlesboro'	16 – 20
6	Barnsley	16 – 19
7	Fulham	16 – 19
8	West Ham	16 – 19
9	Sheffield U	16 – 19

But was Lol Chappell part of Tim Ward's new settled side? Chappell was still running unselfishly, yet despite his encouraging start he had scored only six times in 15 games. Even Norman Smith had scored six.

Chappell's overall Second Division record was 18 goals in 68 games. He would need more than double this rate of scoring to compare with rivals at other clubs – Bradford, Atyeo, Briggs, Johnston, Dwight, Clough, Liddell, Summers, Dick and Rafferty. Tim Ward believed that Chappell had reached the limit of his abilities.

When his luck was in, Chappell would chase paper bags, but when his luck was out he would feel his injuries, and it became harder to sustain his running game. He lived from match to match, wondering whether he would be picked, and from season to season, wondering whether he would be retained. As early as 1952 he had thought he would be released and then he scored four in a late-season friendly against Wellington Town, a game arranged when John Jarman was bought.

Tim Ward knew that for a real chance of promotion they needed a consistent goalscorer. Almost every week he made an unsuccessful enquiry. Newly-promoted Grimsby Town would not part with Ron Rafferty. Nor would Doncaster Rovers sell Bert Tindill. Ward was swift to notice if a player was dropped. He sounded out Sheffield United about Derek Hawksworth and asked Sheffield Wednesday about Roy Shiner. Earlier, he had chased Hartlepools' Ken Johnson and Stockport's Jack Connor, but Ward was cautious about Third Division players, recognising that there were a lot of "overnight sensations".

There was no immediate answer within the club. John Stainsby was stationed in the south and temporarily out of circulation. Players on National Service had to cope with a strange tax position over expenses. They paid tax if the game were at home, but not if it were away. One club flew a player back from Germany and he was out of pocket for home games.

Gordon Duggins was having the headaches and bad patches that the doctor had predicted after his road accident, but Malcolm Graham scored five in four games, coinciding with his switch to full-time professional. Graham was still barracked by sections of the Oakwell crowd and his play could be inconsistent. He preferred playing away and was willing to consider a transfer. The shrewd Joe Richards was aware of this. The best method of strengthening goalscoring with the overdraft at £15,000 was by selling a player first. And this became a possibility when Barnsley received an offer for Malcolm Graham from Newcastle United, who had watched Graham at Huddersfield.

On Wednesday 13th November, Tim Ward and Joseph Richards travelled to Newcastle by train. They met five Newcastle directors as the club were without a manager. Joe Richards, as always, fixed the price – £20,000. Newcastle were unprepared to go that high.

Newcastle had a policy of changing chairman every two years and there were several former chairmen on the board, which led to an unusual debate. Alderman McKeag, an eloquent solicitor and former mayor, asked Richards outside for a chat. They returned after five minutes. The issue was still unresolved. So Stan Seymour asked Tim Ward outside and Seymour explained some of the intricacies of the matter. The meeting ended with no definite outcome. Richards also talked to Wilf Taylor, a Newcastle director on the Football League Management Committee. "He says they'll pay £20,000," Richards told Ward on the journey back to Barnsley, but so far Newcastle had only raised their bid part of the way.

Friday 15th November 1957

Using a system he had inherited from Angus Seed, Tim Ward filed away some more of his scouts' reports. He sat down. His Parker 51 moved fluently across another page of correspondence as he listened to Lily Johnson spelling out the names of the Grimsby Town players. Ward expected at least one team change. Grimsby had just signed Jeff Whitefoot from Manchester United.

Mrs Johnson ended her call to Hibbert, Ashton and Youell, printers of the programme, but the telephone soon rang again.

"It's John Uprichard," she said, handing the receiver to Tim Ward.

"What's the situation for tomorrow?" asked Uprichard.

"Well, we've no injuries from training ... despite Duncan Sharp." Ward paused as Uprichard laughed and then added, "It's the same team, John." It was something Ward never tired of saying.

"Is there anything new on the Graham deal?"

"Not as far as I know," replied Ward cautiously, "There's no further development. Malcolm will be playing tomorrow."

Ward did not say much, even to his friends, but he wasn't especially concerned about the outcome of the Malcolm Graham negotiations. Ward had faith in Graham's ability, although the money would be useful too. As the week had progressed it looked increasingly likely that Newcastle would stick to their original offer. Joseph Richards had sold the Robledos to Newcastle eight years ago, but this time he had gone too high.

Malcolm Graham scored a goal in the Grimsby game and Lol Chappell scored twice, but two late goals from Grimsby's Ron Rafferty meant Barnsley dropped a point in the 3–3 draw. Tim Ward always watched all 22 players, not just his own, and he studied Rafferty with envy. From his various enquiries Ward knew Rafferty would be an ideal centre-forward. Ward's sources of information included Len Noad of the *Weekly News*, a friend from his playing days. Noad would ask how much he wanted to spend. "Nothing," Ward would reply, "But we might be able to go to £6,000." This narrowed it down, Noad's knowledge of the player's character narrowed it further. In the end it would almost certainly be a matter of discovering a player.

One possible way was through Harry Nattrass, who had found Frank Bartlett and Denis Coughlin for a signing-on fee. But Nattrass began to irritate Ward with the sheer number of players he sent down with a recommendation to sign. At the end of one season Ward asked Lily Johnson to draw up a list of them. There had been 68, so the scout was asked to whittle them down.

It was Jimmy Crapnell, the Glasgow scout, who recommended Ward his next centre-forward signing, Rikkie McDonald from Saltcoats Victoria. Ward first watched McDonald in the company of director Arthur Raynor. The two men took the overnight sleeper and then stood to watch the game. There was no shelter from the snow and wind. On their return they reached Barnsley at 3 am.

November 1957

Tim Ward moved some papers along the boardroom table. "We can't put you on full-time wages," he said as he sat down.

"I'm playing as well as the others on a Saturday, aren't I?" replied Duncan Sharp.

"Of course you are, Duncan, but being part-time means you're not always available when we want you – for training and team talks."

"My job keeps me fit," said Sharp, "I get down to Oakwell more than most part-timers."

Sharp always trained very hard, but Tim Ward believed that becoming full-time improved a player's standard. It also gave the club a better guide to the player's injuries and character. Yet Syd Storey felt he played better when part-time and chose that arrangement at Accrington.

"1 know you're fit," said Ward, "But you're earning money elsewhere. You're better off part-time. You're earning more than the others."

Ward and Sharp had never quite hit it off. In 1952–53 they had both been wing-halves for Barnsley A in a disastrous 9–0 defeat at Stocksbridge. The trialist goalkeeper finished that game in tears. Ward had shouted at Sharp during the game and Sharp had shouted back. This had surprised Ward.

Since then, Duncan Sharp had worked his way slowly from the Yorkshire League to the Second Division, and Ward had dealt with him in a diplomatic but roundabout manner, never fully getting to grips with the player's attitude. A comment of Ward's might be witty for Henry Walters but sarcastic for Duncan Sharp.

The issue of part-time wages was left unresolved. It would return. The maximum wage for part-time players was the same as full-timers, so there was scope for bargaining – although others were happy with their part-time terms. Tim Ward went back to his office. He felt he'd had a good week if Duncan Sharp had not come to see him. He thought that if all his players were as little trouble as Bob Wood, Frank Bartlett and Norman Smith then his job would be easy.

Duncan Sharp was disappointed. In training and on match days he gave all his energy for the club. If Tim Ward would treat him right then he felt he would do anything for him. He knew that Joseph Richards appreciated his effort and business-like approach, and John Steele seemed much more on his wavelength.

Tim Ward was always the man in the middle, operating between the policy of the directors and the demands of the players. After almost five years in management Ward did not appear to the players as progressive as he once had. Yet his understanding with Joe Richards and the board had never been stronger.

Ward realised that he had a good set of directors, but like all managers he enjoyed the stories about directors at other clubs. Some were true. Others grew in elaboration as they went the rounds: "I had to send him to watch Tom Finney three times because he didn't think much of him the first time"; "I sent him to watch a centre-forward and he said he'd make a good wing-half because he took a good throw-in"; "If he'd had his way we'd have had more coaches than Wallace Arnold".

The players were also fond of stories about their directors: "He thought we were 2–0 up and didn't realise it was Manchester United in red"; "He was impressed with the half-time team-talk because the opposition were soon down to ten men".

On the whole, the board saw little of the players. It was difficult for a director to know whether his presence would be appreciated. It could be seen as an act of encouragement or simply interference. There were times when players were grateful for advice, especially from an ex-professional like Gordon Pallister, but there were occasions when a director might make an extraordinary observation or offer a different opinion from that of the manager.

It was on the practical side that the directors made their most favourable impact with the players – repair jobs, club houses, offers of employment, contacts, cheap goods and produce, and lifts in cars. After the Aldershot FA Cup game in 1956, Ralph Potter had offered to drive Duncan Sharp and Malcolm Graham home from Barnsley, but his car ran out of petrol at Darton in the early hours. Vice-chairman Arthur Raynor came to the rescue on that occasion. Raynor was a very involved director who respected the difference between his own football with Barnsley Amateurs and the professional game. Potter, Pallister and Raynor were young directors pleased with Tim Ward's approach.

When Joseph Richards became Football League president there was talk of Arthur Raynor becoming Barnsley chairman, but the only noticeable effect was some extra difficulty arranging the weekly board meeting around Richards' London duties. Undoubtedly, Richards' success reflected well on Barnsley. His obstinacy might have been a drawback in recent dealings with Newcastle, and some were surprised at Barrie Betts being refused permission to play in the League for six months after signing for Stockport. Richards sometimes tried to do too much himself, but he supported Tim Ward when the manager needed him. The chairman was especially good at enforcing club rules. "These are not the manager's rules," he would say, "They are club rules." Richards continually wanted details of the club's activities and Raymond Vicary felt it important that he should know everything – although there was one small thing that Vicary kept secret.

When Joseph Richards had provided funds for a bar extension in the Oakwell boardroom, two plaques were hung in recognition. One was inside the bar, the other in the boardroom. Unfortunately the plaques showed different dates – October 1950 and October 1951 – and Vicary fretted in case Richards noticed.

The bar was built into the wall between the boardroom and the main corridor. The directors had a bar committee and took turns as barman. The room was cosy enough for the barman to be involved in conversation and Roy Lax once found himself offered a tip by a visiting director.

The boardroom was a discreet place. It was free from the raucous behaviour of the terraces. There were no political discussions, although if there had been, local MP Roy Mason would have found himself in a Labour minority. Generally there were no reporters allowed, although Joe Richards very occasionally invited one in. Eric Thompson of the *Daily Mail* once remarked that, "If the England team had the brains of us reporters and the guts of Barnsley then we'd win the World Cup".

England, however, were still smarting from a 3–2 home defeat by Northern Ireland. Joseph Richards, like any figure in authority, was open to criticism. After a mid-week game with Derby County Reserves, Derby manager Harry Storer was driven to taking up the issue of England selection. He asked Joseph Richards what right he had to be an England selector. When Richards told him he had been watching football for over 50 years, Storer was ready. "Come off it," he said, "We've got a corner-flag at the Baseball Ground. It's been there for 50 years and still knows absolutely nothing about the game."

There were six months before the World Cup competition in Sweden. Many Barnsley people believed that Arthur Kaye was the obvious man to replace Stanley Matthews. With Tommy Taylor at centre-forward it was an exciting prospect. "Get rid of Haynes," some northerners argued, "He's only good for advertising Brylcreem."

December 1957

Tim Ward stood up as the chairman came into the office. Joe Richards remained standing.

"I hope you've forgotten all about the letter you handed me yesterday."

Ward was taken aback. He hadn't tendered his resignation lightly. "Have you read it?" he asked.

"Yes, of course I have," said Richards quickly.

"You said we could discuss the matter this morning, Mr Chairman."

"There's nothing to discuss. The board's made its decision over Storey. He's to get nothing."

"I'm sorry, Mr Chairman, I find that difficult to accept. He did very well for us last season." He left a short pause. "He's been a credit to the club. I think he deserves £100."

"Oh, I've nothing against Storey but he only played half a season."

"Twenty-nine games in the League, Mr Chairman."

"Twenty-nine … yes, not even a full season."

Ward detected a slight hesitation in his chairman's manner so he shifted to his favourite ground. "That's true, Mr Chairman," he said, "But it's not just the playing side I'm concerned about. Storey's well-known in these parts, very well-respected in the game. We don't want him going off spreading bad things about the club. I feel it would be for the good of Barnsley Football Club if we were able to make a small concession in this case."

Ward waited. He had moved cleverly from "I" to "we" and he could see Joseph Richards considering the advancement of the good name of the club in a favourable light, as he always did. Ward played his last card "And we did get him on a free, Mr Chairman."

A free transfer, and Accrington were paying £250 for him, a sum that Walter Galbraith had indicated would go to the player.

"Very well, Mr Manager, £50," said Richards. Then he added, "For the good of the club."

Having withdrawn his resignation, Tim Ward looked to keep his side together. This meant the Reserves were also settled and they were near the top of the Central League. But they were still deputies, hoping to establish themselves in the first team. Players like wingers Peter Whyke and Jack Lunn were patient and loyal local boys who admired Kaye and McCann and were young enough to wait. Yet young wingers were given first-team chances elsewhere – McHale at Huddersfield and Holliday at Middlesbrough.

This frustrated Joe Hooley. Now 19, Hooley felt that Tim Ward should have fulfilled his promise of first-team football. He began to meet Ward frequently for 10-minute sessions, sometimes three times a week. They could develop into heated, bitter arguments. Ward would raise his voice as quietly as he could, but he had too much dignity to boil over. The youngster had a vision of his future and he was impatient for it to take effect. Tim Ward wanted his players to conform and get on with the job. If they didn't conform they might find it difficult to get in the first team – although many with good character were also excluded. "Hooley, Hooley, Hooley, Lord God Almighty," sang an Oakwell spectator as Christmas approached. Joe Hooley asked for a transfer and he moved to Sheffield United.

Tim Ward also signed Colin Brookes, who had been unable to settle in Manchester. Bert Whalley, the Manchester United coach, visited Brookes in Barnsley and listened sympathetically. Whalley agreed to discuss it with Matt Busby, who then rang Oakwell and delayed a press release for two days. By then Brookes had signed for the Barnsley groundstaff. At 16, he played for Barnsley Reserves as their youngest-ever player. Earlier in the season, when still 15, he had also been Manchester United Reserves' youngest player.

December had started badly for Barnsley with a 7–0 defeat at Cardiff. That game was on television. Tim Ward became annoyed with a player who was smiling at the camera after a goal went in. Barnsley recovered with three points from the next two games, including a 2–1 win over leaders Liverpool. Arthur Kaye was still improving and his four goals in five games took him to nine for the season, equal with Chappell and one ahead of Graham, whose eight goals had come in 14 games.

Wednesday 25th December 1957

Christmas came just once a year. Brass bands took to the Barnsley streets and children leapt from their beds, perhaps expecting to become the proud possessors of a football, boots, kit or a game of "New Footy". But the Barnsley players were not disturbed by their children, because they stayed at Bawtry to prepare for an 11 am game at Notts County. Barnsley always played away on Christmas Day and Good Friday because of their church origins. They dare not risk any transport other than the coach driven by Joe Thorpe, who had also stayed overnight.

It was 36 miles from Bawtry to Nottingham. The coach's radio blared out customary Christmas messages and the players sang along with "Jingle Bells", "White Christmas" and other hardy perennials. The coach arrived at Meadow Lane and the players stood up. Then the next record was announced. "We'll just listen to this one," said someone near the front, so they sat down and heard "Mary's Boy Child" by Harry Belafonte. Joe Thorpe and reserve Brian Summerfield then sorted out the skip.

Frank Beaumont was celebrating his 18th birthday. Still on the groundstaff, he was in the team for his fourth League game. For the third time he opened Barnsley's scoring, heading in a centre from John McCann. Then Bob Wood scored from 25 yards and Barnsley led 2–0 at half-time. By the 84th minute Wills and Loxley had brought the scores level. Arthur Kaye took up the challenge and scored the winner. He appeared to beat everyone in the ground before scoring into an empty net.

After the game each player was given a Christmas present. There were just 11 bottles of sherry so Norman Smith, rested for this match, received nothing. "I thought I was in the first team again," contemplated Smith, "But now I'm not sure." Joseph Richards also sent bunches of chrysanthemums and grapes to the wives of the directors and staff.

The players were famished when Joe Thorpe drove back to Bawtry. Leaving Meadow Lane at 1.30 meant Christmas lunch was over when they arrived at the Crown Hotel. The management were upholding tradition by serving the staff with Christmas lunch. There was nothing immediately ready for the players although eventually a meal of rainbow trout and mashed potatoes was put together. With two holiday games to come there was no real escape from under the trainer's thumb.

Joe Thorpe missed the Queen's first television broadcast and did not eat his Christmas dinner until 7 pm, when about 20 people gathered in his Tower Street home. The next day Thorpe would be driving the Reserves. His duties always prevented him from seeing a home match.

The next day at Oakwell, Norman Smith scored his seventh goal of the season, but Barnsley's performance in the 1–1 draw was not entirely to the liking of the 20,193 crowd. They ended the year with an impressive 3–0 win against Derby County; Frank Beaumont, included in place of Graham, scored again. Norman Smith's early advice to the youngster was to either put the ball in the net or give it to him. And now Beaumont was signed professional. But Peter Whyke, playing in the Reserves as an amateur, was wondering whether he should ask the club if they were intending to sign him. It was the time for New Year resolutions. Tim Ward welcomed 1958 with his thoughts on promotion.

1	Fulham	25 – 32
2	Liverpool	26 – 32
3	West Ham	25 – 31
4	Charlton	25 – 31
5	Barnsley	25 – 30
6	Blackburn	25 – 30

On 4th January 1958, Oakwell staged one of its most memorable matches. Manchester United Reserves made a hazardous journey across the Pennines. There had been heavy falls of snow and the cancellation of local matches raised the Oakwell attendance to 2,500. It was difficult to say how many inches of snow lay on the pitch for it was tightly packed down by Ernest Steele's roller. The spectators looked forward to seeing something from Eric Anderson. He had hardly played in the first team since signing from Liverpool but had scored twice in the previous week's 3–3 draw at Old Trafford in the Central League. There was also the prospect of news from the first team's FA Cup game at Hull, represented by the letter "A" on the half-time scoreboard. Both matches started at 2.15.

The Manchester United team was a mixture of internationals and youngsters: Wood; Greaves, Bent; Goodwin, Blanchflower, McGuinness; Berry, Whelan, Webster, Harrop, Pegg. The Barnsley team was less experienced: Lawson; Thomas, Jones; Price, Hopkins, Houghton; Whyke, Holmes, Anderson, Edgar, Brookes.

Billy Houghton opened the scoring from 30 yards, then Eric Anderson scored a hat trick and Tommy Holmes added a fifth. The crowd rubbed their eyes; at half-time Barnsley were beating the Central League leaders 5–1.

United's assistant manager Jimmy Murphy gave his team a roasting during the interval, particularly the players who had been dropped from the first team and were suspected of not trying their hardest. They'd only been back on the field a few minutes when John Edgar made it 6–1. Then Jackie Blanchflower switched positions with Bob Harrop and the tide turned. Webster, Whelan and Berry all scored. It went to 6–4, 6–5, and then Colin Webster missed an "open goal" before it was all over: 6–5 was an extraordinary result.

On the east coast at Hull, conditions were less severe but more unpredictable. Boothferry Park was the third Hull City ground that Joe Thorpe had driven to. Bob Shotton had taken three pairs of boots for each player to allow for any ground surface. Barnsley had declined the use of floodlights and by four o'clock the game had ended 1–1.

Hull won the replay 2–0 and Arthur Kaye was put out of action by a damaged left ankle. Peter Whyke, still an amateur, was promoted from the Reserves. He learned of his selection from a newspaper placard, Tim Ward's notification having gone to the wrong address. Whyke played two games, during which time he turned professional, but only part-time. He still had his bricklaying apprenticeship to complete.

The Reserves reached fifth position in the Central League, yet their players made only isolated appearances in the first team: Leeson, Thomas, Gillott, Hopkins, Houghton, Whyke, Duggins, Anderson, Edgar, Lunn and Price. Four years had passed since Bryn Price had played his first game for Barnsley Juniors at Middlesbrough. At the end of that game he was greeted by his brother, who was working at Redcar.

After the initial loneliness of living in a new town, Bryn Price had adapted to life in Barnsley. He had married a local girl and his career was progressing. He was called for a Welsh Under 23 trial at Newport, and was so excited that he was halfway to Sheffield before realising that the trial was the following day. And the next time he went to Middlesbrough was for his second Division Two game, marking Alan Peacock. But Price knew that Frank Bartlett would be back in the first team as soon as he was fit.

If Tim Ward had had to choose his most valuable player it would have been Arthur Kaye. He was a crowd puller, and his international class had been recognised by selection for England Under 23s, the Football League and in the original World Cup 40 for Sweden. He had missed only eight games in four seasons and was a difficult man to replace.

Despite losing Kaye, Barnsley remained in the promotion hunt. They started February preparing for a trip to West Ham, who had come from a lowly position in September into second place. West Ham had signed Vic Keeble of Newcastle for £10,000, money that might in turn have been spent on Malcolm Graham. But Keeble, like Kaye, was now injured.

1	Charlton	28 – 37
2	West Ham	28 – 36
3	Blackburn	28 – 35
4	Liverpool	29 – 34
5	Fulham	28 – 33
6	Barnsley	28 – 32

Thursday 6th February 1958

It was late in the afternoon and quiet enough for Tim Ward to hear himself think. As usual he delayed announcing his team until Friday, but he would make just one change, bringing back Frank Bartlett for Bryn Price. It would mean keeping John Edgar out of position on the right wing for the important game at West Ham.

Ward also wondered what he should do about training. He instructed Bob Shotton about what was needed but the final decision rested with the trainer. Sometimes he came out of his office and was surprised to see players still lapping long after he had intended them to see a ball. Other times Shotton would tell the players, "The Boss will want his usual." Then the ball would come out, and often Tim Ward came out too.

The telephone rang. There was never quiet for long.

"John Uprichard," said Lily Johnson.

"Good afternoon, John," said Tim Ward.

"Tim, we've just had a news-flash. It sounds very serious. Manchester United's plane has crashed in Munich. People have been killed. The news is very hazy at the moment."

Uprichard filled in all the known details and promised to keep Ward informed. Ward replaced the receiver. His face was white. Yes, it could be true. Manchester United were returning from Yugoslavia. Ward tried to think who could be on the plane. He picked up the telephone and dialled Joseph Richards' number at Worsbrough Bridge.

"Have you heard the news about Manchester United?" asked Ward.

"Yes," replied Richards, "The Football League have been on." The two men could say little more. They replaced their receivers and waited.

Part-time players and amateurs reported for training and began to learn the grave consequences of the Munich air disaster. Full-time players stayed by their wirelesses. As the confusion cleared, shock submerged the Barnsley people. Supporters and players cried alike.

Tim Ward had earned his living in a physical contact sport. During the war he had served in a medical unit and had grown accustomed to pain and suffering. He was a man who could carry the same expression in victory and defeat. Yet as the evening progressed and the news unfolded he became visibly upset.

Seven players had lost their lives in the crash and an eighth, Duncan Edwards, was to die later in hospital. Three of the dead had their roots in the Barnsley area. One was Tommy Taylor from Smithies, where the joke was that a player needed to be an international to get a Sunday kickabout game. Taylor's transfer to Manchester United had tested the allegiance of some Barnsley supporters. Three bus loads travelled to watch his first game for them.

Also killed were Mark Jones, who had attended Foulston School just a short step across from Syd Storey's house in Ardsley, and David Pegg from Doncaster. In football communities throughout the country the issues of knocks and bruises and preparation for Saturday suddenly seemed very trivial.

Despite some criticism, the Football League schedule continued apart from Manchester United's fixtures. At West Ham, the following Saturday, the teams stood for two minutes' silence before the game.

Then the promotion chase resumed. Barnsley were unlucky to concede a penalty in the first half when the ball appeared to hit John Edgar on the arm as he stood at the edge of the area.

In the 58th minute the whole Barnsley bench appealed for a penalty – all except West Ham's John Bond who happened to be sitting there because his own bench was crowded with injured players. Malcolm Graham's shot seemed to be handled on the line but the referee gave a corner. Soon afterwards John McCann made it 1–1. For West Ham the draw was enough to topple Charlton from the head of the division. For Barnsley it was a point lost.

1	West Ham	29 – 37
2	Charlton	29 – 37
3	Blackburn	29 – 36
4	Liverpool	30 – 36
5	Fulham	28 – 33
6	Stoke	30 – 33
7	Barnsley	29 – 33

Then two defeats made promotion doubtful, and a third in a friendly against Arsenal ended 6–0. Herd, Tapscott and Barnwell each scored two. It was a sobering reflection on First Division standards.

On 8th March snow returned to Barnsley. Snow had been the setting for the magnificent Central League game in January. Snow had hampered Munich airport on the fateful February day. This time it took people by surprise. At 3 pm the weather was fine. The home game against Doncaster started but was overtaken by a blizzard. It was Bryn Jones' first game for Barnsley.

Visibility deteriorated but Oakwell spectators could still spot Jones ploughing through the snow. Like Bryn Price and Duncan Sharp, Jones was tenacious. He was disliked by away crowds for relentless fast and fierce tackling and he preferred difficult conditions. He had been a surprise selection but he seemed to do everything against Doncaster except score the winning goal. The game finished 1–1.

During March Barnsley continued to slump. Kaye was fit again but six games produced only four points. There was irony in two of the home defeats – 3–2 to Huddersfield, a stark contrast to the ecstasy in November, and 3–1 against Lincoln, the day after they'd beaten them away by the same score. Lincoln still needed to win their last six games to stand even a chance of avoiding relegation.

Good Game, Henry

Chapter Ten

Saturday 12th April 1958

There were 45 minutes until kick-off and the Barnsley players were settling into the Visitors' dressing-room at Bristol City. Bob Shotton was in charge, ready to satisfy every request. "Right, lads," said Shotton, "Let's get rid of your comps."

Some players reached into pockets for their two complimentary tickets. There was no urgency. They were a long way from Barnsley.

Some complimentaries would go to the nearest red-and-white scarf that spoke in a Yorkshire accent. Fans such as Saturday Sam were easily recognised by players as they stepped outside the ground.

Bob Shotton started to lay out the Barnsley change strip in its mint condition. Norman Smith picked a penny out of his pocket, spun it into the air and caught it on his foot. From there he flicked it into the top pocket of his suit jacket.

Tim Ward sat quietly on a dressing-room bench. After a long train journey and overnight stay, he had little to say to the players. He had talked to them for a whole season. Yet Ward was closer to home than any of the players. "God's country" was the Cotswolds to Ward.

The dressing-room door opened gingerly. "Everything alright?" asked Peter Doherty, the new manager of Bristol City.

"Peter," said Ward, who jumped from the bench at the sight of his former Derby County colleague. "How's life treating you down here?"

"Not so bad, Tim, not so bad," replied Doherty, "Come and have a chat."

When Doherty was at Doncaster, Ward saw him most weeks. "We've still to get settled. Where are you staying?"

"The Royal."

The two men were very friendly, but there was always the undercurrent of competition. Doherty had taken Bert Tindill from Doncaster to Bristol City for £6,000 at a time that Ward was interested in the player. This Friday, at Bristol station, Ward had noticed a young player from the Barnsley area, obviously waiting to be met by one of the Bristol clubs. Ward stayed to see which one – while the players left in taxis.

"Just a minute, Peter," said Ward as they passed the referee's room, "I'll get a time-check." He knocked and exchanged pleasantries with the referee.

"I've got exactly 2.24," said the official. Ward and Doherty checked their watches. The last 10 minutes before kick-off were a well-timed ritual. If the managers thought the referee had the wrong time they might suggest a telephone call to the speaking clock.

In the dressing-room the players prepared. Duncan Sharp strapped his knees, pulled up his socks and pushed them down again. He was contemplating his opponent, John Atyeo, an England international. The two men worried for a week about each other: the big, burly Atyeo against Sharp, who tackled like an earthquake. It was said that both could score penalties with a medicine-ball.

Norman Smith also strapped his knees, Malcolm Graham reeled rolls of elastoplast around his ankles. Cotton wool was pushed behind the shinpads, which might otherwise rub against the skin and irritate it. Bob Shotton moved around, pampering the players.

"How can you afford to play Malcolm, Bob?"

"Tha soft lad," said one, as another strapping went on, but Shotton would never agree. The player knew best.

"Good luck then, lads," said a Barnsley director as Ward entered. Directors tended to stay in the dressing-room longer before an away game but they left before the manager's team-talk.

"Let's play some football out there," said Tim Ward, "I know it's the end of the season, I know we're safe, but we can show these. Let's see you prove something after the Lincoln game. Now you all know your jobs, go out and do them."

The bell went. Studs clattered against the stone floor and the Barnsley players turned left. They kicked around for a few minutes, then the referee blew and the two captains trotted towards him. They all shook hands and a coin was tossed. "Tails," called Norman Smith as he always did. Tails it was. "As we are," he added.

"As we are, lads," shouted Smith, making his way back towards his goal. Harry Hough threw him a ball. Smith took a shot and the ball sailed wide, hardly a good omen. Frank Bartlett, moving back to right-half, also shot into the crowd. Norman Smith ran to the side of the goal to collect the stray balls.

The balls bobbed down the crowd and Smith controlled them at his feet. He turned round and gazed in surprise. Bert Tindill was boring down on the Barnsley goal. Harry Hough came out but Tindill poked it past him and into the net. Smith looked down at the three balls within his reach. "Wait a minute," he thought, "I'm supposed to be playing in this game."

"Oh no," said a visiting supporter, "1–0, after 15 seconds."

Tindill scored again two minutes later, then Watkins, Tindill again, Watkins again ... after 55 minutes it was 5–0. The Yorkshire reporters held their heads and noted that Barnsley failed to recover from an early shock.

It finished 5–0, and as the Barnsley party walked into the station after the game, John Uprichard listened to Tim Ward's appraisal: "The first goal should never have been. The referee should have checked the number of players on the field. What if we'd had twelve on? And he should have checked that all the balls were off the field. The last goal was offside. Any further offside, he'd have been charged admission. And the third we were standing still. They were moving quicker on the Aldermaston march last week. And the penalty ..." Uprichard smiled. Ward, like most managers, had the ability to turn a 5–0 defeat into a 2–2 draw within an hour of the game.

Sitting in their reserved compartments, the players were deathly quiet after defeat. "Come on then, Lol," said one, eventually, "Give us a chance to win back that money. You haven't spent it, have you?"

"1 nearly did this morning. I wanted to buy a watch but Arthur said I would do better for a guarantee at Benjamin Harral's."

The train was more suited to cards than the bus. The players cut for deal and played incessantly – except for one hand where Norman Smith somehow substituted a blank pack and they had to deal again. Four hours later Lol Chappell was back where he started. When the players reached Doncaster they looked around for copies of the *Green 'Un*, which they could read in Joe Thorpe's coach on the final leg.

Practice matches continued on a Tuesday despite the fact that the fitness of the players was self-evident. Sometimes they were used to add extra bite to a particular player's game; a timid lad might find himself against Duncan Sharp. Bob Shotton made a strict referee, John Steele and Eddie Fleetwood ran the line, while Tim Ward never missed a chance to play.

The practice matches offered the Reserves a chance to parade their skills in front of the manager. The games had always been competitive. Before Tim Ward's time, Bob Shotton had handed out shinpads and the phrase "Save it for Saturday" was not unknown. On one occasion in 1954 a reserve player had chased a first-team player up the Queen's Ground slag heap and then sent him tumbling down from near the top. Tim Ward sent him for an early bath, as he also did with anyone who complained.

When the practice matches ended and players returned to the dressing-rooms there was no real resentment. There were odd comments about how the first goal was miles offside, and was only allowed because it was scored by the Boss' team, but generally the players respected authority. They spent more time planning stunts than complaining. Some had to search all afternoon for a shirt which was up a flag-pole or a shoe placed neatly in the centre-circle on a muddy day with the groundsman hovering.

Early spring brought a new diversion. From November to February watering the pitch was prohibited, but at other times Ernest Steele's hosepipe, which worked from the dressing-room tap, was often lying around. Drenching another player was a custom. On one occasion Olly Hopkins splashed a few; then one of his team-mates approached wearing a shirt and Hopkins waved the hosepipe again. "Oh, look what you've done," said the player, "I'm soaked. Hey, wait a minute, I've put on the wrong shirt ... this looks a bit like yours, Olly."

Due to an administrative error Hopkins' National Service had not been deferred for his apprenticeship. When he came out in 1956 he was two stone over his fighting weight of 13¼ stone. He was a good trainer and discarding the surplus was no problem, but after two years with virtually no football he came back to find himself behind Duncan Sharp in the centre-half queue. But he took everything in good spirit and was well liked by Tim Ward.

Despite the strong emotional element in football, Barnsley had relatively few displays of cross words and violence, but some of the jokes could be near the bone, such as "I've heard a rumour that they're getting rid of you." The basic instability of the job made footballers continually worry about what might happen to their families. The retained list brought more nerves than a big match.

Typing notification to players not retained was one of Lily Johnson's most unpleasant tasks, although it was not as arduous as typing contracts. On 23rd April 1958 there were three free transfers to be confirmed by letter.

Dear

My Directors have decided to grant you a Free Transfer from this Club at the termination of your present Agreement.

We wish you every success for the future.

Yours sincerely,

Secretary

The letters were stamped with Raymond Vicary's signature and the name of the player was written on each – Barry Barber, Brian Summerfield and Lawrence Stafford, all 21-years-old. The letters went by registered post. Tim Ward often took them to the post-office in Regent Street.

The club's finances made them consider releasing players who might fetch money. Joe Thomas had already been sold for £2,000 to Mansfield Town just before the transfer deadline. Now George Spruce, another important member of the championship team, was listed. Thus, two centre-halves, Summerfield and Spruce, would be leaving the club. It left a line of Duncan Sharp, Olly Hopkins, Bryan Matthews and Roy Sawyer, who was signed part-time after impressive performances in the Juniors. Ward also signed Dennis Medlam, Alan Vest and

Peter Lycett.

In addition to George Spruce, who went to Chester, the list surprisingly included two forwards: 23-year-old John Edgar, who fetched £1,500 when signed by Gillingham; and Gordon Duggins, who left for non-League Buxton.

At the 1958 Football League AGM the maximum weekly winter wage was raised from £17 to £20. The wages of the Barnsley players were raised to £18, and for the first time since they returned to Division Two they earned less than the maximum. A handful of first-team players held out. They were kept informed by Harry Hough, representative of the Professional Footballers' Association, as it was re-named by the executive on 18th April.

The key date was 30th June, after which the players would lose money. One by one they re-signed except for Duncan Sharp and Arthur Kaye. Sharp was busy with his newsagency at Lundwood, bought with a small benefit of £200, after tax. This marked eight years of service.

While part-timer Duncan Sharp spent the summer working, Barnsley's full-timers had been barred from casual work and told to rest completely. In other years they had worked as gardeners, handymen and labourers. But the club now thought the summer wage of £14 "pretty fair", to use Ward's words.

Sharp was slightly surprised when John Uprichard called at his newsagency to ask him why he was holding out. Sharp went to Worsbrough Bridge to explain to Joe Richards that it was simply that time had slipped by. That left Arthur Kaye, which was not altogether surprising. Kaye, although recently married, had less responsibilities than other players. Besides, he was the Barnsley star, though if he got £20 then the others would have to. Harry Hough had recently confirmed that full-time first-team players would be paid the same.

Arthur Kaye was close to full international honours. He came so near to selection for Sweden that he bought £50 worth of clothes in anticipation. He was named in both the last 40 and the last 22, and Tim Ward hinted he was in. When omitted from the final party, he was left with a set of fruitless preparations. Ward was also aggrieved, especially since he thought Kaye a far better winger than Peter Brabrook of Chelsea, who did go.

Kaye never thought to ask for a transfer. He felt sure the club would increase his wages. Yet when he finally signed at the end of July, it was for the same terms. Harry Hough saw Tim Ward soon after this and asked if the contracts were to be changed, thinking that Kaye must have signed for more.

It was a disillusioning experience for Hough, Ward, and especially Arthur Kaye, who was already a little cool towards the club. Kaye was a quiet man. He thought rather than spoke, but he had thought hard about his job and his club. Why were players sold in the early 1950s? Why were players not bought in recent years, particularly other forwards? What would he and McCann have been like if someone of Tommy Taylor's class had been in the middle? And why had Lol Chappell had to prise his benefit slowly from the board?

Kaye felt let down by both sides. He had met the blunt, business-like approach of Joe Richards and the resolute interpretation of Tim Ward. His team-mates had not been totally behind him. Undoubtedly Kaye was in the best bargaining position. He was offered more perks than others, small as those were: offers of two pairs of trousers if the maker's name were displayed, a television and chickens at Christmas, and a fiver pushed in his jacket-pocket by a businessman. He also got half a crown when a collieryman left £2 for Norman Smith to share out after a good run. Kaye was the crowd's idol, but he started training on the same wages. And he found it difficult to work at it with his customary vigour.

Saturday 23rd August 1958

There was one minute remaining in the game at Ninian Park, Cardiff. Football fanatics throughout the country waited for news of the season's first fixtures. The results would be used as pointers. Barnsley fielded the team that had won so devastatingly at Huddersfield the previous season. Tim Ward chose it as his best for this game at Cardiff, which was still goalless.

"It was about now that Frankie Bartlett scored his Cup winner," thought Ward, automatically forgetting last season's 7–0 hiding at the same ground. A cross from John McCann passed across the face of the penalty area and reached Malcolm Graham's right foot. Graham looked up during the flight of the cross and glimpsed Cardiff centre-half Danny Malloy some yards away. Recent words from John Steele swiftly went through Graham's mind: "If you get the chance, if you have the time, get it onto your left foot." It was typical of Steele to encourage a player to play to his strength.

Malcom Graham had the chance and he had the time. He brought the ball down, coaxed it across to his left foot and hit it into the net. A goal in the last minute and Barnsley started with two points. For the next few days at least, the talk around Barnsley would be promotion.

The season progressed in a bizarre manner. There was another last-minute 1–0 win, this time against Huddersfield, but three defeats produced a total of 21 goals. Barnsley were "doubled" 7–4 and 3–1 by Bristol City and they went down 5–1 at Leyton Orient.

Then came an evening game at home to Charlton Athletic. It was 1–1 when Gordon Jago handled in the area after 27 minutes. Jackie Lunn, deputising for Arthur Kaye, ran up for the penalty. It was just like his fitness test that same morning. He struck the ball firmly with his left foot and it hit the net to the goalkeeper's right. Tim Ward immediately turned to his trainer: "Hey, that's not right. He was hitting them with his right this morning." Ten minutes later Johnny Summers missed a penalty for Charlton and from that point the game developed into a personal triumph for Malcolm Graham. He scored his second before half-time, then again in the 65th and 69th minutes. He broke through looking for his fifth in the 71st minute only to be tripped by Jago. The penalty fell to Lunn, who switched it to the goalkeeper's left – as he generally did with a second kick. The game finished 7–1, giving Barnsley six points from six games.

Barnsley lost the next three and conceded another 10 goals. In the return at Charlton they were losing 4–0 by the 33rd minute. Charlton left-half Billy

Kiernan shook his head at that point. "Hey, Frank," he said to Frank Bartlett, whom he had only met on the football field, "This is ridiculous." But it was typical of football.

A run of only one defeat in nine games ended with two defeats in December against clubs chasing promotion: Fulham (5–2) and Sheffield Wednesday (1–0). The latter was a scrappy local derby at Oakwell in front of 23,075 people. It left Barnsley halfway up the division, preparing for a long trip to Swansea.

Journeys to south Wales were always a problem. There was an hour and a half's wait between trains on Birmingham station, and on one occasion a player had been arrested there for taking two cream cakes from the canteen. Only the intervention of Joseph Richards had saved the good name of the club. A rail trip meant an overnight stay, which was not always ideal. Players slept better in their own beds and were often glad to get back to their wives promptly. The one compensation of the train was that they would almost certainly arrive on time. The Football League stipulated to referees that they should not attempt to drive more than 100 miles to a match, and they frowned upon car breakdowns as a reason for lateness. But Barnsley were considering the idea of a day trip by coach to Swansea.

Financially it was a mixed period for the club. If you had floodlights then there was extra revenue available from winter friendlies and later kick-off times. Barnsley did not. The floodlight fund stood at less than half the £20,000 needed. The policy of keeping players certainly stabilised the club in Division Two, but the faces were becoming very familiar to the crowd and the queue for benefits steadily grew. Joe Richards knew that the 4% Football League levy on receipts – which went towards the players' Provident Fund – would soon be lifted due to higher attendances, and the board felt able to raise players' wages to the maximum of £20 a week. On the other hand, Bob Wood and Frank Bartlett had to leak news of their dissatisfaction to the *Daily Herald* before the club would pay their benefits.

It was not the only worry for Bob Wood. Despite Tim Ward's protestations that he was doing a good job at inside-forward, Wood wanted to return to wing-half. He wanted to rely more on skill and run less, preferring to come on to the ball and face the challenge. Wood accepted that the team needed his strength up front but he wondered just how long he would have to provide it. It had been three months already and other inside-forwards in the club wondered why they were overlooked, all except Norman Smith, who like Jack Lunn was booked for a cartilage operation. Billy Houghton took Wood's left-half position.

On the Thursday before the Swansea game Harry Hough was last out of the dressing-room for training. He stared at the team-sheet before he left. The team was straightforward – the only change was Swift for Jones – but Hough was annoyed at the arrangements. He recalled Tim Ward's Tuesday meeting to discuss travel. Admittedly Duncan Sharp had said that he preferred travelling on Saturday morning, but Hough could not remember any others in favour. Yet a Saturday coach trip had been decided and players were expected to report to Oakwell by 7.30 am. Harry Hough took down the notice, screwed it up and threw it on the floor. Then he went out and led the lapping until Tim Ward brought him in for a dressing-down.

Saturday 13th December 1958

Joe Thorpe drove the bus to Swansea. Four seasons ago, on the way to the Third Division championship, Barnsley had travelled 3,000 miles for 23 away games, about as many as Lol Chappell was expected to run in a season. The Swansea trip meant they had overtaken this total before Christmas. Extra travelling and overnight stops were a further strain on finances.

These players were experienced travellers. They knew the length of the journeys and did not make foolish arrangements for Saturday evening. Nor did they need Joe Thorpe to tell them that Swansea was in Wales, or that Aston Villa was not in Liverpool, as some youths first assumed. Yet even the experienced players were surprised at today's arrangements. Last season they had stayed Friday and Saturday nights in a Cardiff hotel. They were quiet at the start of the journey but soon livened up.

"Murraymints, Murraymints," sang one player, "Too good to hurry mints."

"Hey, I wonder if Andy Graver will be playing against us again," said another. Duncan Sharp looked up from the *Financial Times*. Graver seemed to play against Barnsley four times a season, and he often scored a goal. Lincoln City had twice sold him, to Leicester and to Stoke, and twice bought him back at a reduced price.

On the field Duncan Sharp feared no man. Off the field he suffered physically before some matches. He had been sick prior to playing against Don Kitchenbrand of Sunderland, yet marked him tightly. Then he had been too ill to play against Fulham and Olly Hopkins had deputised. Tim Ward now regularly kept a centre-half as 12th man, often Hopkins, but Roy Sawyer at Bristol Rovers and Sunderland. The reserve at Swansea was Bryan Matthews, who had played several Central League games at centre-half.

"Do you want to stop for a cup of tea?" asked Tim Ward.

"Yes, Boss," said several of the players.

"Where are we?"

"Stratford."

"I'll look out for Shakespeare."

"Who does he play for?"

"He keeps the pub on Wellington Street."

"It's your deal, Malcolm, if you've got any wages left."

Joe Thorpe drove through Stratford before pulling the bus into a transport cafe. More than one player thought it peculiar that the manager chose to ignore the picturesque town itself. The wheels ploughed through a puddle of water. It was wet, muddy and mid-December. Not the best time for tourists.

At Vetch Field, Swansea, Bob Wood scored an early goal to justify his selection in the forwards. Then Mel Nurse equalised from a penalty, an incident the players remembered at half-time.

"It was over the line, Boss, when Allchurch crossed it."

"I thought he'd blown, Boss, when I caught it."

"Should always play to the whistle."

"Did you see that linesman flagging? I thought he was going to take the penalty the way he put the ball on the spot."

"Aye, he flagged so much he set off two trains on Swansea station."

"We always get Welsh linesmen here."

This was a familiar complaint, one the Huddersfield manager Bill Shankly had raised at a recent managers' meeting. But Alan Hardaker pointed out that the Welsh teams had to put up with English linesmen when they came to England.

"Forget about it, lads, we can do it this half." But they didn't. Mel Charles scored an 87th minute winner that lingered through the long journey home. The bus was quiet for 20 minutes before the talking started. Tim Ward read out the results and a few checked pools coupons, which had only recently been allowed to footballers. It was around 4 am when they reached Oakwell.

Tim Ward maintained his policy of joining in as much as possible at training and it was while playing against winger Reg Bonson one evening that he decided to sign him as a part-time professional. Bonson had played occasionally in the 1951 Barnsley Boys team that included John Edgar and Reg's brother, Joe Bonson, who had played for Wolves and Cardiff. Reg Bonson's first spell at Oakwell, as an amateur, hardly led to a game so he left to concentrate on his motor mechanics course and his athletics, both of which were interrupted by a spell stationed at Suez in REME.

In 1956 Bonson had bought a pair of contact lenses and these proved efficient, though they were rare in football. The lenses covered the whole of each eye, never falling out or collecting mud underneath, even when his head was pushed in the dirt by an opponent. Contact lenses had progressed swiftly from the early 1950s when Barnsley full-back Eddie Bannister often complained of mud or bubbles behind his. Bannister's team-mates might see him grovelling around the pitch looking for a missing lens, but the ultimate drawback became evident one day when a lens fell out and Bannister made a crunching tackle on referee Bill Evans from Liverpool, one of the first referees to sprint into position. The Barnsley players had to spend some time mollifying Evans.

Reg Bonson carried his contact lenses in a cuff-link box and before training he took off his glasses in preparation. On one occasion he opened the case but there were no lenses. Instead there sat a pair of cuff-links. "It's about time you tied your eyes together, Reg," said Henry Walters, "But doesn't that chain cut into your nose?" The players roared with laughter.

Tim Ward enjoyed the joke too. When at Derby, Ward had played with Jack Howe, whose eyesight was very poor. When he left the Huddersfield pitch on a gloomy day in 1946, Howe's colleagues thought his career was finished. He'd had trouble telling the pitch from the terracing. But Howe became the first League player to wear contact lenses and later played for England.

The winter months were the worst for training but some would never miss.

Malcolm Hirst, for instance, loved training so much that when on holiday he rose at 6 am to keep in trim without spoiling the family's enjoyment of the break. Tim Ward found playing a relaxation from the administrative and man-management aspects of his job. If he could, he would spend all day in football boots, with the full-timers in the morning, the groundstaff in the afternoon, and the part-timers in the evening.

December 1958

Two big lamps shone over the car-park at the Pontefract Road end of Oakwell. Moving lightly over the rough cindered surface, Tim Ward collected a short pass and glimpsed a young opponent approaching from behind his left shoulder. Ward slowed, temptingly. He feigned to backheel the ball with his right foot, his foot seeming to disappear through the ball without moving it. He then whipped the ball forward with the same right foot and took three paces forward. Smiling, he looked back at the youngster, who was rooted to the spot. Even when a player knew it was coming, it was difficult not to fall for this trick. Ward called it the "Alex James stutter". He had learned it in the army, practising for hours after seeing it used by Arsenal's Reg Lewis, who had picked it up from James himself.

Barnsley players were expected to learn by watching their seniors. Ward and Steele recognised the importance of craft, disguise and ability to wrong-foot opponents. "If only you could control the ball a bit better," the speedy Reg Bonson was told, "then you'd be a world-beater." No-one actually talked him through the techniques but there were plenty of displays.

Tim Ward was still a skilful player. He could be very clever with the ball. Yet his success as a manager was based on encouraging team-work. In matches he wanted the easy pass, simple and direct. In practice matches he sometimes annoyed players with the reverse. John McCann found himself in the odd early bath after complaining about Ward's spinning or swerving passes.

"What do you reckon your time is for the hundred yards?" Tim Ward asked one player, after training had finished.

"Dunno, Boss," he replied, wondering if he could compare with Reg Bonson.

"Well, I'll tell you what. I'll bring in a calendar tomorrow and we'll time you."

A few players laughed and Ward picked one out. "I thought you made two good runs tonight," he said.

"I did that, Boss."

"One up the tunnel and one down it."

"Who won the Cup last year?"

"Bolton."

"No, Aston Villa, Bolton won it this year. Who won the Cup and haven't played in the competition since?"

"Oh, I don't know that. Who? Blackburn Olympic?"

"No, Bolton. They don't come in till the third round."

Tim Ward picked up a football boot and threw it across the room. A couple of players ducked but Ward had kept hold of the laces, and he pulled the boot back as if it were a yo-yo. There was a lot of ribbing all round.

Just before Christmas the players were practising on the rough surface of the Pontefract Road car-park. No-one held back, and the centre-halves were among the most combative. Olly Hopkins and Bryan Matthews challenged for a 50–50 ball. They collided. Matthews crashed down and hit his head on the floor. Immediately he had double-vision. He walked towards the treatment-room in a daze. It was the third time he'd had a head injury recently.

The club policy in these circumstances would always be to send someone home with the player. On this occasion there was some confusion and Matthews set off alone. He was sick on the bus and collapsed at home. He was taken to the brain unit at Sheffield and then to Beckett Hospital, Barnsley. Although a few players came to see him there were no visitors from the club.

All in all he was in hospital for about eight days. His mother had rung the club on the day of the injury but the news took some time to filter through. It was Christmas. Communications were bad and there were other hectic matters to deal with, such as the transfer of Malcolm Graham to Cardiff City. This was arranged, but Graham turned down the move on Christmas Eve.

Not every injured player would expect to receive a visit from the club, but it was normal procedure for anyone in hospital to be taken a basket of fruit from Ernest Dennis' shop. For some reason Bryan Matthews was left to make his recovery with no word from the club, which naturally upset him; after four weeks he returned to Oakwell and explained that he wouldn't be able to play again.

Bryn Price's progress had been interrupted at the end of the previous season. Against Leeds United Reserves he suffered a broken collar bone – an injury that had dogged him as a youth. Now recovered, he found his Central League place threatened by England Youth international David Barber. In the first team at right-half was Frank Bartlett, the newly-appointed captain. Everyone agreed Bartlett would be selected, even on crutches, if only to retain the continuity of his example.

Henry Walters was another wing-half considered a good example and he was now the guiding influence on the Reserves. Walters also kept them entertained, and in return the Reserves teased him about his age. The younger players called him "Dad" and even spectators threw in an occasional comment, such as "Who's that old crow?" If the H-bomb was mentioned, Barnsley players might look quizzically at Walters and ask, "How does it compare with the bow and arrow, Henry?" Or they would remind him that shinpads went inside the socks, "Not like in your day, Henry." Walters' hair was thinning on top, but anyone commenting on this would be met with a typical reply: "It's where the manager keeps patting my head and saying, 'Good game, Henry'."

With the competition at wing-half, Walters was often moved to full-back where his lack of speed was sometimes exposed against Central League fliers such as Bannister of Bolton. If anyone complained at half-time that he wasn't doing much of a job on the winger, Walters would reply innocently, "But I'm catching him on the way back." Alternatively, Walters might come into the dressing-room blowing his nose and complaining about the draught he kept experiencing as the player went past him.

Walters had only been into Ward's office to complain once in six years, and then only because he hadn't been given a game at all. Bryn Price was getting a game every week but not in the first team. He had been more than once to the manager's office on that account. When the team-sheets went up for Boxing Day, Bryn Price found he wasn't in any of the teams. There was a proviso that all players should report 40 minutes before the kick-off but Price tucked into a large Christmas dinner until there was a knock at the door. It was director Arthur Raynor, who explained that Price was needed for the Reserves after all, because of a late absentee.

Bryn Price collected his coat and Arthur Raynor drove him to Oakwell. They could have heard a pin drop in the car. Price was in disgrace and yet he played well in the match. "You must have a cooked dinner before every game," Joe Richards said to him afterwards.

A Real Sort-out

Chapter Eleven

Saturday 3rd January 1959

1–1 at Huddersfield. It was anybody's game with a few minutes left. Huddersfield were down to ten men. Stan Howard ran into the Barnsley penalty area and Duncan Sharp came across to tackle. Howard went down. The ball went out.

"Penalty."

"Goal-kick."

The penalty was given and Derek Hawksworth scored.

Into the last minute; Huddersfield goalkeeper Ray Wood came for a long cross and the usual bundle of players met in the penalty area. They went down like skittles and the ball bobbed away. Lol Chappell chased it to the left of the area. He lunged with his left leg and the ball looped over his right shoulder. It floated temptingly towards goal. Players scuttled back. It looked a goal. Then Huddersfield centre-half John Coddington threw up a hand and scooped the ball from under the crossbar. "Penalty." It was given.

Arthur Kaye, who had missed the last game with stomach trouble, placed the ball on the spot. He ran briskly and struck the ball hard, as he normally did. The ball thudded against an upright. There was a scramble and the game was over. Barnsley had lost 2–1. It was a bad start to the New Year.

The penalty saga was a contrast to the August game against Huddersfield at

Oakwell. Then Les Massie had missed an important 85th minute penalty when the scores were level. In fact, in the first fortnight of the season Denis Law, Massie and Hawksworth all missed penalties for Huddersfield.

Arthur Kaye appeared to have solved Barnsley's penalty problems, Since September 1956 he had scored 13 out of the 16 he had taken. Curiously, this latest miss was his second at Leeds Road, and it put Huddersfield above Barnsley in the League.

1	Sheffield Wednesday	25 – 39
2	Fulham	25 – 34
3	Liverpool	25 – 34
14	Huddersfield	25 – 22
15	Barnsley	25 – 22
16	Sunderland	26 – 22
17	Brighton	25 – 22
18	Scunthorpe	25 – 21
19	Grimsby Town	24 – 19
20	Leyton Orient	26 – 19
21	Lincoln City	25 – 16
22	Rotherham	25 – 14

The third round of the FA Cup matched Barnsley with Brentford, which meant an extra trip to London. As usual, all the arrangements would be left to Dean and Dawson, travel agents in Regent Street South. They took care of transport and booked 10 rooms in the Great Northern Hotel – six with twin beds for the players, and singles for the officials.

Although some of Britain's first motorway, the M1, was almost complete, the party travelled by train. The hotel was close to King's Cross station, yet Bob Shotton always hailed a porter and a taxi for transporting the skip, the big basket of kit. Just after the war Barnsley players were given Gladstone bags numbered from one to twelve. This eliminated the need for a porter's trolley as the players could carry their own boots, shirt, shorts, shinpads, socks and towel. But the Gladstone bags caused other headaches. They were regularly left on trains, and players disembarked to a chorus: "Have you got your cases? Don't forget your cases."

In the dressing-room, a player might say to another amidst much mirth, "I'll have my boots now, it was good of you to bring them down. I put them in your bag." Dave Lindsay once unwittingly carried two bricks to London. Other players might reach the dressing-room to find that they had left the hotel with sheets and spoons stashed in their kit. Another trick was to put a bag behind the bathroom door and then tell a player he must have left it on the train. The idea of cases was eventually dropped.

Dean and Dawson also booked seats for the players to see a Friday-night show. The week-ends in London gave the players an early chance to see one of the epic Hollywood productions of the day, such as "Ben Hur", "The Ten Commandments" or "Oklahoma". Before the Brentford game, however, they went to see the Christmas show at the Palladium.

Saturday 10th January 1959

The bone-hard Griffin Park pitch took away some of the magic of the FA Cup. The players took a close look. John McCann walked to the furthest corner. Here he could inspect the left wing, and quickly light a cigarette away from the eagle eye of Bob Shotton. Meanwhile a small group paced towards the centre-circle. The two inside-forwards did not relish their battle here. Bob Wood knew he would feel his thigh and Malcolm Graham his knee, which would be strained by the constant thud on the iron grass. The balance of the smaller players might sway the game.

"Just look at this pitch," said Henry Walters, the reserve and deputy for Duncan Sharp if necessary, "Pantomime last night and now circus today."

In the dressing-room the discussion about the pitch continued. The appearance of the warm sun was complicating the issue, with the pitch becoming patchy. In such circumstances captains were beginning to toss up in the dressing-rooms. This meant that goalkeepers in particular could choose boots to suit their part of the field.

"What boots do you think I should wear, Bob?" asked the players.

"Well I brought four pairs."

"Which are best, Bob?"

"Hey, I'm not playing. It's up to you. Why don't you try them on the pitch?"

Some players were too self-conscious to do this. A crowd of 16,890 was gathering for the FA Cup tie. Brentford were promotion contenders in the new Division Three and had finished runners-up in the last season of Division Three (South). They were a traditional bogey team for Barnsley, who had won only one of 14 League fixtures against them. And Brentford had a dangerous pair of forwards in Jim Towers and George Francis, who had scored 51 goals between them the previous season.

People always said the FA Cup was a great leveller and Tim Ward knew the pitch was too. It was often in the interest of the underdog to play in bad conditions.

As the buzzer went and the players filed out, there was the closest thing to a moment's relaxation for Tim Ward, Bob Shotton and Henry Walters. They collected the sponge, water, spare shorts, four extra tie-ups and more spare boots than usual.

"What sort of toffees have you bought for us, Henry?"

"Oh, I see. I suppose I'll have to buy buttered brazils if I want this job regularly."

"I can tell you the score before we start."

"0–0. I know that one. It's always 0–0 before we start."

There was one goal in the first-half. It came in the 20th minute from Towers of Brentford, while Malcolm Graham was off injured. At half-time there was still a debate about boots. The ball was impossible to control.

"Come on, Bob, what boots do we need?"

"I'm not playing, lads, I've not been on the pitch." Besides the four sets of boots, Shotton had brought the usual two sets of shirts and shorts in case they were needed at half-time. Some players changed boots, unsure of what they would face. They faced Towers and Francis in form. It was Francis who scored the only goal of the second-half, beating Hough to McLeod's centre in the 73rd minute. Barnsley lost 2–0 and went out of the FA Cup.

Afterwards, there were the usual murmurs about whether the game should have been played. "What's the idea?" asked Joe Richards, when he passed Bob Shotton coming out of the ground, "The players could hardly stand up out there."

"They can wear what they want, Mr Chairman," replied Shotton, who showed Richards the big sack with all the boots.

"Well, I'll be ... and some are blaming you."

Joseph Richards concealed his obvious disappointment and prepared for a night out in town. He was well-known in London restaurants such as the Caprice and the Coq D'Or, and he would often take his fellow directors to the restaurant and a show. Edmundo Ros was a favourite artist.

There was still no first-team opportunity for Bryn Price and he requested a transfer. His confidence had grown in five years at Barnsley. He was joined on the transfer list by Colin Swift and Peter Gillott, full-backs who were currently kept out of the first team by John Short and Bryn Jones.

Colin Swift had been ill with influenza. He delayed his come-back until he felt fully fit, worried about attracting extra blame for a poor first game. When Swift declared himself fit, he was picked for the A team. Tim Ward sometimes found it difficult to be sympathetic to such problems as his own career had been free from major illness or injury. He believed in fighting the trivial. "He's got a cold," Ward might say of a player, but in a voice that clearly indicated disapproval.

Peter Gillott's request came nearly six years after his selection for England Youth. He had played five first-team games since, making appearances in each of the four Second Division seasons. His longest run was two games in 1957–58. Gillott had sometimes struggled at the higher level, but it came back to Joe Hooley's argument – an extended opportunity was needed. Gillott had watched the careers of full-backs take shape – Thomas, May, Hudson, Betts, Roscoe, Swift, Short, Jones – and now he decided that there was no place at Barnsley for him.

After the 5–0 defeat at Sheffield United on 7th February, Tim Ward made four changes. One of them was the dropping of Harry Hough.

I'm blaming you for all five goals," he told him in the corridor after the game, "You've got too confident."

Dropping a player was a delicate decision for a manager. There was no clear procedure. A quiet word might be resented by one player: "He didn't have the courage to tell me in front of the others." Yet a public announcement might cause embarrassment or anger. Tim Ward's methods varied. Sometimes he would pull a player aside during a training session. Or he would call a player into the board-room, perhaps saying he was "resting" him. Like most managers, Ward disliked giving bad news. But he was prepared for standard retorts, such as "I know I had a bad game but there were others worse than me." Fred Westgarth of Hartlepools had a unique way of telling a player he was dropped. He would simply send him across the road for the result of the 2.30 race.

Tim Ward's own experience of being dropped was exceedingly limited. Although Ward was an international, he had worked at his football, thinking about his weaknesses, improving all the time until age overtook him. He was sensitive enough to try different solutions for dropping different players, but finding the right one was not easy.

The players looked for tell-tale signs. They considered the teams for the Tuesday practice match. They noticed if someone was called aside. They looked in the pigeon-holes to see if their boots had been shined by Bob Shotton. They noticed whether key individuals said "Good morning" or not. Sometimes they still learned from the paper-seller: "Tuppence, lad, I see tha's dropped."

When Brighton visited Oakwell on St Valentine's Day, Barnsley had Don Leeson in goal. Bob Wood finally resumed at wing-half, Rikkie McDonald made his debut at centre-forward and Norman Smith returned without a single cartilage. But Barnsley still lost 2–0, in front of a thinning crowd.

The tide began to turn a little with a 3–3 draw at Grimsby, but conceding a late equaliser to a side several places below made Tim Ward feel that his side had lost a point rather than gained one. He had at least been able to play his favourite forward line – Kaye, Smith, Chappell, Graham, McCann – and his entire team showed a noticeable improvement. It was the first time they had scored more than once since Christmas.

Blundell Park had always seemed a friendly ground. After the match there were about 20 parcels of fish in the dressing-room for the visitors. Until recently three had also been left in the referee's room. One referee had reported the practice to the Football League, considering it tantamount to a bribe. Now an experienced official might by taken by surprise and have to apply at the manager's office: "Er, I told the wife not to buy any meat this week-end and …" There was always a Barnsley comedian who suggested that his club were mean compared to Grimsby, adding, "We should leave 20 sacks of coal for our visitors."

The improvement was short-lived. Losing away to Stoke and dropping a home point to Bristol Rovers took Barnsley down into the bottom six.

17	Barnsley	31 – 25
18	Lincoln	32 – 23
19	Scunthorpe	32 – 23
20	Grimsby	30 – 22
21	Leyton Orient	32 – 22
22	Rotherham	30 – 19

It was now nine League games since a win and Tim Ward's thoughts turned to the awkward Easter programme, which included two games against a powerful Liverpool team. Ward knew that the traditional remedy was to go for experienced players who would do the easy thing every time. He chose Henry Walters at right-back against Scunthorpe but Barnsley lost 1–0.

Ward began to have reservations about his experienced players. He could see Harry Hough becoming more involved with PFA activities, Bob Wood suffering from a troublesome knee injury and Norman Smith, while always willing, coming back from a long lay-off. His most pressing headache was Arthur Kaye, who was not his normal self. Ward found it difficult to know how to approach him. His star player had been disillusioned with the club since the wages problem, and there were other difficulties. Kaye seemed less hungry to get on the field. He was even missing training, a complete contrast to the dedication of the early days, when he ran on his own at night and followed a diet of fresh and dried fruits and honey.

It would be simple just to leave him out, but there were several aspects to consider. To have Arthur Kaye in the Reserves was not good for business, and his general popularity in the town was undiminished by some relatively ineffectual performances. When Ernest Steele's son, Hedley, became the team's regular mascot there was no doubt which shirt he wanted, even though the no. 7 he wore was several sizes too large. Attendances had fallen below 6,000 and it was the beginning of the familiar pattern – no money, no new players, no results, no fans, less than no money.

Tim Ward was also concerned about the advice he was receiving. He leaned by nature towards the opinions of John Steele and often took him aside for a talk. But Bob Shotton was the senior trainer, and although Ward did his best to involve him in discussions he knew there must have been times when Shotton felt left out. Now Shotton was telling Ward that some players weren't trying. Ward found it difficult to accept, but then perhaps he was too trusting. "The players are getting lazier," said Shotton, "They should be stopped from bringing cars to the ground." Certainly a stricter attitude towards Kaye might have lessened the problems, but perhaps it had gone too far now.

In contrast to the usual remedy of experience, Ward plumped for youth. The Juniors were top of the Northern Intermediate League. Barnsley Boys were in the English Schools' Trophy semi-final for the sixth time since the war. Youngsters might be raw, unsure of the seriousness of the situation, but they could at least compensate for staleness and complacency. For the Easter Friday game at Liverpool, Ward picked David Barber at left-half, Frank Beaumont at inside-left and Peter Whyke at outside-right. They were unperturbed by the 52,546 partisan crowd but went down 3–2, conceding two late goals to Billy Liddell, who was making his 466th appearance for Liverpool, a record on Merseyside. The next day, at Derby, Ward rested his three youngsters and Barnsley lost 3–0.

Monday 30th March 1959

Liverpool at home on Easter Monday. It would be a hard and important match. John McCann arrived at Oakwell early. He explained that his groin strain was too bad for him to play. It had been touch-and-go all Easter, and it was the last thing Tim Ward wanted because McCann had been a star in what was proving a problem season.

Ward's first thought was to play Colin Brookes at outside-left. Brookes had been kept available, but rather than stay idle he had asked Norman Rimmington for a game in the A team. So Tim Ward walked hurriedly to the Queen's Ground. It was exactly 2 pm but as Ward walked up the rise he could see the game had already started.

While Ward considered the outside-left spot, John Steele went to Duncan Sharp's house. The big centre-half was not feeling fit. As Sharp sat on the sofa, Steele went through a rigmarole of persuasion. Eventually he collected Sharp's jacket and put it round him. Sharp set off for Oakwell. He might not have done so for Tim Ward.

When the Barnsley players ran onto Oakwell they included regular right winger Arthur Kaye, who hadn't scored for three months, and makeshift left winger Norman Smith. In the first half Barnsley created more scoring chances but Liverpool took a one-goal lead. Then Dick White's back pass gave Lol Chappell a run at goal, but his shot was too close to Tommy Younger, who soon afterwards pushed a header from Holmes onto the underside of the bar. Younger also saved from Kaye. Bartlett hit the post. Then John Short's back pass let in Jimmy Melia for his second goal of the game.

The Barnsley players trudged off tired and dejected after three losses in four days. They sat and said even less than in the usual silences after defeat. Only the crowd seemed loud.

"Get some new players."

"Spend some money. Get some players bought."

"I'd do better leaving early to get cheap vegetables from the market."

"Never agen! I'm not coming agen!"

"You'll be here next Saturday to see Sunderland."

"Nah, they didn't come to see me when I was bad. I wouldn't pay them in washers. I'll go and watch Wakefield Trinity. They need that Fox down here to kick a few goals."

17	Leyton Orient	36 – 28
18	Scunthorpe	37 – 28
19	Lincoln	37 – 27
20	Grimsby	36 – 26
21	Barnsley	36 – 25
22	Rotherham	35 – 24

It meant 12 games without a win. It was easy for spectators to criticise the players' lack of fight and forget that they had their own personal lives to sustain. The twenties were a time of adjustment and sometimes insecurity. Last season had brought the tragedy of Munich. This season had brought the sudden death of Bristol Rovers full-back Harry Bamford in a road accident. Then on 29th March, West Brom assistant trainer W G Richardson died during a charity game. But a week later came news that stunned the football world. Birmingham right-back Jeff Hall died of polio. He was 29-years-old. Barnsley immediately arranged inoculations for all their staff and the game with Sunderland on 4th April was played with both teams wearing black arm-bands.

It suited many footballers to settle down and marry young. They were smart, in good physical condition and healthy. They always looked as though they'd just stepped out of the bath – and they usually had. It was rare that they were caught in dirty overalls. They were also easily recognised and much in demand on social occasions. Many faced the prospect of living away from home at some stage of their career. Yet while many sought support through marriage a small element stayed clear. Norman Smith, for instance, felt football was a single man's sport. He had seen too much injury and too many retained lists to think otherwise. Footballers could spend afternoons at home but there were few week-ends that they could spend entirely with their families.

For those wishing to marry, there was the question of fixing a day. Saturdays were sacred during the season, so Bryn Jones selected Easter Tuesday, after which he spent a two-day honeymoon in Doncaster before returning to training. When he looked at the team-sheet his name was missing. "You've been rested," said the other players knowingly. It was the standard joke.

Wednesday 15th April 1959

"Do you fancy coming tonight, Colin?" asked Bob Shotton as he arranged boots for the County Cup game at Sheffield United, "You can help me out."

"Yes please," said a delighted Colin Brookes, who was now a regular Reserve team player despite still being on the groundstaff.

"Would you like your Dad to come too?" continued Shotton.

"Oh, yes," said Brookes, thinking this was a little odd. He knew the coach was usually the sanctuary of the players. People were very careful with such invitations.

Colin Brookes returned to Oakwell at 5 pm. The team-sheet was in the dressing-room but Brookes stayed outside since a schoolboy team were changing. The schoolboys often used the facilities' end. Clarrie Hirst, secretary of Barnsley Schools FA and a teacher at nearby Grove Street school, worked closely with Ward and Ernest Steele.

"All the best," said John McCann, appearing suddenly from the dressing-room. Colin Brookes felt the first signs of excitement. And then Bob Shotton emerged.

"You're playing tonight, Colin," said Shotton, "John's got a groin strain. We knew earlier but didn't want you to worry."

Barnsley lost the game 2–1 but Colin Brookes played soundly, having one shot well saved by Alan Hodgkinson. Sheffield United full-backs Cecil Coldwell and Graham Shaw offered him advice, which they would never have done in a League game. It was an interlude in Barnsley's intense relegation struggle, for they had lost another two games.

Five home matches without scoring a goal. The latest was a 2–0 defeat by Sunderland. Then Andy Graver turned up again, scoring a goal to help Lincoln beat Barnsley 2–1 at Sincil Bank. He had done the same in a January friendly.

In the League match, Ron Smillie played at outside-right for Lincoln, directly against his Barnsley Boys colleague Colin Swift. Ten years. "Whatever happened to Angus Seed's dream?" thought Smillie. His home-town club were bottom of the division.

18	Leyton Orient	38 – 30
19	Lincoln	39 – 29
20	Grimsby	38 – 26
21	Rotherham	37 – 26
22	Barnsley	38 – 25

Saturday 18th April 1959

"Give it him," came an order from the Barnsley crowd.

"Come on, ref, he's wasting time," shouted the occupants of the Barnsley trainer's box. The ball had gone out for a throw-in in front of them.

"Put it down, it's the other way," shouted referee Jack Kelly of Chorley.

It was the heat of battle. Fulham were leading 3–2 at Oakwell and it was close to time. Barnsley were hoping for a point. It might be a vital point. They had already equalised twice, but Frank Bartlett's own-goal had put Fulham in the lead for the third time.

Jimmy Hill tucked the ball under his arm and walked 30 yards towards the referee. When he arrived the book was out. But there was still time for a goal … and it fell to Graham Leggatt of Fulham. It ensured promotion for them, while another defeat meant more worry for Barnsley. Still bottom, three games to play.

Two days passed and Swansea Town arrived at Oakwell. Tim Ward made one change. He brought in Tommy Holmes at inside-left. It was Holmes who had marked Ivor Allchurch in a game three years ago when Barnsley picked up two vital points. It was the type of memory that stuck in a manager's mind; but where was Lol Chappell, whose two goals had helped win the game in 1956?

Chappell was still running, but it was so much harder in a bad spell. He had scored 14 times in the first 27 games of the season. But after returning in place of Rikkie McDonald, Chappell had managed only one goal in nine matches. He still played with injuries. A specialist at Beckett Hospital treated his arthritis and warned that he might be in a wheel-chair in 10 years. But Chappell still chased. If he scored a goal he was likely to get two.

So it proved on the Monday evening against Swansea. Lol Chappell scored twice in a 3–1 Barnsley win. Including FA Cup ties and friendlies, it broke a run of 18 games without a win. It was Don Leeson's 15th appearance yet his first winning bonus. And it took Barnsley from the bottom of the table. But only 4,882 people saw the game.

			For	*Against*	*Goal Average*
17	Scunthorpe	42 – 33			
18	Leyton Orient	39 – 32			
19	Lincoln	40 – 29	62	90	.689
20	Rotherham	40 – 29	42	67	.623
21	Barnsley	40 – 27	54	83	.651
22	Grimsby	40 – 26	58	85	.682

The season had reached the stage where each day brought results for other teams that were just as important as Barnsley's. On the Tuesday the news was mixed. Lincoln City lost 1–0 at Bristol City but Grimsby Town beat Leyton Orient 4–1. Grimsby's win put their goal average out of Barnsley's reach and it left Barnsley bottom, but still only a point behind with a game in hand. And that game in hand would be at home to Leyton Orient. Only two went down.

			For	*Against*	*Goal Average*
18	Leyton Orient	40 – 32			
19	Lincoln	41 – 29	62	91	.681
20	Rotherham	40 – 29	42	67	.623
21	Grimsby	41 – 28	62	86	.721
22	Barnsley	40 – 27	54	83	.651

First came the last full Saturday's fixtures; At 4.40 it looked grim. By then Barnsley had lost 5–0 to a Sheffield Wednesday side already promoted. Then the other results came through to redeem the situation. Lincoln, Grimsby and Rotherham had all lost – Lincoln by the odd goal in three, Grimsby and Rotherham both by 4–0.

			For	*Against*	*Goal Average*
19	Lincoln	42 – 29	63	93	.677
20	Rotherham	41 – 29	42	71	.592
21	Grimsby	42 – 28	62	90	.689
22	Barnsley	41 – 27	54	88	.614

Grimsby were definitely down. Rotherham's defeat left one escape route still open for Barnsley. Barnsley had to beat Leyton Orient and Rotherham had to lose at home to Huddersfield.

The disappointing result was that of Lincoln. True, they had lost but even in defeat they had gained precious goals on Barnsley. If only Lincoln had lost 5–0 and Barnsley 2–1, then any win against Leyton Orient would have been enough. Now, the Reds would have to win 6–0, 7–1, 7–2 or 8–3 to move above Lincoln. It was typical of the end-of-season drama. The committed fans were polishing up their maths.

Wednesday 29th April 1959

"You worry about winning tonight," said Bill Shankly over the telephone. "We'll do Rotherham for you."

"Thanks, Bill," said Tim Ward, "I know your seasons go all the way." He hung up.

The two men knew each other well from playing together for the Starlights team, and it was some comfort at times like this to know that people outside the club wanted you to stay in the division. There were quite a few clubs who would be sorry to lose the Grimsby fixture – a hospitable club with the bonus of free fish. Ironically, Barnsley might not want Rotherham to go down, for with them would disappear two well-attended games. But whatever happened, one of them had to drop.

Ward turned his attention to team selection. It was one of the occasions when he put up an extended list of names on the notice-board with a view to selecting 11 when the players reported. The biggest question-mark was against Arthur Kaye, who had played poorly against Sheffield Wednesday. When Ward approached him Kaye was hesitant. The manager wanted a ready answer and promptly pencilled in Jackie Lunn's name on the team-sheet, which he then pinned up. Kaye was upset and made his way up to watch from the stand. A few heads turned and wondered what he was doing there.

Tim Ward walked thoughtfully to the dressing-room. He never said much before a game but today he had rehearsed a careful speech. He took a moment to compose himself before going in. He had to relax the players and the best way to do that was to appear calm himself. It would be no use if they saw sweat form on his brow.

"Relax, lads, we all know we shouldn't be where we are. We're due some good luck. Let's build on the good things we've started to get together."

He took care to say no more than usual otherwise it would put pressure on the players. They didn't need more pressure, the importance of the game was self-evident.

As he made his way to the bench Ward tried to remember whether there was anything else Raymond Vicary had asked him to do; had he forgotten any of the complimentary tickets? The sight of the ground and the players kicking in brought other thoughts to his mind; how hard would the opposition be trying, how hard would some of his own players be trying, what would Third Division football really mean?

Friday 1st May 1959

Tim Ward woke on Friday morning, stepped out of bed, and walked straight to the front door. It was his wife's birthday and he had to pull the "Daily Express" from under a pile of cards. He flipped to the back page.

"Well look at that," he said aloud, though no-one else was up, "Rotherham lost." But it did not matter, Barnsley were down anyway. They had lost 3–1 to Leyton Orient. Six years and Tim Ward was back where he came in. Rotherham's defeat stirred the memory of all the "ifs and buts" the season had brought. Andy Graver, Roy Shiner, Mel Charles had all scored late goals that cost Barnsley a point. If only Arthur Kaye's penalty had scraped in at Huddersfield. Then there was the extraordinary visit he'd received at the back-end of the season. An opposition player had come into his office about an hour before one game and announced that if his side's bonuses were guaranteed then Barnsley could look forward to two points. Ward told him without hesitation that if they lost, they lost. Only when he was alone again did the manager stop to consider whether the offer had been serious.

Ward knew that such offers were made, though not necessarily to managers or whole teams, but you could try the goalkeeper or a couple of experienced defenders who might give away a penalty or two. He himself had received an anonymous letter before the away game at Southport in September 1954, promising £25 if the game were won. He had shown it to Joe Richards who told him to send it to Fred Howarth at Football League headquarters, just to be on the safe side. Barnsley had won 2–0 and for several days Ward waited to see if anything would arrive, but nothing did. Pools punters were generally assumed to be responsible for such approaches.

On this recent occasion Ward decided not to trouble the chairman. It was too petty and he knew he had an honest board, whose only response to the suggestion would have been indignation. He felt the benefit of the directors' integrity himself. Some managers would already have had the sword hanging over their heads: "If we go down you find another job." There were never any such intimations at Oakwell.

As Ward took stock of all that had happened during the season, he could not help feeling a sense of irony. At the top of Division Two were Sheffield Wednesday, nine points clear of the third-placed club. It was the fourth time in ten seasons that they had won promotion to the First Division. In contrast to Barnsley they were a big club with a relatively sound financial basis, yet a year before Tim Ward might have become their manager. He was in for the job, and they asked him back to the interview room to confirm that his mind was set on a five-year contract against the three-year term they were offering. Ward had said that it was. The position went to Harry Catterick, who five years before had applied unsuccessfully for the vacancy at Barnsley. Now Catterick had become a First Division manager at the first attempt, while Ward was back where he started, except that the Third Division no longer had a north and south separation.

Another thing that had changed was Ward's style of life. He was more involved in the town than he would have expected to be as a player. He had taken up cricket at Stainborough in the summer of 1953. He had acquired shares in the football club and local business. He was a member of the Rotary Club and began to mix socially with the professional people of the town. He was much sought after as a speaker at functions. Most significant of all he was no longer living in a club house. As a manager he was a reasonable prospect for a mortgage, whereas building societies tended to frown on footballers with their one-year contracts. The Ward family had moved to a £2,750 bungalow in Intake Lane, Gawber. "It's an awful lot of money to pay for a house," Ward had said, "I'd expect 20 goals a season for that." Ward always thought in football terms, in seasons rather than in years. The job monopolised his thoughts. He visited Oakwell every day and even at home the telephone rang persistently.

He was now experienced in all aspects of a manager's responsibilities and particularly capable in the administrative duties that some other managers wished written out of their contracts. While his personality did not win him friends amongst some sections of the playing staff, he was a track-suit manager who had done his best to bring a new dimension to the football.

Those who had appreciated the "rough and ready" style of Brough Fletcher would find it difficult to like the "gentlemanly" Tim Ward. Those who admired the open friendliness and professional distance of Angus Seed would find something to complain of in his successor. But Ward had put Barnsley back in Division Two and consolidated. In 1957–58 they took 40 points, which was more than Seed had averaged in his six full seasons after the war.

There were things to worry about aside from relegation. There was a squad of players who had perhaps been together too long. Ward had experienced difficulties with senior players who had developed their own views on matters, a process encouraged by the increasing strength of the Professional Footballers' Association. Some points of friction were related to long service itself; several players were entitled to benefits within the space of one or two seasons. The club could not find the money easily. Financial problems had contributed to preventing tours and delaying the acquisition of floodlights, two areas which Ward had hoped to exploit in his earlier days.

What of the future? At least they would still get fish once a season since Grimsby were also down. The most immediate concern for Tim Ward was facing the directors. He was not especially worried about the possibility of losing his job, although there had been 394 managerial changes in 13 seasons since the war. Ward had faith in the fact that he was only the second Barnsley manager in that period. Only three managers had been with the same club since 1945 – Matt Busby at Manchester United, Billy Walker at Nottingham Forest, and Bill Anderson at Lincoln.

His faith proved justified. When the first board meeting after relegation was completed the directors approached Ward one by one and shook his hand sincerely, asking him to stay for a drink. They had accepted their manager's explanations: two or three players had not produced their best form; Bob Wood and Norman Smith had been injured; other players had wanted to sit out with minor injuries; and the slide had started late and taken grip. Had the situation seemed serious at Christmas, Ward could have bought players as other clubs did. Leyton Orient had signed Brown, Baily and Johnston. Rotherham had bought Cooper.

The Barnsley board accepted the reasons and looked to the future. Financially they had been caught out. Relegation seemed to have come from nowhere, typical of the unpredictable nature of football. The manager would stay, but what of the players? The club must have money, and only the sale of the best players could prevent a large loss. Also, since the supporters might view the same faces as failures, new players were needed to bring back the crowds. An end-of-season Central League game against Aston Villa had attracted 226 and collected £9 in receipts. The average attendance at Reserve games was about a thousand.

The plan for the future would have to be built around youth, with a sharp reduction in playing staff. Lower attendances next season would mean that the wage bill would have to be cut. To complicate matters, National Service was ending and the club could no longer hold players on token wages.

For six years the club had been on the rise. Financial losses had been endured in the quiet hope of reaching the First Division. Now the 1950s were fading away. The affluence of football in the post-war boom had given way to the affluence of the family – cars, televisions, electric gadgets, hire purchase. Britain was motorised. Cinemas and football clubs were among the victims. It was the end of an era for Barnsley football, and the effect on the players was devastating.

The retained list was minimal. The transfer list was huge. As usual, Barnsley sent details to the Football League, who produced a booklet for circulation. The Barnsley transfer list was a match for any other club. The relegation season ended with 36 professionals on Barnsley's books, plus six groundstaff boys. But when the players reported back for training, less than three months later, the number of professionals was down to 19, and only 12 were full-time. The groundstaff was brought up to seven.

Retained
David Barber
Frank Bartlett
Frank Beaumont
Lol Chappell
Malcolm Graham
Alan Green
Olly Hopkins
Bill Houghton
Arthur Kaye
Don Leeson
Jackie Lunn
John McCann
Roy Sawyer
Duncan Sharp
John Short
John Stainsby
Colin Swift
Henry Walters
Peter Whyke

Transfer List
Eric Anderson
Peter Gillott
Tommy Holmes
Harry Hough
Rikkie McDonald
Bryn Price
Norman Smith
Bob Wood

Groundstaff
George Jagger
Jeff Sacre
Malcolm Senior
Clem Wood

Free Transfers
David Cade
Dennis Coughlin
Malcolm Hirst
Bryn Jones
John Lawson
Peter Lycett
Bryan Matthews
Dennis Medlam
Alan Vest

Signed Professional
Colin Brookes
Ron Gregory

Oakwell saw its first big transfers for six years. Although retained, Arthur Kaye, Malcolm Graham and John McCann were all sold to higher division clubs, but the fees were far lower than Barnsley would have demanded a year before. Blackpool paid £13,500 for Kaye, while the left-wing pair were part of a very complicated deal with Bristol City.

On Monday 5th May Joe Richards and Tim Ward spent four hours in talks with Bristol City chairman Harry Dolman and manager Peter Doherty. That evening Ward rode back to Bristol in Dolman's Rolls-Royce, with Doherty driving. In the end, £14,500 passed from Bristol City to Barnsley. The evaluations of £7,000 for Graham and £15,000 for McCann were reduced by £7,500 in respect of Bert Tindill who joined Barnsley. The money for McCann would be paid over five years.

Two of Barnsley's most experienced players, Harry Hough and Norman Smith, also left the club. "We're having a real sort-out," Tim Ward told Smith, "We're putting you on the list, Norman, but it's for your own good. We're asking £750 so you'll get an accrued share." Eventually, however, both Smith and Hough had to bargain for their share. "We have to buy new players and we can't give all our money away," Joe Richards told the players.

Hough received half the £1,000 paid by Bradford Park Avenue. He found this very disappointing. With 12 seasons service Hough knew that he qualified for a £1,000 benefit. Norman Smith did slightly better. He received £500 of the £750 Shrewsbury Town paid for him to become player/coach, but only after meetings with Richards and the full board.

In almost every deal concerning a transfer-listed player, there was some setback to Barnsley's urgent need for cash. Mansfield Town turned down Bob Wood when the player told them of his recurrent knee trouble. Wood returned home to Scotland and discovered he needed a cartilage operation.

There were plenty of offers from progressive non-League Clubs. Chelmsford paid £1,000 for Peter Gillott and Eric Anderson went to Macclesfield but Bryn Price rejected an attractive-sounding offer from Headington United manager Arthur Turner, a friend of Tim Ward. Price and his wife did not wish to move. Price signed for Buxton and bought an A30 for travelling. Both Bryn Price and Tommy Holmes appealed to the Football League Management Committee for a reduction in transfer fee. Price went on a free transfer rather than £1,000, while Holmes' fee came down from £1,500 to £750, and he signed for Halifax Town.

The saddest of the free transfers was Bryan Matthews, who eventually received £500 compensation for the premature end to his promising career; but it was the release of Bryn Jones that surprised the players most. Jones himself was surprised and shocked when he learned from the placards of the big clear-out. He had moved and the club did not have his new address. Jones, who had made 15 first-team appearances, moved to York City and bought a Lambretta to travel the 38 miles. David Cade was the only other free transfer to stay in the Football League. He moved to Bradford Park Avenue.

It took a long time for the dust to settle on the registration forms at Oakwell. Then Raymond Vicary worked on the next season's Northern Intermediate

League fixtures and referees, while a printers' strike kept away all except the local journalists.

Vicary and Ward occasionally took advantage of the quiet by playing bowls on Walter Drewry's Co-op ground or table-tennis in the gymnasium. Vicary always played with an extra-large bat. He enjoyed his relaxation and certainly earned it. Some players called him "Little Sport" after a cartoon character in the *Sheffield Star*. They never let him forget the time he used the sun-ray lamp in the dressing-room. Rather than lift the head of the lamp and lie on the masseur's table, Vicary had laid a towel on the floor and stretched out on it as if it were a Majorcan beach. Not that Vicary went to Majorca, although 3 ½ million Britons were now taking holidays abroad each year. Vicary more likely went to Butlin's at Ayr, while Ward still regularly visited the YMCA at Skegness.

The summer gave Ernest Steele a chance to nurture the Oakwell grass without Lol Chappell pounding over every blade. If there were times when Chappell wished the earth would swallow him up, even he was unprepared when a big hole appeared in the Queen's Ground in the summer of 1959; it was caused by subsidence.

The hole grew three feet wide and stretched across the Queen's Ground, running dangerously close to Walter Drewry's beloved Co-op cricket square. In one place it was 36 feet deep. When people threw stones down they listened, heard nothing and shouted, "Any of you miners want a game?"

Barnsley was always affected by the coalfield, the divine influence from below. Subsidence moved houses. Cracks appeared from nowhere. Doors shifted and keys failed to fit. Some people swore they could lay in bed at night and hear the eerie sounds of miners working below. At Birdwell house building had stopped. At Darton the railway station was sinking. At Tankersley houses were evacuated.

The Coal Board filled in the hole on the Queen's Ground, but it re-appeared and the whole sequence of events had people talking of Quatermass. One day Ernest Steele felt the ground give way when he was walking his dog, and it began to crack as he stepped back. It took Steele 2 ½ hours to cut the grass of the football pitch and he walked seven miles, treading gingerly over the Queen's Ground.

Tim Ward didn't want to lose a player down a Queen's Ground crevasse; after all, players were disappearing everywhere else. Lol Chappell and Duncan Sharp asked for transfers, and when Chappell signed for Doncaster Rovers for £4,000 it meant that all of Ward's first-choice forwards had left the club: Kaye, Smith, Chappell, Graham and McCann. Ward had already decided that his young players would need an experienced guide before the season started at home to bogey team Brentford.

Jimmy Baxter had been retained by Preston to coach and play in the second team, and he and his family were happily settled in Lancashire. At the beginning of June he was down in Barnsley on holiday, visiting his wife's relatives, when he received an unexpected call from Doncaster manager Jack Bestall, who expressed an interest in signing him. Baxter was invited to look at a club house, after which he decided to think the matter over for a few days.

Then quite by chance Jimmy Baxter ran into Tim Ward. It occurred to Ward that if Baxter were available he might be just the man to help the youngsters along at Oakwell. John Steele was not in favour, bearing in mind that Baxter was not only 34-years-old, but had spent much of his last two years on the treatment table. But Ward felt that age and injury could be overcome by a player whose main quality was skill.

Tim Ward telephoned Preston manager Cliff Britton and the two men agreed a small fee for Baxter. Ward contacted the player and Jimmy Baxter agreed to see him. "Fine," said Ward, "Do you know where the ground is?"

Jimmy Baxter laughed. It was almost exactly 14 years since Angus Seed had travelled to Scotland to sign the boy miner. Now Baxter met Ward and accepted the Barnsley captaincy and the chance of first-team football.

Season-by-season Statistics

Appendix

1953–54 DIVISION THREE (NORTH)

AUG 19	Bradford City	a	0–1	15030	Ho	Th	My	Sm	Sp	No	Ka	Lu	Wo	Br	Pa
22	Port Vale	a	0–0	14242	Ho	Th	My	Sm	Sp	No	Ka	Lu	Ke	Br	Pa
26	Chester	a	1–1	7110	Ho	Th	My	Sm	Sp	No	Ka	Lu	Ke	Br(1)	Pa
29	BRADFORD PA	H	2–1	7369	Ho	Th	My	Sm(1)	Sp	No	SM	Lu	Ke	Br(1)	Pa
SEP2	CHESTER	H	3–0	9859	Ho	Th	My	Sm	Sp	No	SM	Lu(1)	Ke(1)	Br	Pa(1)
5	CHESTERFIELD	H	4–1	12537	Ho	Th	My	Sm	Sp	No	SM	Lu(3)	Ke	Br	Pa(1)
7	Crewe Alex	a	2–3	8850	Ho	Th	Hu	Sm	Sp	No	SM	Lu(1)	Ke(1)	Br	Pa
12	Darlington	a	1–1	6911	Ho	Th	Wa	Sm	Sp	No	SM	Lu	Ch(1)	Br	Pa
16	CREWE–ALEX	H	1–1	10126	Ho	Th	Hu	Wa	Sp	No	SM	Lu	Ch(1)	Br	Se
19	HARTLEPOOLS	H	3–2	10659	Ho	Th	My	Wa	Sp	No	Se(1)	Lu	Ch(1)	Br(1)	Pa
23	SOUTHPORT	H	2–1	9102	Ho	Th	My	Wa	Sp	Ar	SM	Lu(1)	Ch	Br(1)	Se
26	Gateshead	a	0–0	10196	Ho	Th	My	Wa	Sp	Ar	SM	Lu	Ch	Br	Se
OCT3	WORKINGTON	H	4–2	10899	Ho	Th	My	Sm	Sp	Wa	SM	Lu(2)	Ch(1)	Br(1)	Pa
10	Halifax	a	2–1	8000	Ho	Th	My	Sm	Sp	Wa	SM	Lu(1)	Ch(1)	Br	Se
17	CARLISLE	H	1–1	11271	Ho	Th	My	Sm	Sp	Wa	SM	Lu	Ch	Br(1)	Se
24	Accrington	a	0–3	8500	Ho	Th	My	Sm	Sp	Wa	SM	Lu	Ch	Br	Bt
31	GRIMSBY TOWN	H	0–0	8341	Ho	Th	My	Sm	Sp	Wa	Ka	Wo	Ch	Br	Bt
NOV7	Stockport	a	0–3	6400	Ho	Th	My	Sm	Sp	Wa	Ka	Wo	Ch	Br	Bt
14	ROCHDALE	H	2–1	8053	Ho	Th	My	Sm	Sp	Wa	Ka(1)	Lu	Ch	Br(1)	Wd
28	MANSFIELD	H	2–1	9150	Ho	Th	My	Sm	Sh	Wa	Ka(1)	Lu	Ch	Br(1)	Wd
DEC5	Barrow	a	1–0	6217	Ho	Th	My	Sm	Sp	Wa	Ka	Lu	Ch	Br(1)	Wd
19	PORT VALE	H	0–1	11330	Ho	Th	My	Sm	Sp	Jk	Ka	Lu	Ch	Br	Bt
25	York City	a	2–0	5136	Ho	Th	My	Sm	Sp	Wa	Ka	Lu	Ch(2)	Br	Bt
26	YORK CITY	H	2–1	9536	Ho	Th	My	Sm	Sp	Wa	Ka.	Wo	Ch(1)	Br(1)	Bt
JAN1	Southport	a	2–5	5350	Ho	Th	My	Sm	Sp	Wa	Ka	Lu	Ch(2)	Br	Bt
2	Bradford PA	a	2–0	11141	Ho	Th	My	Sm	Sp	Wa	Ka	Lu	Ch	Br(2)	Wd
9	BRADFORD CITY	H	4–2	8629	Ho	Th	My	Sm	Sp	Wa	Ka	Lu	Ch(2)	Br(1)	Wd(1)
16	Chesterfield	a	1–1	8399	Ho	Th	My	Sm	Sp	Wa(1)	Ka	Lu	Ch	Br	Wd
23	DARLINGTON	H	5–1	7860	Ho	Th	My	Sm	Sp	Wa	Ka(1)	Lu	Ch	Br(4)	Wd
FEB6	Hartlepools	a	1–0	7026	Ho	Th	My	Sm	Sh	Wa	Ka	Lu	Ch(1)	Br	Wd
20	Workington	a	0–2	12400	Ho	Th	My	Sm	Sp	Wa	Ka	Lu	Ch	Br	Wd
27	HALIFAX	H	1–2	9030	Ho	Th	My	Sm	Sp	Wa	Ka	Lu(1)	Ch	Br	Wd
MAR3	Tranmere	a	1–0	3168	Ho	Th	My	Sm	Sp	Wa	Ka	Lu(1)	Ch	Br	Wd
6	Carlisle	a	4–2	4921	Ho	Th	My	Sm	Sp	Wa	Ka	Lu	Ch(3)	Br(1)	Wd
13	ACCRINGTON	H	5–0	8040	Ho	Th	My	Sm	Sp	Wa	Ka(2)	Lu	Ch(2)	Br(1)	Wd
20	Grimsby Town	a	1–0	6399	Ho	Th	My	Sm	Sp	Wa	Ka	Lu	Ch	Br(1)	Wd
27	STOCKPORT	H	4–1	9274	Ho	Th	My	Sm	Sp	Wa(1)	Ka	Lu	Ch(1)	Br(2)	Wd
31	GATESHEAD	H	0–2	12863	Ho	Th	My	Sm	Sp	Wa	Ka	Lu	Ch	Br	Wd
APR3	Rochdale	a	1–1	6127	Ho	Th	My	Ar	Sp	Wa	Ka	Lu(1)	Ch	Br	Wd
10	WREXHAM	H	3–0	8676	Ho	Th	My	Ar	Sp	Wa	Ka	Lu	Ke(2)	Br(1)	Bt
16	Scunthorpe	a	0–6	10274	Ho	Th	My	Ar	Sp	Wa	Ka	Lu	Ch	Br	Bt
17	Mansfield	a	0–2	10031	Ho	Th	Hu	Jk	Sp	Wa	Ka	Lu	Ch	Br	Wd
19	SCUNTHORPE	H	0–1	10762	Ho	Th	Hu	Jk	Sp	Wa	Ka	Lu	Ch	Br	Wd
21	TRANMERE	H	3–0	5794	Ho	Th	My	Jk	Sp	Wa	Ka(1)	Lu	Ch(1)	Br(1)	Wd
24	BARROW	H	3–2	6826	Ho	Th	My	Jk	Sp	Ar	Ka	Lu(2)	Ch(1)	Br	Wd
28	Wrexham	a	1–1	6500	Ho	Th	My	Jk	Sp	Wa	Ka	Lu	Ch(1)	Br	Wd

APPEARANCES

Brown (Br) 46, Hough (Ho) 46, Thomas (Th) 46, Spruce (Sp) 44, Lumley (Lu) 43, May (My) 41, Chappell (Ch) 38, Walters (Wa) 37, Norman Smith (Sm) 34, Kaye (Ka) 33, Wardle (Wd) 22, Gavin Smith (SM) 12, Normanton (No) 10, Pattison (Pa) 10, Bartlett (Bt) 9, Doug Kelly (Ke) 7, Ron Archer (Ar) 6, Jackson (Jk) 6, Smillie (Se) 6, Hudson (Hu) 4, Bob Wood (Wo) 4, Sharp (Sh) 2.

GOALS

Brown 24, Chappell 22, Lumley 14, Kaye 6, Kelly 4, Walters 2, Pattison 2, Norman Smith 1, Wardle 1, Smillie 1.

1954–55 DIVISION THREE (NORTH)

AUG21	OLDHAM	H	2–2	11277	Ho	Th	My	Sm	Sp	Wa	Ka	Lu(1)	Ch	Br(1)	Wd
23	Bradford PA	a	0–1	12644	Ho	Th	My	Sm	Sp	Wa	Ka	Lu	Ke	Br	Wd
28	Halifax	a	1–1	10000	Ho	Th	My	Sm	Sp	Wa	Ka	Lu	Ch	Br(1)	Wd
SEP1	BRADFORD PA	H	2–1	12571	Ho	Th	My	Sm	Sp	Wa	Ka	Wo	Ch	Br(1)	Pa(1)
4	YORK CITY	H	1–0	11338	Ho	Th	My	Sm(1)	Sp	Wa	Ka	Wo	Ch	Br	Pa
9	Scunthorpe	a	0–1	12140	Ho	Th	My	Wo	Sp	Wa	Ka	Lu	Ch	Br	Wd
11	Southport	a	2–0	4095	Ho	Th	My	Jk	Sp	Wa	Ka(1)	Wo	Ch	Br(1)	Se
15	SCUNTHORPE	H	1–0	16331	Ho	Th	My	Jk	Sp	Wa	Ka	Wo	Ch	Br(1)	Pa
18	BARROW	H	3–0	12032	Ho	Th	My	Jk	Sp	Wa	Ka	Wo(1)	Ch(2)	Br	Pa
22	ACCRINGTON	H	1–2	13904	Ho	Th	My	Ar	Sp	Wa	Ka	Wo	Ch(1)	Br	Wd
25	Workington	a	0–1	7831	Ho	Th	My	Jk	Sp	Wa	Ka	Ar	Ch	Br	Se
27	Accrington	a	3–2	12295	Ho	Th	My	Jk	Sp	Wa	Ka	Lu(1)	Ch	Br(1)	Bt
OCT2	MANSFIELD	H	1–0	13856	Ho	Th	My	Jk	Sp	Wa	Ka	Lu	Ch	Br	Bt(1)
9	Rochdale	a	0–3	11552	Ho	Th	My	Jk	Sp	Wa	Ka	Lu	Ch	Br	Bt
16	TRANMERE	H	4–1	10668	Ho	Th	My	Jk	Sp	Wa	Ka	Lu(1)	Ch(3)	Br	Wd
23	Stockport	a	0–1	7250	Ho	Th	My	Jk	Sp	Wa	Ka	Lu	Ch	Br	Se
30	HARTLEPOOLS	H	0–0	10041	Ho	Th	My	Jk	Sp	Wa	Se	Lu	Ch	Br	Bt
NOV6	Gateshead	a	4–0	5076	Ho	Th	My	Sm	Sp	Jk	Se	Lu	Ch	Wo(1)	Bt(3)
13	DARLINGTON	H	4–1	8318	Ho	Th	My	Sm	Sp	Jk	Ka	Lu	Ch(3)	Wo(1)	Bt
27	CREWE ALEX	H	3–1	9042	Ho	Th	My	Sm	Sp	Wa	Ka	Lu	Ch(3)	Wo	Bt
DEC4	Carlisle	a	4–2	5000	Ho	Th	My	Sm	Sp	Wa	Ka	Lu(1)	Ch(1)	Wo(1)	Bt(1)
18	Oldham	a	1–4	8803	Ho	Th	My	Sm	Sp	Wa	Ka	Lu	Ch(1)	Wo	Se
25	Grimsby Town	a	3–1	10200	Ho	Be	My	Sm	Sp	Jk	Ka	Lu	Ch(1)	Wo	Bt(2)
27	GRIMSBY TOWN	H	1–3	16531	Ho	Be	My	Sm	Sp	Wa	Ka	Lu	Ch	Wo	Bt(1)
JAN1	HALIFAX	H	3–0	13036	Ho	Th	My	Sm(1)	Sp	Wo	Ka	Lu	Br(1)	Gr	Bt(1)
8	WREXHAM	H	4–2	10619	Ho	Th	My	Sm	Sp	Wo(1)	Ka	Lu(1)	Br(1)	Gr(1)	Bt
15	York City	a	3–1	7711	Ho	Th	My	Sm	Sp	Wo	Ka	Lu	Ch(1)	Br(1)	Bt(1)
29	Wrexham	a	0–3	6607	Ho	Th	My	Sm	Sp	Wo	Ka	Lu	Ch	Br	Bt
FEB5	Barrow	a	1–3	4602	Ho	Th	My	Sm	Sp	Wo	Ka	Lu	Br(1)	Gr	Bt
12	WORKINGTON	H	3–1	6147	Ho	Th	My	Sm	Sp	Jm	Ka	Lu	Br	Wo	Bt(3)
19	Mansfield	a	1–1	4020	Ho	Th	My	Sm	Sp	Jm	Ka	Lu	Br(1)	Wo	Bt
MAR5	Tranmere	a	1–0	5000	Ho	Th	My	Sm	Sp	Jm	Se	Lu	Br	Wo(1)	Bt
12	STOCKPORT	H	2–0	9411	Ho	Th	My	Sm	Sp	Jm	Ka	Lu	Br(2)	Wo	Bt
19	Hartlepools	a	3–0	8231	Ho	Th	My	Sm	Sp	Jm	Ka(1)	Lu	Br	Wo(1)	Bt(1)
26	GATESHEAD	H	3–0	6194	Ho	Th	My	Sm	Sp	Jm	Ka(2)	Lu	Br	Wo(1)	Bt
APR2	Darlington	a	1–0	6760	Ho	Th	My	Sm	Sp	Jm	Ka	Lu(1)	Ch	Wo	Bt
9	CHESTERFIELD	H	3–0	17141	Ho	Th	My	Sm	Sp	Jm	Ka	Lu	Ch(2)	Wo(1)	Bt.
11	BRADFORD CITY	H	1–0	18808	Ho	Th	My	Sm	Sp	Jm	Ka	Lu	Ch(1)	Wo	Bt
12	Bradford City	a	2–0	18514	Ho	Th	My	Sm	Sp	Jk	Ka(1)	Lu	Ch	Wo(1)	Bt
16	Crewe Alex	a	2–1	5450	Ho	Th	My	Sm	Sp	Wo	Ka	Lu	Ch	Br(1)	Bt(1)
23	CARLISLE	H	3–1	13510	Ho	Th	My	Sm	Sp	Jm	Ka	Lu	Ch(2)	Wo	Bt
25	Chesterfield	a	1–3	13238	Ho	Th	My	Sm	Sp	Jm(1)	Ka	Lu	Ch	Wo	Bt
27	SOUTHPORT	H	0–0	13848	Ho	Th	My	Sm	Sp	Jm	Ka	Lu	Br	Wo	Bt
30	Chester	a	2–0	6566	Ho	Th	My	Sm	Sp	Wa	Ka	Lu(1)	Br(1)	Wo	Bt
MAY3	ROCHDALE	H	2–0	11606	Ho	Th	My	Sm	Wa	Be	Ka	Lu	Ch	Wo(2)	Br
4	CHESTER	H	4–2	9974	Ho	Th	My	Sm	Be	Hm	Ka	Lu(1)	Ch	Br(3)	Se

APPEARANCES

Hough (Ho) 46, May (My) 46, Thomas (Th) 44, Spruce (Sp) 44, Kaye (Ka) 43, Lumley (Lu) 39, Wood (Wo) 35, Smith (Sm) 34, Chappell (Ch) 34, Brown (Br) 33, Bartlett (Bt) 30, Walters (Wa) 23, Jackson (Jk) 14, Jarman (Jm) 12, Smillie (Se) 8, Wardle (Wd) 6, Pattison (Pa) 4, Betts (Be) 4, Graham (Gr) 3, Archer (Ar) 2, Kelly (Ke) 1, Holmes (Hm) 1.

GOALS

Chappell 21, Brown 18, Bartlett 15, Wood 12, Lumley 8, Kaye 5, Smith 2, Pattison 1, Graham1, Jarman 1, Holliday (Accrington) 1, Mitton (Carlisle) 1.

1955–56 DIVISION TWO

AUG20	LEEDS UNITED	H	2–1	19253	Ho	Th	Be	Sm	Sp	Jm	Ka(1)	Wo(1)	Ch	Lu	Br
25	Notts County	a	2–2	16000	Ho	Th	Be	Wo	Sp	Jm	Ka	Lu	Ch	Gr(1)	Br(1)
27	Fulham	a	1–5	22500	Ho	Sw	Be	Wo	Sp	Jm	Ka	Lu	Ch	Gr(1)	Br
31	NOTTS COUNTY	H	3–1	16546	Ho	Sw	Be	Wo	Sp	Jm	Ka(1)	Lu	Ch	Gr(2)	Br
SEP3	BURY	H	3–3	17070	Ho	Sw	Be	Wo	Sp	Jm	Ka	Lu	Br(1)	Gr(2)	Bt
5	Rotherham	a	0–0	18000	Ho	Sw	Be	Wo	Sp	Jm	Ka	Lu	Br	Gr	Bt
10	Leicester	a	0–0	22950	Ho	Sw	Be	Wo	Sp	Jm	Ka	Lu	Br	Gr	Bt
14	ROTHERHAM	H	3–2	19331	Ho	Sw	Be	Wo	Sp	Jm	Ka	Lu	Br(1)	Gr(1)	Bt(1)
17	Middlesbrough	a	1–1	27000	Ho	Sw	Be	Wo	Sp	Jm	Ka	Lu	Br(1)	Gr	Bt
24	BRISTOL CITY	H	0–0	19447	Ho	Sw	Be	Jk	Sp	Jm	Ka	Lu	Br	Wo	Bt
OCT1	West Ham	a	0–4	20500	Ho	Sw	Be	Jk	Sp	Jm	Ka	Lu	Br	Wo	Bt
8	LINCOLN CITY	H	1–0	14719	Ho	Sw	Be	Jk	Wa	Wo	Ka	Lu(1)	Ch	Br	Bt
15	Blackburn	a	1–5	22200	Ho	Sw	Be	Jk	Wa	Wo	Ka	Hm	Ch	Br(1)	Bt
22	PLYMOUTH	H	1–2	11245	Ho	Sw	Be	An	Wa	Jm	Ka	Lu	Br	Wo(1)	Bt
29	Nottm Forest	a	0–1	11262	Ho	Sw	Wa	An	Sh	Jm	Ka	Lu	Br	Wo	Bt
NOV5	SHEFF WED	H	0–3	21554	Ho	Sw	Wa	An	Sh	Wo	Ka	Lu	Br	Ed	Bt
12	Doncaster	a	1–1	12507	Ho	Sw	Be	An	Sh	Wa	Ka	Lu	Br(1)	Wo	Bt
19	BRISTOL ROV	H	4–3	11625	Ho	Sw	Be	An	Sh	Wa	Ka	Lu	Br(2)	Wo(1)	Bt(1)
26	Stoke City	a	1–2	17728	Ho	Sw	Be	An	Sh	Wa	Ka	Lu	Br	Wo(1)	Bt
DEC3	HULL CITY	H	2–1	13967	Ho	Sw	Be	Wo	Sh	Wa	Ka(1)	Lu	Ch	Br(1)	Bt
10	Liverpool	a	1–1	26241	Ho	Sw	Be	Wo	Sh	Wa	Ka	Lu	Ch	Br(1)	Bt
17	Leeds United	a	1–3	23000	Ho	Sw	Be	Wo	Sh	Wa	Ka	Lu	Ch	Br	Bt(1)
24	FULHAM	H	3–0	14943	Ho	Sw	Be	Wo	Sh	Wa	Ka	Lu	Ch(2)	Br	Bt
26	Port Vale	a	2–1	19130	Ho	Sw	Be	Wo(l)	Sh	Wa	Ka	Lu	Ch	Br	Bt(1)
27	PORT VALE	H	1–2	21949	Ho	Sw	Be	Wo	Sh	Wa	Ka	Lu	Ch	Br(1)	Bt
31	Bury	a	0–3	12972	Ho	Sw	Be	Wo	Sh	Wa	Ka	Lu	Ch	Br	Bt
JAN14	LEICESTER	H	0–1	13196	Ho	Sw	Be	Wo	Sh	Wa	Ka	Gr	Du	Br	Bt
21	MIDDLESBROUGH	H	0–4	15849	Ho	Sw	Be	Wo	Sh	Wa	Ka	Gr	Ch	Br	Bt
FEB4	Bristol City	a	0–2	19349	Ho	Sw	Be	Ar	Sh	Wa	Ka	Br	Du	Gr	Bt
17	WEST HAM	H	1–1	8367	Ho	Sw	Be	Ar	Sh	Wa	Ka	Br	Ch	Wo	Gr(1)
18	Bristol Rov	a	1–1	20995	Ho	Sw	Be	Ar	Sh	Wa	Ka	Bt	Ch	Wo(1)	Gr
25	BLACKBURN	H	2–1	11597	Ho	Sw	Be	Ar	Sh	Wa	Ka	Bt	Ch(2)	Wo	Gr
MAR3	Plymouth	a	0–3	11000	Ho	Sw	Be	Ar	Sh	Wa	Ka	Bt	Ch	Wo	Gr
10	LIVERPOOL	H	0–5	13678	Ho	Sw	Be	Ar	Sh	Wa	Ka	Bt	Ch	Wo	Gr
14	Sheff Wed	a	0–3	31577	Ho	Th	Sw	Ar	Sh	Wa	Ka	Br	Ch	Wo	Gr
24	DONCASTER	H	2–2	9811	Ho	Th	Gi	Ar	Sh	Wa	Ka(2)	Bt	Ch	Br	Gr
31	Lincoln	a	0–4	11787	Ho	Th	Be	Ar	Sp	Wa	Ch	Bt	Du	Br	Gr
APR2	SWANSEA TOWN	H	3–2	12106	Ho	Th	Be	Hm	Sp	Wa	Se	Wo(1)	Ch(2)	Br	Bt
7	STOKE CITY	H	1–0	9690	Ho	Th	Be	Hm	Sp	Wa	Se	Wo	Ch	Br	Bt(1)
14	Hull City	a	1–4	8931	Ho	Th	Be	Hm	Sp	Wa	Se	Ka(1)	Ch	Wo	Bt
21	NOTTM FOREST	h	1–1	11334	Ho	Th	Be	Hm	Sp	Wa	Ka	Wo(1)	Ch	Br	Mc
28	Swansea Town	a	1–3	12000	Ho	Th	Be	Sm	Sp	Wa	Ka(1)	Bt	Ch	Br	Mc

APPEARANCES

Hough (Ho) 42, Kaye (Ka) 39, Betts (Be) 38, Wood (Wo) 38, Brown (Br) 37, Bartlett (Bt) 35, Swift (Sw) 33, Walters (Wa) 31, Chappell (Ch) 27, Lumley (Lu) 25, Sharp (Sh) 22, Graham (Gr) 19, Spruce (Sp) 17, Jarman (Jm) 13, Thomas (Th) 10, Archer (Ar) 9, Anderson (An) 6, Holmes (Hm) 5, Jackson (Jk) 4, Smillie (Se) 3, Duggins (Du) 3, McCann (Mc) 2, Smith (Sm) 2, Edgar (Ed) 1, Gillott (Gi) 1.

GOALS

Brown 11, Graham 8, Wood 8, Kaye 7, Chappell 6, Bartlett 5, Lumley 1, Greenwood (Fulham) 1.

1956–57 DIVISION TWO

AUG18	Port Vale	a	0–0	14326	Ho	Be	Th	Sm	Sp	Wa	Ka	Wo	Ch	Gr	Br
22	SWANSEA TOWN	H	2–3	13530	Ho	Be	Th	Sm	Sp	Wa	Ka(1)	Wo	Ch	Gr	Br(1)
25	MIDDLESBROUGH	H	1–3	11567	Ho	Be	Th	Sm	Sp	Wa	Ka	Wo	Ch(1)	Gr	Br
29	Swansea Town	a	3–2	19000	Ho	Be	Th	Sm	Sp	Wa(2)	Ka(1)	Wo	Ch	Gr	Bt
SEP1	SHEFF UNITED	H	1–6	21114	Ho	Be	Th	Sm	Sp	Wa	Ka(1)	Wo	Ch	Gr	Bt
5	LINCOLN CITY	H	5–2	9287	Ho	Th	Sw	Sm(1)	Sp	Wa	Ka	Sy(1)	Ch(1)	Gr(1)	Mc(1)
8	Bristol City	a	2–1	19635	Ho	Th	Sw	Sm	Sp	Wa	Ka	Sy	Br(1)	Gr	Mc(1)
15	BLACKBURN	H	3–3	14529	Ho	Th	Sw	Sm	Sp	Wa	Ka(2)	Sy	Br	Gr(1)	Mc
22	West Ham	a	0–2	19500	Ho	Th	Sw	Sm	Sp	Wa	Ka	Sy	Hi	Gr	Mc
29	NOTTM FOREST	H	1–1	15529	Ho	Th	Sw	Bt	Sp	Wa	Ka	Sy	Du	Gr	Mc(1)
OCT6	Leicester	a	2–5	27270	Ho	Th	Sw	Bt–	Sp–	Wa	Ka(1)	Sy	Du(1)	Gr	Mc
13	BRISTOL ROV	H	0–2	14983	Ho	Th	Sw	Bt	Sp	Wa	Ka	Sy	Du	Gr	Mc
20	Doncaster	a	2–5	14971	Ho	Th	Sw	Bt	Sp	Wa	Ka	Sy	Ch(1)	Gr(1)	Mc
27	LIVERPOOL	H	4–1	13941	Ho	St	Sw	Bt	Sp	Hm	Ka(1)	Sy(1)	Ch	Gr	Mc(2)
NOV3	Leyton Orient	a	0–2	17374	Ho	St	Sw	Bt	Sp	Hm	Ka	Sy	Ch	Gr	Mc
10	HUDDERSFIELD	H	0–5	15105	Ho	St	Sw	Bt	Sp	Hm	Ka	Sy	Ch	Gr	Mc
17	Bury	a	2–1	9713	Ho	St	Sw	Bt	Sp	Wa	Ka	Sy	Du(2)	Gr	Mc
24	GRIMSBY TOWN	H	2–0	11281	Ho	St	Sw	Bt	Sp	Wa	Ka(2)	Sy	Du	Hm	Mc
DEC1	Notts County	a	2–3	11000	Ho	St	Sw	Bt	Sp	Wa	Ka	Sy	Du(2)	Ed	Mc
8	STOKE CITY	H	2–2	11626	Ho	St	Sw	Bt	Sp	Wa	Ka(1)	Sy	Du	Ed	Mc(1)
15	PORT VALE	H	2–0	9603	Ho	St	Sw	Bt	Sp	Wa	Ka(1)	Sy(1)	Du	Ed	Mc
22	Middlesbrough	a	2–1	11147	Ho	St	Sw	Bt	Sp	Wa	Ka	Sy	Du	Ed(1)	Mc(1)
25	Rotherham	a	0–0	14235	Ho	St	Sw	Bt	Sp	Wa	Ka	Sy	Du	Ed	Mc
26	ROTHERHAM	H	1–1	10939	Le	St	Sw	Bt	Sp	Wa	Ka	Sy	Du(1)	Wo	Mc
29	Sheffield Utd	a	0–5	25960	Ho	St	Sw	Bt	Sp	Wa	Ka	Sy	Du	Wo	Mc
JAN12	BRISTOL CITY	H	3–0	13439	Ho	St	Sw	Bt(1)	Sh	Wa	Ka(1)	Hm	Ch	Ed(1)	Mc.
19	Blackburn	a	0–2	21100	Ho	St	Sw	Bt	Sh	Wa	Ka	Wo	Ch	Ed	Mc
FEB2	WEST HAM	H	1–2	15816	Ho	St	Sw	Bt	Sh	Wa	Ka	Hm	Du	Ed(1)	Mc
9	Nottm Forest	a	1–7	25844	Ho	St	Sw	Bt	Sp	Wa	Ln	Hl	Ch	Ed(1)	Mc
23	Bristol Rov	a	1–1	14004	Ho	St	Sw	Bt	Sh	Wa	Ka	Sy	Ch	Hm(1)	Mc
27	LEICESTER	H	2–0	11109	Ho	St	Sw	Bt	Sp	Wa	Ka	Sy(1)	Ch(1)	Hm	Mc
MAR2	DONCASTER	H	3–1	16185	Ho	St	Sw	Bt	Sp	Wa	Ka(1)	Ed	Ch	Gr(2)	Mc
9	Liverpool	a	1–2	30672	Ho	St	Sw	Bt	Sp	Wa	Ka	Sy	Ch	Hm	Mc(1)
16	LEYTON ORIENT	H	3–0	12427	Ho	St	Th	Bt	Sp	Wa	Ka(1)	Sy	Ch(1)	Hm(1)	Mc
23	Huddersfield	a	0–2	16772	Ho	St	Sw	Bt	Sp	Wa	Ka	Sy	Ch	Hm	Mc
30	BURY	H	1–1	10107	Ho	St	Sw	Bt	Sp	Wa	Ka	Sy	Ch(1)	Gr	Mc
APR6	Grimsby Town	a	1–4	10307	Ho	St	Sw	Wo	Sp	Wa	Ka(1)	Ed	Ch	Gr	Mc
13	NOTTS COUNTY	H	1–1	7566	Ho	St	Sw	Wo	Sp	Wa	Ka	Ed	Ch	Gr(1)	Mc
19	Fulham	a	0–2	17000	Ho	St	Th	Wo	Sp	Wa	Ka	Sy	Ch	Hm	Mc
20	Stoke City	a	0–3	11600	Ho	St	Th	Wo	Sp	Wa	Ka	Sy	Ch	Gr	Mc
22	FULHAM	H	1–1	8410	Ho	Th	Gi	Pr	Sp	Wa	Ka	Wo(1)	Ch	Hm	Mc
27	Lincoln City	a	1–4	7295	Ho	Th	Sw	Wo	Sp	Wa	Ka	Sy	Ch	Hm(1)	Mc

APPEARANCES

Hough (Ho) 41, Kaye (Ka) 41, Walters (Wa) 39, Spruce (Sp) 38, McCann (Mc) 37, Swift (Sw) 32, Bartlett (Bt) 29, Storey (Sy) 29, Short (St) 27, Chappell (Ch) 26, Graham (Gr) 22, Thomas (Th) 19, Holmes (Hm) 14, Wood (Wo) 14, Duggins (Du) 13, Edgar (Ed) 12, Smith (Sm) 9, Betts (Be) 5, Brown (Br) 5, Sharp (Sh) 4, Hirst (Hi) 1, Leeson (Le) 1, Hooley (Hl) 1, Price (Pr) 1, Gillott (Gi) 1, Lunn (Ln) 1.

GOALS

Kaye 15, McCann 8, Chappell 6, Graham 6, Duggins 6, Storey 4, Edgar 4, Holmes 3, Brown 2, Walters 2, Smith 1, Bartlett 1, Wood 1.

1957–58 DIVISION TWO

AUG24	BRISTOL ROV	H	2–2	12673	Ho	St	Sw	Bt	Sh	Wo	Ka	Ad	Ch(1)	Bm(1)	Mc
28	Ipswich	a	0–3	20468	Ho	St	Sw	Bt	Sh	Wo	Ka	Ad	Ch	Bm	Mc
31	Derby County	a	4–1	22376	Ho	St	Sw	Bt	Sh	Wo	Ka(1)	Ad	Ch(3)	Sm	Mc
SEP2	IPSWICH	H	5–1	12185	Ho	St	Sw	Bt	Sh	Wo(1)	Ka(3)	Ad(1)	Ch	Sm	Mc
7	SWANSEA TOWN	H	1–0	15780	Ho	St	Sw	Bt	Sh	Wo	Ka(1)	Ad	Ch	Sm	Mc
9	Blackburn	a	1–3	12900	Ho	St	Sw	Bt	Sh	Wo	Ka	Ad	Ch	Sm(1)	Mc
14	Fulham	a	1–1	25000	Ho	St	Sw	Bt	Sh	Wo	Ka	Ad	Ch(1)	Gr	Mc
18	BLACKBURN	H	0–2	12711	Ho	St	Sw	Bt	Sh	Hn	Ka	Ad	Ch	Gr	Mc
21	MIDDLESBROUGH	H	1–1	11491	Ho	St	Sw	Bt	Sh	Hn	Ka	Sm	Du	Bm(1)	Gr
28	WEST HAM	H	1–0	12119	Ho	St	Sw	Bt	Sh	Hn	Ka	Sm(1)	Ch	Ed	Mc
OCT5	Sheff Utd	a	0–0	25473	Ho	St	Sw	Bt	Sh	Hn	Ka	Sm	Ch	Ed	Gr
12	Leyton Orient	a	1–2	15149	Ho	St	Sw	Bt	Sh	Hn	Ka	Sm	Ch(1)	Ed	Mc
19	CHARLTON	H	4–1	15059	Ho	St	Sw	Bt(1)	Hp	Wo(1)	Ka	Sm(1)	Ch	Gr(1)	Mc
28	Doncaster	a	1–1	18971	Ho	St	Sw	Bt	Sh	Wo	Ka	Sm	Ch	Gr(1)	Mc
NOV2	ROTHERHAM	H	3–0	18838	Ho	St	Sw	Bt	Sh	Wo	Ka	Sm(2)	Ch	Gr(1)	Mc
9	Huddersfield	a	5–0	21667	Ho	St	Sw	Bt	Sh	Wo(1)	Ka	Sm(1)	Ch	Gr(2)	Mc(1)
16	GRIMSBY TOWN	H	3–3	16091	Ho	St	Sw	Bt	Sh	Wo	Ka	Sm	Ch(2)	Gr(1)	Mc
23	Stoke City	a	1–3	17555	Ho	St	Th	Bt	Sh	Wo	Ka(1)	Sm	Ch	Gr	Ln
30	BRISTOL CITY	H	4–1	13449	Ho	St	Gi	Bt	Sh	Wo	Ka(1)	Sm	Ch	Gr(2)	Mc(1)
DEC7	Cardiff City	a	0–7	8000	Ho	St	Gi	Bt	Sh	Wo	Ka	Sm	Ch	Gr	Mc
14	LIVERPOOL	H	2–1	15205	Ho	St	Sw	Bt	Sh	Wo	Ka(1)	Sm	Ch(1)	Gr	Mc
21	Bristol Rov	a	1–1	13355	Ho	St	Sw	Bt	Sh	Wo	Ka(1)	Sm	Ch	Gr	Mc
25	Notts County	a	3–2	11343	Ho	St	Sw	Bt	Sh	Wo(1)	Ka(1)	Bm(1)	Ch	Gr	Mc
26	NOTTS COUNTY	H	1–1	20193	Ho	St	Sw	Bt	Sh	Wo	Ka	Sm(1)	Ch	Gr	Mc
28	DERBY COUNTY	H	3–0	21689	Ho	St	Sw	Bt	Sh	Wo(1)	Ka	Sm	Ch(1)	Bm(1)	Mc
JAN11	Swansea Town	a	2–4	9961	Ho	St	Sw	Bt	Sh	Wo	Wh	Sm	Ch(2)	Gr	Mc
18	FULHAM	H	1–0	14263	Ho	St	Sw	Bt(1)	Sh	Wo	Wh	Sm	Ch	Ad	Mc
FEB1	Middlesbrough	a	1–3	19280	Ho	St	Sw	Pr	Sh	Wo	Ed	Sm	Ch	Gr(1)	Mc
8	West Ham	a	1–1	27182	Ho	St	Sw	Bt	Sh	Wo	Ed	Sm	Ch	Gr	Mc(1)
22	STOKE CITY	H	1–2	14182	Ho	St	Sw	Bt	Sh	Wo	Ed	Sm	Ch(1)	Gr	Mc
MAR1	Charlton	a	2–4	25760	Ho	St	Sw	Bt	Sh	Wo	Ed	Sm	Ch(1)	Gr(1)	Mc
8	DONCASTER	H	1–1	11476	Ho	Jo	Sw	Bt	Sh	Wo	Ka	Sm	Ch(1)	Gr	Mc
15	Rotherham	a	1–4	11389	Ho	Jo	Sw	Bt(1)	Sh	Wo	Ka	Sm	Ch	Gr	Mc
22	HUDDERSFIELD	H	2–3	16409	Ho	Jo	Sw	Bt	Sh	Wo	Ka(1)	Sm	Ch	Gr(1)	Mc
29	Grimsby Town	a	1–2	9632	Le	Jo	Sw	Bt	Sh	Wo	Ka	Ed(1)	Ch	Gr	Mc
APR5	LEYTON ORIENT	H	3–0	8732	Ho	Sw	St	Bt	Sh	Wo	Ka	Sm(1)	Ch(2)	Gr	Mc
7	Lincoln City	a	3–1	7001	Ho	St	Sw	Bt	Sh	Wo	Ka	Ed(1)	Ch(2)	Gr	Mc
8	LINCOLN CITY	H	1–3	11394	Ho	St	Sw	Bt	Sh	Wo	Ka	Sm(1)	Ch	Gr	Mc
12	Bristol City	a	0–5	18002	Ho	St	Sw	Bt	Sh	Wo	Ka	Sm	Ch	Gr	Mc
19	CARDIFF CITY	H	1–1	8861	Ho	St	Sw	Bb	Sh	Wo(1)	Ka	Bm	Ch	Gr	Mc
23	SHEFF UTD	H	0–2	8720	Ho	St	Sw	Bt	Sh	Bb	Ln	Sm	Ch	Gr	Mc
26	Liverpool	a	1–1	26440	Ho	St	Sw	Bt	Sh	Bb	Ln	Sm	Ch	Gr	Mc(1)

APPEARANCES

Hough (Ho) 41, Sharp (Sh) 41, Chappell (Ch) 41, Bartlett (Bt) 40, Swift (Sw) 39, McCann (Mc) 39, Short (St) 38, Wood (Wo) 35, Kaye (Ka) 34, Smith (Sm) 34, Graham (Gr) 32, Eric Anderson (Ad) 9, Edgar (Ed) 9, Beaumont (Bm) 6, Houghton (Hn) 5, Jones (Jo) 4, David Barber (Bb) 3, Lunn (Ln) 3, Gillott (Gi) 2, Whyke (Wh) 2, Duggins (Du) 1, Hopkins (Hp) 1, Thomas (Th) 1, Price (Pr) 1, Leeson (Le) 1.

GOALS

Chappell 19, Kaye 11, Graham 11, Smith 9, Wood 6, McCann 4, Beaumont 4, Bartlett 3, Edgar 2, Anderson 1.

1958–59 DIVISION TWO

AUG23	Cardiff City	a	1–0	23000	Ho	St	Sw	Bt	Sh	Wo	Ka	Sm	Ch	Gr(1)	Mc
27	BRISTOL CITY	H	4–7	14187	Ho	St	Sw	Bt	Sh	Bb	Ka	Sm	Ch(4)	Gr	Mc
30	HUDDERSFIELD	H	1–0	17573	Ho	St	Sw	Bt	Sh	Hn	Ka	Sm	Ch(1)	Gr	Mc
SEP3	Bristol City	a	1–3	28353	Ho	St	Sw	Bt	Sh	Hn	Wh	Hm(1)	Ch	Gr	Mc
6	Leyton Orient	a	1–5	13288	Ho	St	Sw	Bt	Sh	Hn	Ka	Hm	Ch(1)	Gr	Mc
10	CHARLTON	H	7–1	11749	Ho	St	Sw	Bt	Sh	Wo	Ln(2)	Sm	Ch(1)	Gr(4)	Mc
13	Rotherham	a	0–3	12548	Ho	St	Sw	Bt	Sh	Wo	Ln	Sm	Ch	Gr	Mc
18	Chariton	a	0–4	10364	Ho	St	Gi	Bt	Sh	Wo	Ka	Bm	Ch	Gr	Mc
20	SHEFF UTD	H	1–3	16779	Ho	St	Sw	Bt	Sh	Hn	Ka	Sm	Ch	Wo(1)	Mc
27	Brighton	a	1–1	24311	Ho	St	Sw	Bt	Sh	Hn	Ka	Gr	Ch	Wo	Mc(1)
OCT4	GRIMSBY TOWN	H	3–1	10157	Ho	St	Sw	Bt	Sh	Hn	Ka(1)	Gr	Ch(2)	Wo	Mc
11	DERBY COUNTY	H	0–0	11885	Ho	St	Sw	Bt	Sh	Hn	Ka	Gr	Ch	Wo	Mc
18	Bristol Rov	a	2–0	20249	Ho	St	Sw	Bt	Sh	Hn	Ka(1)	Gr	Ch	Wo(1)	Mc
25	IPSWICH	H	3–0	11657	Ho	St	Sw	Bt	Sh	Hn	Ka(1)	Wo	Ch(1)	Gr	Bm(1)
NOV1	Scunthorpe	a	0–1	13013	Ho	St	Sw	Bt	Sh	Hn	Ka	Gr	Ch	Wo	Mc
8	STOKE CITY	H	2–1	12080	Ho	St	Sw	Bt	Sh	Hn	Ka(1)	Gr	Ch	Wo(1)	Mc
15	Sunderland	a	2–2	24390	Ho	St	Sw	Bt	Sh	Hn	Ka(1)	Gr(1)	Ch	Wo	Mc
22	LINCOLN CITY	H	2–2	10380	Ho	St	Sw	Bt	Sh	Hn	Ka	Gr(1)	Ch	Wo	Mc(1)
29	Fulham	a	2–5	18790	Ho	St	Jo	Bt	Hp	Hn	Ka(1)	Gr(1)	Ch	Wo	Mc
DEC6	SHEFF WED	H	0–1	23070	Ho	St	Jo	Bt	Sh	Hn	Ka	Gr	Ch	Wo	Mc
13	Swansea Town	a	1–2	10238	Ho	St	Sw	Bt	Sh	Hn	Ka	Gr	Ch	Wo(1)	Mc
20	CARDIFF CITY	H	3–2	7731	Ho	St	Sw	Bt	Sh	Hn	Ka	Gr(1)	Ch(2)	Wo	Mc
26	Middlesbrough	a	1–3	31518	Ho	St	Jo	Bt	Sh	Hn	Ka(1)	Gr	Ch	Wo	Mc
27	MIDDLESBROUGH	H	1–0	14813	Ho	St	Jo	Bt	Sh	Hn	Wh	Gr	Ch(1)	Wo	Mc
JAN3	Huddersfield	a	1–2	17933	Ho	St	Jo	Bt	Sh	Hn	Ka	Gr	Ch	Wo(1)	Mc
31	ROTHERHAM	H	1–1	13334	Ho	St	Jo	Hm	Sh	Hn	Ka	Bm	Ch(1)	Wo	Mc
FEB7	Sheff Utd	a	0–5	17966	Ho	St	Jo	Bt	Sh	Hn	Ka	Bm	Ch	Gr	Mc
14	BRIGHTON	H	0–2	8402	Le	St	Jo	Bt	Sh	Wo	Ka	Sm	Md	Gr	Mc
21	Grimsby Town	a	3–3	8130	Ho	St	Sw	Bt	Sh	Hm(1)	Ka	Sm	Ch	Gr	Mc(2)
28	Stoke City	a	1–2	13015	Le	Jo	Sw	Bt	Sh	Hm	Ka	Sm	Ch(1)	Gr	Mc
MAR7	BRISTOL ROV	H	0–0	5503	Le	St	Sw	Bt	Sh	Hm	Ka	Sm	Ch	Gr	Mc
14	Ipswich	a	1–3	11125	Le	Jo	Sw	Bt	Sh	Hm(1)	Ka	Sm	Ch	Gr	Mc
21	SCUNTHORPE	H	0–1	5987	Le	Wa	Sw	Bt	Sh	Bb	Wh	Sm	Ch	Gr	Mc
27	Liverpool.	a	2–3	52546	Le	St	Sw	Bt	Sh	Bb	Wh	Hm(1)	Ch	Bm(1)	Mc
28	Derby County	a	0–3	18523	Le	St	Sw	Bt	Sh	Hn	Ka	Sm	Ch	Hm	Mc
30	LIVERPOOL	H	0–2	7517	Le	St	Sw	Bt	Sh	Bb	Ka	Hm	Ch	Bm	Sm
APR4	SUNDERLAND	H	0–2	10153	Le	St	Sw	Bt	Sh	Bb	Ka	Hm	Ch	Bm	Mc
11	Lincoln City	a	1–2	9392	Le	St	Sw	Bt	Sh	Bb	Ka	Hm	Bm(1)	Gr	Mc
18	FULHAM	H	2–4	7969	Le	St	Sw	Bt	Sh	Bb	Ka	Bm(1)	Ch	Gr	Mc(1)
20	SWANSEA TOWN	H	3–1	4882	Le	St	Sw	Bt(1)	Sh	Bb	Ka	Bm	Ch(2)	Hm	Mc
25	Sheff Wed	a	0–5	17917	Le	St	Sw	Bt	Sh	Bb	Ka	Bm	Ch	Hm	Mc
29	LEYTON ORIENT	H	1–3	7780	Le	St	Sw	Bt(1)	Sh	Bb	Ln	Bm	Ch	Hm	Mc

APPEARANCES

Bartlett, (Ba) 41, Sharp (Sh) 41, Chappell (Ch) 40, McCann (Mc) 40, Short (St) 39, Kaye (Ka) 35, Graham (Gr) 33, Swift (Sw) 32, Hough (Ho) 28, Houghton (Hn) 23, Wood (Wo) 23, Holmes (Ho) 15, Smith (Sm) 14, Leeson (Le) 14, Beaumont (Bm) 12, Jones (Jo) 11, David Barber (Bb) 10, Whyke (Wh) 4, Lunn (Ln) 3, Gillott (Gi) 1, Hopkins (Hp) 1, McDonald (Md) 1, Walters (Wa) 1.

GOALS

Chappell 17, Graham 9, Kaye 7, McCann 5, Wood 5, Holmes 4, Beaumont 4, Lunn 2, Bartlett 2.